Mountain Biking

COLORADO'S SAN JUAN MOUNTAINS

D0683690

Help Us Keep This Guide Up to Date

Every effort has been made by the author and editors to make this guide as accurate and useful as possible. However, many things can change after a guide is published—new products and information become available, regulations change, techniques evolve, etc.

We would love to hear from you concerning your experiences with this guide and how you feel it could be improved and be kept up to date. While we may not be able to respond to all comments and suggestions, we'll take them to heart and we'll make certain to share them with the author. Please send your comments and suggestions to the following address:

The Globe Pequot Press
Reader Response/Editorial Department
P.O. Box 480
Guilford, CT 06437

Or you may e-mail us at:
editorial@globe-pequot.com

Thanks for your input, and happy travels!

Mountain Biking

COLORADO'S SAN JUAN MOUNTAINS

Robert Hurst

FALCON®
Guilford, Connecticut
An imprint of The Globe Pequot Press

Photographers Robert Hurst

Maps designed and produced by Beachway Press

Library of Congress Cataloging-in-Publication Data

Hurst, Robert (Robert J.)
    Mountain biking Colorado's San Juan Mountains /
Robert Hurst.
        p. cm. – (A Falcon guide)
    Includes index.
    ISBN 0-7627-2346-7
    1. All terrain cycling—San Juan Mountains (Colo. and
N.M.)—Guidebooks. 2. San Juan Mountains (Colo. and
N.M.)—Guidebooks. I. Title. II. Series.

GV1045.5.S24 H87 2002
796.6'3'097883—cd21
                                    2002019896

Manufactured in the United States of America
First Edition/First Printing

Acknowledgments

First and foremost, I need to thank my family. Without the material and moral support given by my brother, grandmother, and parents, this book would have crashed and burned. There is no possible way I could have finished it without their help. I love you guys. This book is for you.

Many thanks go to Ryan Croxton and Scott Adams, especially for their patience with my snail's pace (a rate of production I happen to share with the ancient masters). You can't rush art, man!

Thank you to Steve Fassbinder, for demystifying some local secrets and for letting us surf the couch.

Melody Miller at the Colorado Division of Wildlife was very helpful, taking time out of her busy schedule to meet me in person and set me straight on some closures—on a Sunday morning. She was also a great source of information about black bears. The folks at the reference department of the Durango Public Library were also above and beyond the call. Also the guys at work, who had to work extra hard in my absence, and I know how they hate workin'.

And to anyone else I bitched at or crapped on or inconvenienced in any way while trying to get this thing done: thank you, and I'm sorry. (You all know where you can go.)

Finally, I want to thank all my cool friends who went out and rode these great trails with me. Looking forward to many more adventures with you guys.

Table of

Contents

Telluride

The Art of Mountain Biking

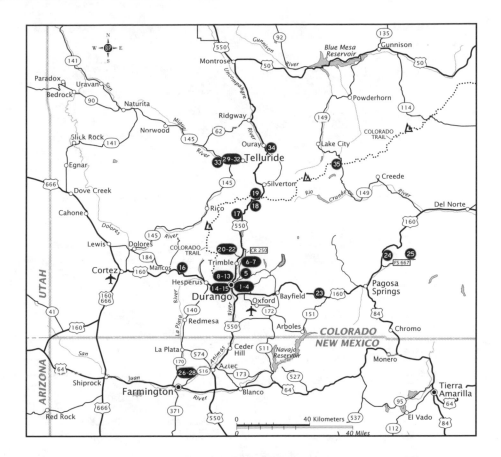

RIDES AT A GLANCE

Ride Profiles

1. Chapman–Rim Trail Loop

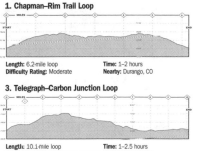

Length: 6.2-mile loop
Difficulty Rating: Moderate
Time: 1–2 hours
Nearby: Durango, CO

2. Ridge Loop

Length: 5.3-mile loop
Difficulty Rating: Difficult
Time: 1–2.5 hours
Nearby: Durango, CO

3. Telegraph–Carbon Junction Loop

Length: 10.1-mile loop
Difficulty Rating: Moderate to Difficult
Time: 1–2.5 hours
Nearby: Durango, CO

4. Sale Barn–South Rim–Cowboy Loop

Length: 7.0-mile loop
Difficulty Rating: Moderate
Time: 1–2.5 hours
Nearby: Durango, CO

RIDES AT A GLANCE

5. Missionary Ridge

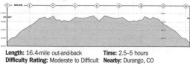

Length: 16.4-mile out-and-back **Time:** 2.5–5 hours
Difficulty Rating: Moderate to Difficult **Nearby:** Durango, CO

6. : Stevens Creek–Missionary Ridge–Haflin Canyon Loop

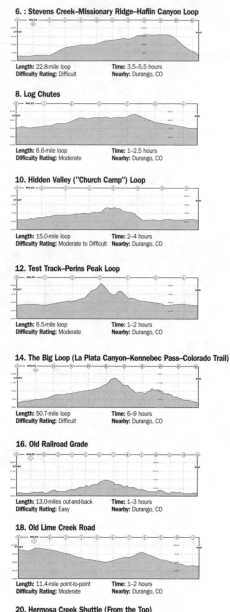

Length: 22.8-mile loop **Time:** 3.5–5.5 hours
Difficulty Rating: Difficult **Nearby:** Durango, CO

7. Stevens Creek Mini-Loop

Length: 7.2-mile loop **Time:** 45 minutes–1.5 hours
Difficulty Rating: Moderate to Difficult **Nearby:** Durango, CO

8. Log Chutes

Length: 6.6-mile loop **Time:** 1–2.5 hours
Difficulty Rating: Moderate **Nearby:** Durango, CO

9. Colorado Trail–Dry Fork–Hoffheins Loop

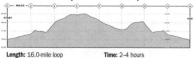

Length: 16.0-mile loop **Time:** 2–4 hours
Difficulty Rating: Moderate to Difficult **Nearby:** Durango, CO

10. Hidden Valley ("Church Camp") Loop

Length: 15.0-mile loop **Time:** 2–4 hours
Difficulty Rating: Moderate to Difficult **Nearby:** Durango, CO

11. Animas City Mountain

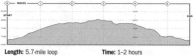

Length: 5.7-mile loop **Time:** 1–2 hours
Difficulty Rating: Difficult **Nearby:** Durango, CO

12. Test Track–Perins Peak Loop

Length: 6.5-mile loop **Time:** 1–2 hours
Difficulty Rating: Moderate **Nearby:** Durango, CO

13. Trans–Test Track Loop

Length: 6.4-mile loop **Time:** 1–2 hours
Difficulty Rating: Difficult **Nearby:** Durango, CO

14. The Big Loop (La Plata Canyon–Kennebec Pass–Colorado Trail)

Length: 50.7-mile loop **Time:** 6–9 hours
Difficulty Rating: Difficult **Nearby:** Durango, CO

15. Smelter Hillclimb

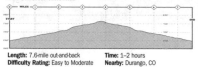

Length: 7.6-mile out-and-back **Time:** 1–2 hours
Difficulty Rating: Easy to Moderate **Nearby:** Durango, CO

16. Old Railroad Grade

Length: 13.0-miles out-and-back **Time:** 1–3 hours
Difficulty Rating: Easy **Nearby:** Durango, CO

17. Purgatory 1990 World Championship Course Sampler

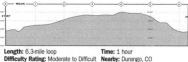

Length: 6.3-mile loop **Time:** 1 hour
Difficulty Rating: Moderate to Difficult **Nearby:** Durango, CO

18. Old Lime Creek Road

Length: 11.4-mile point-to-point **Time:** 1–2 hours
Difficulty Rating: Moderate **Nearby:** Durango, CO

19. Molas Pass to Coal Bank Pass

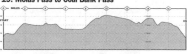

Length: 17.7-mile point-to-point **Time:** 3.5–5 hours
Difficulty Rating: Difficult **Nearby:** Durango, CO

20. Hermosa Creek Shuttle (From the Top)

Length: 19.5-mile point-to-point **Time:** 2–5 hours
Difficulty Rating: Moderate **Nearby:** Durango, CO

21. Hermosa Creek Out-and-Back (From the Bottom)

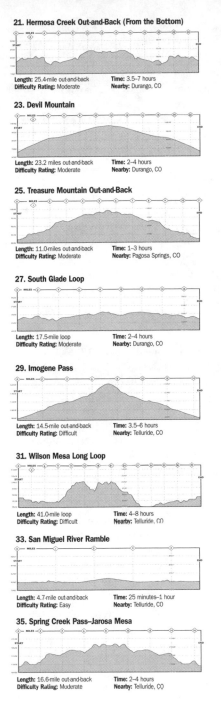

Length: 25.4-mile out-and-back
Difficulty Rating: Moderate
Time: 3.5–7 hours
Nearby: Durango, CO

22. Jones Creek–Dutch Creek Loop

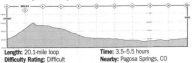

Length: 19.5-mile loop
Difficulty Rating: Difficult
Time: 3.5–6 hours
Nearby: Durango, CO

23. Devil Mountain

Length: 23.2 miles out-and-back
Difficulty Rating: Moderate
Time: 2–4 hours
Nearby: Durango, CO

24. Windy Pass Loop

Length: 20.1-mile loop
Difficulty Rating: Difficult
Time: 3.5–5.5 hours
Nearby: Pagosa Springs, CO

25. Treasure Mountain Out-and-Back

Length: 11.0-miles out-and-back
Difficulty Rating: Moderate
Time: 1–3 hours
Nearby: Pagosa Springs, CO

26. North Glade Loop

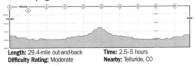

Length: 20.1-mile loop
Difficulty Rating: Moderate to Difficult
Time: 2.5–5 hours
Nearby: Durango, CO

27. South Glade Loop

Length: 17.5-mile loop
Difficulty Rating: Moderate
Time: 2–4 hours
Nearby: Durango, CO

28. Kinsey–Seven Sisters Loop

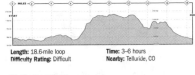

Length: 10.6-mile loop
Difficulty Rating: Moderate to Difficult
Time: 1–2.5 hours
Nearby: Durango, CO

29. Imogene Pass

Length: 14.5-mile out-and-back
Difficulty Rating: Difficult
Time: 3.5–6 hours
Nearby: Telluride, CO

30. Galloping Goose

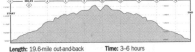

Length: 29.4-mile out-and-back
Difficulty Rating: Moderate
Time: 2.5–5 hours
Nearby: Telluride, CO

31. Wilson Mesa Long Loop

Length: 41.0-mile loop
Difficulty Rating: Difficult
Time: 4–8 hours
Nearby: Telluride, CO

32. Western Deep Creek Loop

Length: 18.6-mile loop
Difficulty Rating: Difficult
Time: 3–6 hours
Nearby: Telluride, CO

33. San Miguel River Ramble

Length: 4.7-mile out-and-back
Difficulty Rating: Easy
Time: 25 minutes–1 hour
Nearby: Telluride, CO

34. Engineer Pass

Length: 19.6-mile out-and-back
Difficulty Rating: Moderate to Difficult
Time: 3–6 hours
Nearby: Telluride, CO

35. Spring Creek Pass–Jarosa Mesa

Length: 16.6-mile out-and-back
Difficulty Rating: Moderate
Time: 2–4 hours
Nearby: Telluride, CO

HOW TO USE THIS BOOK

Take a close enough look and you'll find that this little guide contains just about everything you'll ever need to choose, plan for, enjoy, and survive a ride in the state of Colorado. We've done everything but inflate your tires and put on your helmet. Stuffed with 256 pages of useful southwest Colorado-specific information, *Mountain Biking Colorado's San Juan Mountains* features 35 mapped and cued rides and 37 honorable mentions, as well as everything from advice on getting into shape to tips on getting the most out of mountain biking with your children or your dog. And as you'd expect with any Outside America™ guide, you get the best maps man and technology can render. With so much information, the only question you may have is: How do I sift through it all? Well, we answer that, too.

We've designed this guide to be highly visual, for quick reference and ease-of-use. What this means is that the most pertinent information rises quickly to the top, so you don't have to waste time poring through bulky ride descriptions to get mileage cues or elevation stats. They're set aside for you. And yet, it doesn't read like a laundry list. Take the time to dive into a ride description and you'll realize that this guide is not just a good source of information; it's a good read. And so, in the end, you get the best of both worlds: a quick-reference guide and an engaging look at a region. Here's an outline of the guide's major components.

WHAT YOU'LL FIND IN THIS GUIDE

Let's start with the individual chapter. To aid in quick decision-making, we start each chapter with a **Ride Summary**. This short overview gives you a taste of the biking adventure at hand. You'll learn about the trail terrain and what surprises the route has to offer. If your interest is piqued, you can read more. If not, skip to the next Ride Summary. The **Ride Specs** are fairly self-explanatory. Here you'll find the quick, nitty-gritty details of the ride: where the trailhead is located, the nearest town, ride length, approximate riding time, difficulty rating, type of trail terrain, and what other trail users you may encounter. Our **Getting There** section gives you dependable directions from a nearby city right down to where you'll want to park. The **Ride Description** is the meat of the chapter. Detailed and honest, it's the author's carefully researched impression of the trail. While it's impossible to cover everything, you can rest assured that we won't miss what's important. In our **Miles/Directions** section we provide mileage cues to identify all turns and trail name changes, as well as points of interest. The **Ride Information** box is a hodgepodge of information. In it you'll find trail hotlines (for updates on trail conditions), park schedules and fees, local outdoor retailers (for emergency trail supplies), and a list of maps available to the area. We'll also tell you where to stay, what to eat, and what else to see while you're hiking in the area. Lastly, the **Honorable Mentions** section details all of the rides that didn't make the cut, for whatever reason—in many cases it's not because they aren't great rides, instead it's because they're over-crowded or environmentally sensitive to heavy traffic. Be sure to read through these. A jewel might be lurking among them.

We don't want anyone, by any means, to feel restricted to just the routes and trails that are mapped here. We hope you will have an adventurous spirit and use this guide as a platform to dive into southwest Colorado's backcountry and discover new routes for yourself. One of the simplest ways to begin this is to just turn the map upside down and ride the course in reverse. The change in perspective is fantastic and the ride should feel quite different. With this in mind, it will be like getting two distinctly different rides on each map.

For your own purposes, you may wish to copy the directions for the course onto a small sheet to help you while riding, or photocopy the map and cue sheet to take with you. Otherwise, just slip the whole book in your backpack and take it all with you. Enjoy your time in the outdoors and remember to pack out what you pack in.

5	Interstate Highway	✝	Airfield	𝕩	Hiking Trail
8	U.S. Highway	✈	Airport	✚	Hospital
3	State Road	🚲	Bike Trail	⛏	Mine
CR 23	County Road	🚫	No Bikes	🏛	National Monument
T 145	Township Road	)(	Bridge	☼	Overlook
FS 45	Forest Road	🚌	Bus Stop	♣	Park
	Paved Road	▲	Campground	🎋	Picnic
	Paved Bike Lane	♨	Campsite	🅿	Parking
	Maintained Dirt Road	☰	Cattle Guard	✕	Quarry
------	Unmaintained Jeep Trail	†	Cemetery	((A))	Radio Tower
- - - -	Singletrack Trail	✝	Church	🧗	Rock Climbing
━ ━ ━	Highlighted Route	🖎	College	🏫	School
···▲···	Colorado Trail	⟿	Direction Arrows	🏠	Shelter
··········	Special Trail	🎿	Downhill Skiing	🛒	Shopping Center
- - -	Ntl Forest/County Boundaries	♨	Fire Tower	♂	Spring
━ ━ ━	State Boundaries	⤙	Fishing	★	Trailhead
━·━·━	Railroad Tracks	♦	Forest HQ	🏠	Visitor Center
━··━	Power Lines	🖎	4WD Trail	🦅	Wildlife Refuge
∿∿∿	Rivers or Streams	↕	Gate	◆◆	Most Difficult
	Water and Lakes	↕	Golf Course	◆	Difficult
	Marsh	▲	Highpoint	□	Moderate
				●	Easy

1 Area Locator Map

This thumbnail relief map at the beginning of each ride shows you where the ride is within the state. The ride area is indicated with a star.

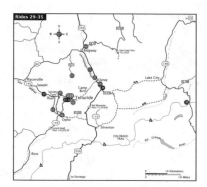

2 Regional Location Map

This map helps you find your way to the start of each ride from the nearest sizeable town or city. Coupled with the detailed directions at the beginning of the cue, this map should visually lead you to where you need to be for each ride.

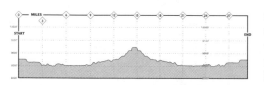

3 Profile Map

This helpful profile gives you a cross-sectional look at the ride's ups and downs. Elevation is labeled on the left, mileage is indicated on the top. Road and trail names are shown along the route with towns and points of interest labeled in bold.

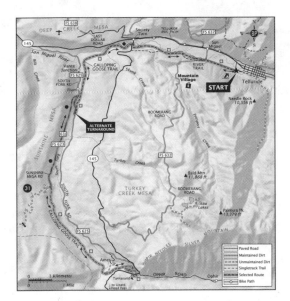

4 Route Map

This is your primary guide to each ride. It shows all of the accessible roads and trails, points of interest, water, towns, landmarks, and geographical features. It also distinguishes trails from roads, and paved roads from unpaved roads. The selected route is highlighted, and directional arrows point the way. Shaded topographic relief in the background gives you an accurate representation of the terrain and landscape in the ride area.

Ride Information *(Included in each ride section)*

🕿 Trail Contacts:

This is the direct number for the local land managers in charge of all the trails within the selected ride. Use this hotline to call ahead for trail access information, or after your visit if you see problems with trail erosion, damage, or misuse.

🕐 Schedule:

This tells you at what times trails open and close, if on private or park land.

$ Fees/Permits:

What money, if any, you may need to carry with you for park entrance fees or tolls.

🅝 Maps:

This is a list of other maps to supplement the maps in this book. They are listed in order from most detailed to most general.

Any other important or useful information will also be listed here such as local attractions, bike shops, nearby accommodations, etc.

Introdu

Introduction

urango is the best place in the universe to ride a mountain bike, and I don't want to hear any backtalk about that. I know about Moab, and I know about Crested Butte, and I can tell you that both spots put together don't add up to a Durango.

Disguised as a modest-looking smelter town on piles of gray shale, Durango is at the epicenter of a mind-blowing web of trails. From alpine tundra to sandy deserts, a tremendous variety of terrain is accessible by bicycle, directly from town. Locals rarely get around to riding it all. And if one ever were to get bored with the trails around Durango—*not bloody likely*—one could branch off into nearby hotbeds of singletrack in Pagosa Springs, Farmington, and Telluride.

If you're a card-carrying trail-junky like myself, you've come to the right place, and the right guidebook. No way is this a complete accounting of all the rides around here, but within these pages you'll find a bunch of excellent jeep road routes and the vast majority of great singletrack in southwest Colorado. In addition to a raging exposé of the Durango core, many of the outlying trails have been included as a kind of bonus. Along the way I give up a few of the tastiest local secrets (the legal ones) and I will probably catch some static for that. Here are the keys to the Ferrari, don't smash it up.

If I had to pick a favorite among all these trails, well, it would be nearly impossible. There are so many great sections. The high-altitude Colorado Trail, and Hermosa Creek, of course, are right up there. The gambler's descent in Haflin Canyon, which lots of guys claim to have ridden flawlessly from top to bottom (although nobody really believes them), is a good one. There's Church Camp, and the roller coaster Farmington trails. Treasure Mountain near Pagosa. In Telluride, the Deep Creek and Wilson Mesa trails are always callin' my name. Dutch Creek, Jones Creek, Dry Fork. Stevens Creek. Pass Creek. I know I'm forgetting some of those creeks. Test Track, with the man-made jumps. Missionary Ridge, Raider Ridge, the brand-new South Rim Trail, Carbon Junction...

But there is this one trail I guess you could say is my favorite. One thing, though. *It's not on the list.* Not in this book, or any book. I'll give you a hint about where it is. No I won't. Let's just say it's up there somewhere, very high, very thin, and rarely ridden. I'd like to keep it that way. Some things are sacred.

Finally, let's not forget what this sport is all about. Don't let racing, training, or a love for trails themselves (my disease) cloud the issue. So much is missed through the steely, downward-pointed eyes of the fitness Nazi. The best advice I could give any mountain biker is to just sit in the woods. Watch, listen, and learn. What you will most likely hear, when the ringing of imaginary cash registers subsides, is a squirrel telling you to get lost. The wind coming at you through the pines, smooth and ominous. An elk bugle. Or one of the most beautiful sounds of all, complete silence. When was the last time you heard that? With just a little sitting-still time, you could find yourself visited by mule deer, elk, bobcats, coyotes, pumas, mountain goats, black bears, lynx, turkeys, ptarmigans, porcupines, marmots, big horn sheep, pikas, horses, cattle, Fear Not birds, beavers, chipmunks, loud squirrels, rabbits, voles, grouse, skunks, and llamas. Okay, no llamas. Mountain bikers should spend more time getting to know these colorful characters, less time scaring them off.

I hope this book helps you find your new favorite trail(s). Keep the rubber side down, and enjoy every moment. Never forget how lucky you are to be riding trails in southwest Colorado.

Robert Hurst
Durango, Colorado

The Rides

Durango
COLORADO

The Rides

1. Chapman–Rim Trail Loop
2. Ridge Loop
3. Telegraph–Carbon Junction Loop
4. Sale Barn–South Rim–Cowboy Loop
5. Missionary Ridge
6. Stevens Creek–Missionary Ridge–Haflin Canyon Loop
7. Stevens Creek Mini-Loop
8. Log Chutes
9. Colorado Trail–Dry Fork–Hoffheins Loop
10. Hidden Valley ("Church Camp") Loop
11. Animas City Mountain
12. Test Track–Perins Peak Loop
13. Trans–Test Track Loop
14. The Big Loop (La Plata Canyon–Kennebec Pass–Colorado Trail)
15. Smelter Hillclimb
16. Old Railroad Grade
17. Purgatory 1990 World Championship Course Sampler
18. Old Lime Creek Road
19. Molas Pass to Coal Bank Pass
20. Hermosa Creek Shuttle (From the Top)
21. Hermosa Creek Out-and-Back (From the Bottom)
22. Jones Creek–Dutch Creek Loop
23. Devil Mountain
24. Windy Pass Loop
25. Treasure Mountain Out-and-Back
26. North Glade Loop
27. South Glade Loop
28. Kinsey–Seven Sisters Loop

Honorable Mentions

A. Horse Gulch Road
B. Just Haflin Loop
C. First Fork Trail
D. Missionary Ridge Road
E. Beaver Meadows–First Notch Loop
F. First Fork Road
G. Colorado Trail–Dry Fork Loop from Town
H. Madden Peak
I. Menafee Mountain
J. Dolores River Canyon
K. Transfer Campground
L. Bear Creek Trail
M. Colorado Trail Shuttle
N. Indian Trail Ridge
O. Bolam Pass–Hotel Draw Loop
P. Purgatory–Elbert Creek Loop
Q. Harris Park Loop
R. The Ultimate Shuttle
S. Molas–Silverton Loop
T. Silverton to Clear Lake
U. Stony Pass
V. Engineer Pass–Cinnamon Pass–Lake City Loop
W. Fawn Gulch–Mill Creek Loop
X. Reservoir Hill
Y. Chris Mountain & Turkey Springs

Dropped off and getting ready for the Colorado Trail Shuttle.
See Honorable Mentions M

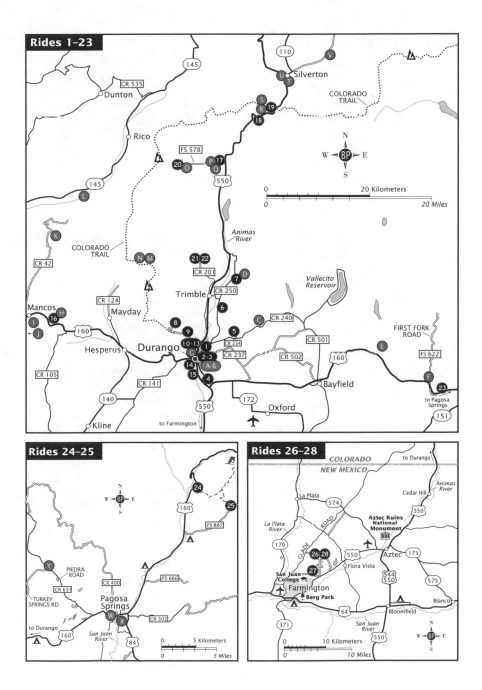

Durango

Rides 1–23

CR 535
Dunton
Rico
FS 578
CR 42
COLORADO TRAIL
CR 124
Mancos
Mayday
Hesperus
CR 105
CR 141
CR 140
Kline

110
145
Silverton
COLORADO TRAIL
S 19
18
N
W—BP—E
S
0   20 Kilometers
0   20 Miles

20 O P 17 Q
550
Animas River
N M
21 22
CR 201
Trimble
CR 250
8
9
10-13
C
2-3
A-B
14
15
4
550
172
Oxford
to Farmington

7 D
6
5
CR 234
CR 237
Vallecito Reservoir
CR 240
CR 501
CR 502
160
Bayfield

FIRST FORK ROAD
FS 622
E
F
23
to Pagosa Springs
151

K
L
H
16
I
J
160

Rides 24–25

N
W—BP—E
S
24
160
25
FS 667
Y
PIEDRA ROAD
CR 63
TURKEY SPRINGS RD
CR 400
FS 666
Pagosa Springs
W X
CR 302
to Durango
160
San Juan River
84
0   5 Kilometers
0   5 Miles

Rides 26–28

COLORADO
NEW MEXICO
to Durango
Animas River
La Plata
574
Cedar Hill
550
La Plata River
GLADE ROAD
Aztec Ruins National Monument
170
26 28
550
173
27
San Juan College
Flora Vista
544 550
575
Farmington
Berg Park
Aztec
Blanco
64
Bloomfield
371
San Juan River
550
N
W—BP—E
S
0   10 Kilometers
0   10 Miles

Durango

Aaah, Durango. All of us who love mountain biking eventually end up here.

In the 1980s, when the sport was still in diapers, there seemed to be some kind of rule which stated no mountain bike publication could be printed without a write-up on Durango, proclaiming its status as One of the World's Greatest Mountain Biking Towns. With their monthly torrent of ink and glossy pictures, the magazines could only *hint* at the vast network of far reaching singletracks that almost surround this place. Singletrack—challenging, smooth, rough, high, and long—was the fuel of the Durango Mountain Bike Rush. Like prospectors looking for gold, many of the world's top racers and trail-loving enthusiasts relocated to Durango to form a unique community in this ideal training ground. The sport of mountain biking wasn't born here, but it was raised here. The first ever World Championships of mountain bike racing were held at the nearby Purgatory Ski Area (now renamed Durango Mountain Resort) in 1990, and the competition was dominated by Durango residents.

Over time, the novelty wore off a bit. Juli Furtado and some of the other famous racers moved away, looking for a change, and the magazine guys finally got tired of writing about Durango. But the trails remain, as nice as they always were, and still ready for action. In fact, the trail network has grown significantly since the glory days (due primarily to the efforts of a local group called Trails 2000). Durango is still the king of mountain biking towns.

Durango has all varieties of terrain for the mountain biker. Beginners and dirt road *aficionados* will find plenty to their liking. Let's face it, though: *It's all about singletrack.* Trail-lovers have a lot to work with here, right out the back door. An extensive network surrounds Telegraph Hill and The Ridge, and smaller systems await at Test Track and Church Camp, just beyond the perimeter. To the north, prime singletrack runs all over Missionary Ridge and through Hermosa Canyon. To the west, the Colorado Trail comes down out of the mountains and spawns a few gorgeous connectors. Even with all the goods nearby, locals and visitors to town do well to venture forth into the outlying areas. Carve out some time for a roadtrip up to Molas Pass, down to Farmington, or into the shadows below Wolf Creek Pass, east of Pagosa Springs.

In addition to trails, Durango has the amenities to satisfy all but the snootiest of city-lovers. And it's a college town, with all the implications. It's also a nuts-and-bolts, blue-collar town, where you can get a good, cheap meal and live in an affordable house or apartment—a near impossibility in many Colorado mountain communities. Not surprisingly, Durango is being suburbanized, mainstreamed, and Californicated as the population grows. Expansive parking lots and luxury homes are popping up on the outskirts, much to the chagrin of the old-timers—retired miners, railroad workers, smelter operators, and schoolteachers who remember when Durango was neither a college town nor a mountain bike town, but a gritty, industrial burg beneath the smelter's toxic cloud. These days, Durango has a young, renewed feel, as lots of folks have moved in to raise their children next to the Animas, among the trails. Who can blame them?

Getting around Durango

☎ AREA CODES

The **970** area code services a large area encompassing all of Southwestern Colorado—including Durango, Pagosa Springs, and Telluride—and most of the northern half of the state as well. (The Denver/Boulder metro area uses **303** and **720**. The **719** area code services the greater south-central and southeastern part of the state, including Colorado Springs, Pueblo, Buena Vista, Leadville, Alamosa, and Del Norte.) The area code for Farmington, NM is **505**.

🚗 ROADS

For current information on statewide weather, road conditions, and closures, contact the **Colorado Department of Transportation** (CDOT) at their toll free hotline 1–877–315–ROAD (only in-state callers). Denver metro area and out-of-state callers can still access the hotline by calling (303) 639–1111. The same information can also be found by visiting CDOT's website at *www.dot.state.co.us* or *www.cotrip.org*

✈ BY AIR

The **Durango-La Plata County Airport** is located about 14 miles southeast of Durango, off of Colorado Highway 172 (the road to Ignacio) and is served by four airlines: United Express (serving Denver with ten daily flights), American Airlines, America West Express (offering three daily non-stop flights to Phoenix), and Rio Grande Air. For more information, contact its website at *www.durangoairport.com*, or call (970) 247–8143.

To book reservations online, check out your favorite airline's website or search one of the following travel sites for the best price: *www.cheaptickets.com*, *www.expedia.com*, *www.previewtravel.com*, *www.orbitz.com*, *www.priceline.com*, *travel.yahoo.com*, *www.travelocity.com*, or *www.Trip.com*—just to name a few.

🚌 SHUTTLES

A few companies provide shuttle service from the Durango-La Plata County Airport. **Durango Transportation** operates on a regular schedule from the airport to Durango; for information concerning this company, call (970) 259–4818. Rental cars are also available.

🚆 BY RAIL

The only rail service to Durango is on the **Durango-Silverton Narrow Gauge tourist train**, a steam-powered time machine, which operates on a regular schedule between Durango and Silverton from May through October. In the winter months, the train goes from Durango to Cascade Canyon, and then comes back. To make reservations call 1–888–872–4607, or click on *www.durangotrain.com*. Consider hauling your bike to Silverton for a day of riding. The train will carry up to 200 pounds of your equipment for 15 dollars.

🚍 BY BUS

There is sporadic **Greyhound** service to and from Durango. Call 1–800–231–2222 or visit *www.greyhound.com* for more information.

Once in Durango, you can get around on the **Durango Loop** public bus service which connects the north City Market on the north end, Bodo Industrial Park on the south, Fort Lewis College to the east, and the Crestview neighborhood on the west. The fare is one dollar (fifty cents for seniors). Call (970) 259–LIFT for detailed route and schedule information. Each bus can carry two bicycles.

❓ VISITOR INFORMATION

For general information on Durango, visit the website of the **Durango Chamber of Commerce**: *www.durango.org*, or call (970) 247–0312. There is also plenty of good info at *www.durango.com*.

For Pagosa Springs information, call the **Pagosa Springs Chamber of Commerce** at (970) 264–2360 or visit their website at *www.pagosaspringschamber.com*.

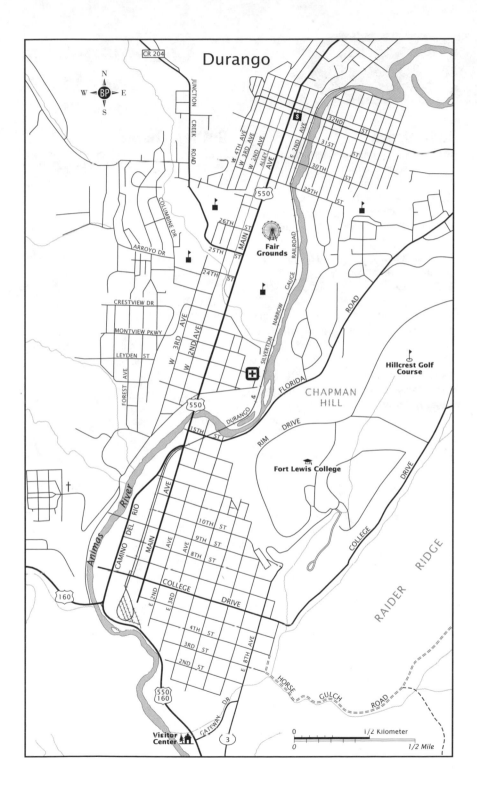

Chapman–Rim Trail Loop

Ride Specs

Start: From the base of Chapman Hill, on Florida Road, in Durango
Length: 6.2-mile loop
Approximate Riding Time: 1–2 hours
Technical Difficulty: Moderate: nothing too wicked on this smooth singletrack route, unless it's wet, then forget it
Physical Difficulty: Moderate: relatively short and mellow, almost easy
Trail Surface: 96% singletrack, with some widetrack and a tiny bit of pavement
Lay of the Land: The series of mesas and ridges east of town, covered in scrub oak, ponderosa pine, and the Fort Lewis College campus
Elevation Gain: 686 feet
Land Status: City park and private property
Other Trail Users: Walkers

Getting There

In Durango: Start at the base of Chapman Hill. To find it, head east on 15th Street from Main Avenue (U.S. 550/U.S. 160) for two blocks, then turn left at the Y-intersection onto Florida Road. About a half mile up this road, you'll notice a towrope leading up the slope on your right, and a huge shed at the base that is actually an ice rink. Park here in a sizable lot.

Public Transportation: The Durango Lift North/Crestview bus stops along the northbound side of Florida Road, Monday to Saturday, at seven minutes past the hour until 6:07 PM. (5:07 PM. on Saturdays).

D urangoans are blessed with the opportunity of cycling from their doorsteps to any one of a number of tasty singletrack trails within a matter of minutes, and this moderate loop starting at Chapman Hill is a prime example of that.

Chapman Hill is named for Colton Chapman, one of a group of rabid skiing enthusiasts who lived in Durango in the early 1940s. Like skiers everywhere, this group decided they needed some assistance getting to the top of their local hill and started to build a tow-cable. Chapman took charge of the operation. Later, he was known to promote skiing among kids in town, helping them make skis out of old barrels. (This led to the Great Barrel Shortage of '47.)

As a ski hill, Chapman is pitiful. Somewhat better for sledding. It gets a lot of sun and not much snow. If they think up some new extreme sport that involves gravity and *mud*, Chapman will be at the epicenter. For quite some time now, of course, cyclists have claimed the hill, and epic velo-dramas have been played out here. The annual Iron Horse Mountain Bike Classic, one of the biggest mountain bike events in the world, uses Chapman as a start/finish for its cross-country races and as a staging area for its festival, expo, and dual slalom. The muddy, rocky slope of Chapman Hill has been marked with the tread patterns of the greatest cyclists in the world, as well massive crowds of courageous sport class racers. Now it's your turn.

From the base of Chapman Hill, angle northeast (to the left and slightly up, if you're standing at the bottom of the hill looking up the tow rope) and find the Lion's Den singletrack contouring across into the scrub oak. Just into the brush, the trail passes an intersection with the steep, rocky track that heads immediately for the top of Chapman Hill. Taking a much gentler and longer route, your trail flows north above the houses, rolling quickly. Soon you'll find a few generous switchbacks, which ease the ascent, and, after about one mile of singletrack climbing, there's an inviting bench where the Lion's Den Trail splits into north and south forks (the North Fork is a shortcut to the Lion's Den). Take a right onto the South Fork and contour, quickly and smoothly, up to the Rim Trail.

The Rim Trail is a tame but pleasant singletrack which tours pretty much the entire length of the mesa's rim. The trail is sandwiched between Rim Drive and the steep slope falling away to the Animas River floodplain (upon which, by the way, Durango is a sitting duck for the 500-year flood). From the rim, the views of town and the mighty La Plata Mountains are unobstructed and top-notch. This track's unsurprising popularity with pedestrians and their masters (dogs) could force you into slower speeds than you would like—save the thrill-seeking for a different ride, or at least wait until you reach the less-populated back side of this loop.

The Rim Trail improves steadily from a trail rider's standpoint—that is, it gets tougher—as it rolls around to the south side of the round mesa. (Notice the tempting option at mile 2.5: the smooth singletrack of the Centennial Nature Trail, which corkscrews back to town-level.) After about 2.6 miles, the Rim Trail drops somewhat seriously to 8th Avenue on the most technical terrain of the ride. Across 8th Avenue,

John Tomac crushes all as he gives 140% in the Iron Horse MTB Classic on Chapman Hill.

11

MilesDirections

0.0 START from the parking lot at the base of Chapman Hill. It's important that you find the correct trail. While facing up the hill, look left and slightly up for a hint of a trail headed northeast, away from the ski hill. This trail, the Lion's Den Trail, contours across the slope, above the houses.

0.3 Stay right and up as a spur intersects on the left.

0.8 Stay right again, switching back here.

1.1 The incline mellows at a fork in the Lion's Den Trail. (The North Fork leads directly to the glorified pagoda on the edge of the mesa.) Veer right onto the South Fork. There is also a bench here trailside.

1.4 Turn right onto the Rim Trail.

1.8 Arrive at the top of Chapman Hill and an intersection with the Chapman Hill Widetrack, which descends sharply to the base. *[Option. Take a sharp right onto this widetrack and descend to the top of the dual slalom course. Rip it at your own risk, keeping in mind that this stuff is tougher than it's often made to look by daredevils with BMX background. Or use this rough widetrack to descend all the way to the base along the edge of Chapman Hill, bypassing the course and its jumps.]*

2.0 Pass another bench.

2.4 Pass yet another bench, or take a rest, of course.

2.5 Pass the intersection with a sweet-looking track headed down to the right, the Centennial

Nature Trail. *[Option. This trail twists back to town and pops out at the eastern dead-end of 10th Street.]*

2.6 Descend sharply to 8th Avenue.

2.8 Cross the paved road and turn left onto the singletrack just opposite. You're not on the actual rim anymore, but this is a continuation of the Rim Trail.

3.0 The trail curls sharply to the right.

3.1 The trail joins a widetrack. Continue right.

3.3 The widetrack curls back all the way left, then morphs into twisty singletrack. The trail is usually lined with rocks through here.

4.0 Stay left, passing a spur (which descends to College Avenue).

4.1 Cross a spur.

4.2 The trail veers hard to the left.

4.3 The trail joins Fort Lewis Drive for a block or so, then crosses to the north side at a cairn.

4.6 Cross Rim Drive and rejoin the Rim Trail. Turn right. *[Option. Turn left onto the Rim Trail, and find the top of the Chapman Hill widetrack and dual slalom course, or one of the other optional escape chutes.]*

5.1 Back at the first bench (mile 1.1), continue left and downhill at the intersection.

6.2 Finish the ride at the base of Chapman Hill.

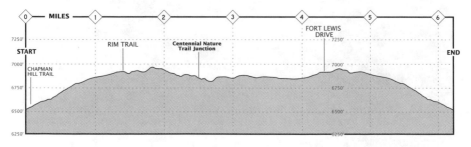

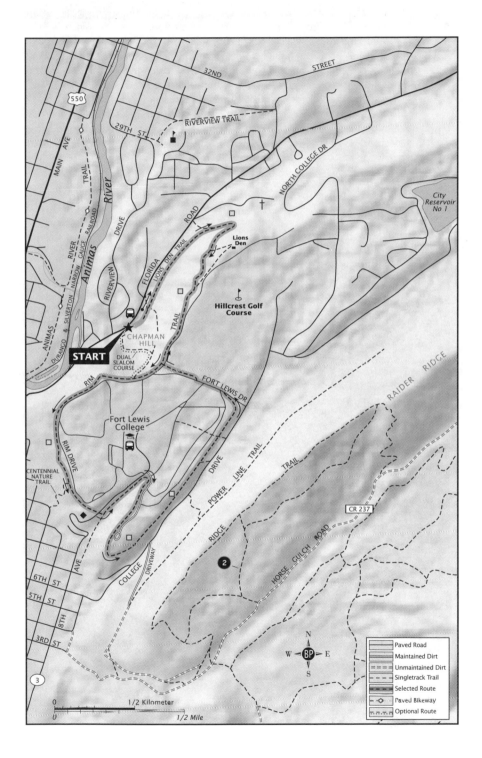

32ND STREET

550

29TH ST

RIVERVIEW TRAIL

NORTH COLLEGE DR

City Reservoir No 1

Animas River

Main Ave

Riverview Trail

River

Silverton Narrow Gauge Railroad

Durango & Silverton

Animas

Drive

Florida Road

Lions Den Trail

Lions Den

Hillcrest Golf Course

Trail

CHAPMAN HILL

START

DUAL SLALOM COURSE

RIM

FORT LEWIS DR

RAIDER RIDGE

Fort Lewis College

Rim Drive

College Driveway

Drive

Power Line Trail

Ridge

Trail

Horse Gulch Road

CR 237

CENTENNIAL NATURE TRAIL

2

6TH ST

5TH ST

Ave

8TH

3RD ST

3

N
W · BP · E
S

	Paved Road
	Maintained Dirt
	Unmaintained Dirt
	Singletrack Trail
	Selected Route
	Paved Bikeway
	Optional Route

0   1/2 Kilometer
0   1/2 Mile

pick up the singletrack headed left (northeast) and follow this strip as it hugs a little brook and curves around to the south again, where it joins a mellow widetrack. This widetrack runs out to the end of a finger on the mesa, then turns about 170 degrees, again facing northeast. From here the route thins into a moderately twisty single-track—called the Campus Loop in some circles—that winds through a ponderosa pine woodland on the northern edge of the mesa. The forest provides a cool, shady retreat from the *concrete jungle* that is Durango. (Sometimes you just gotta get away!) Deer and various other creatures are a common sight in this section. As you head through the woods, the route can be confusing as it crosses and winds directly past doubletracks and half-trails. Stay on the groomed singletrack that has been lined with babyhead rocks.

Snow in October.

Still on the north slope of the mesa, the trail exits the woods and crosses a field of tall grasses (also a few spur trails), paralleling College Drive below. Then the thin singletrack cuts left and west across the mesa, crossing a paved road or two, and links back up with the Rim Trail by mile 4.6. This completes the singletrack loop around the entirety of Fort Lewis College. From here, cruise back to the base on the same trail you rode up originally, the final descent becoming the highlight of the ride, in my opinion. Or, use the Chapman Hill dual slalom course, pulling a Truck Driver, Superman, or, better yet, a Flare over the double jump.

Fort Lewis hasn't always been a college. Established in 1880, it began as a genuine military fort, located west of Durango in Hesperus. Since its soldiers were never called on to "restrain" the Utes or striking miners—the familiar targets of American military force at the time—the government was unable to justify Fort Lewis' military existence. By 1891 it was officially deactivated and turned over to the Department of the Interior for an Indian school. Twenty years later it became a high school, then a two-year junior college committed to agriculture and mining. Finally, in 1956, the school was relocated to the mesa over Durango and was transformed into a four-year, degree-granting liberal arts college. Some time later, Fort Lewis acquired its reputation as one of the nation's most dedicated party schools.

Fearing the usual suspects—change and communists—many in Durango's old guard fought hard to keep Fort Lewis College out of town. Today, I think almost everyone would agree that the marriage of school and town is a good one.

This ride barely leaves town and is therefore one of the least adventurous in the book. Then again, the route is composed almost entirely of singletrack trails, and some of the sections are moderately challenging. Overall, the concentration of fast singletrack on this loop more than makes up for the lack of adventure.

Ride Information

Trail Contacts:

Trails 2000, P.O. Box 3868, Durango, CO 81302, (970) 259–4682 or *www.trails 2000.com. Trails 2000 is a highly effective non-profit that builds and maintains trails around Durango.*

Schedule:

May through October, due to mud. Try it in the off-season at your own considerable risk.

Maps:

USGS maps: Durango East, CO

Ridge Loop

Ride Specs

Start: From the bottom of Horse Gulch Road, located near the intersection of East 8th and 3rd Avenue

Length: 5.3-mile loop

Approximate Riding Time: 1–2.5 hours

Technical Difficulty: Difficult: technical thrills on the ridgetop, not great for beginners

Physical Difficulty: Moderate to Difficult: rough, steep climbs, but overall a short ride

Trail Surface: 80% singletrack and 20% dirt road

Lay of the Land: Rocky, ponderosa pine-covered ridge overlooking Durango

Elevation Gain: 1,130 feet

Land Status: BLM and La Plata County lands

Other Trail Users: Hikers and joggers

Getting There

In Durango: Start on Horse Gulch Road, which can be found at the dead end of 3rd Street in southeast Durango. One good way to get there is to head east from Main Avenue (U.S. 550/U.S. 160) on College Drive (6th Street) to East 8th Avenue. Take a right on East 8th to 3rd Street, then a left on 3rd Street. The street dead-ends in one block, and there you will find the dirt Horse Gulch Road continuing east. Park here, if possible, or along one of the streets nearby. Better still, ride to the trailhead from anywhere in town.

Public Transportation: The Durango Lift FLC South bus stops at the corner of 8th Avenue at 3rd Street, Monday to Saturday, at four minutes past the hour until 6:04 P.M. (5:04 P.M. on Saturdays).

Above Durango, even above the mesa-top campus of Fort Lewis College, looms Raider Ridge. And all along The Ridge is a sweet technical trail that is perfect if you're looking for an excellent, quick mountain bike ride from town. As such, it's no surprise that The Ridge is one of the most popular, time-honored destinations of local cyclists.

Access The Ridge mini-network via Horse Gulch Road. There are lots of ways to attack the many singletracks between The Ridge and Horse Gulch. For this particular route, a clockwise loop incorporating most of the trails, aim first for the Ridge Trail that winds to the summit of Raider Ridge on the west side. There are a few spurs leading from Horse Gulch Road up to the Ridge Trail at about mile 0.5. The main Ridge Trail is easy to find by simply heading up the singletrack across the road from the Telegraph trailhead, at mile 0.7. The Ridge Trail is climbing east-northeast here. Make sure you don't head west immediately from Horse Gulch Road, or find yourself riding along beneath the power lines that skirt the northwest side of The Ridge (the Power Line Trail). At mile 0.8, just one or two tenths of a mile from the road, depending on which spur you used, your trail switches left and goes west—don't get confused. So begins a rough, steep climb to the ridgetop. Most folks will need to walk portions of the half-mile climb.

When you gain the spine of Raider Ridge, within one mile from the start, you'll know it. The whole town, campus included, comes into view below, with the La Platas rising dramatically beyond. Here the trail is an expert's delight, dipping and diving along the edge, twisting through and over large rocks. The 1.8-mile long portion on The Ridge is a Durango classic, a must-do. Don't count on it, but the highline trail could be passable year round. The preponderance of rocks (and sun) up there keeps the hellish Durango-area mud partially at bay.

At mile 2.9, take a sharp right onto the Traverse Trail, descending gently. (The Ridge Trail continues straight here and bombs roughly down to Horse Gulch Road.)

Cruising on the ridge is sooo cool.

The southwest-bound Traverse winds pleasantly for a time, then morphs into a rocky widetrack. At mile 3.8, the route joins a widetrack called Rocky Road and descends on a solid, slippery bed of—you guessed it, genius—rock. Instead of following the Rocky Road all the way down to Horse Gulch, extend your trail surfing by turning right onto the Sport Loop, another Iron Horse race section. This track meanders over to the Ridge Trail, the trail you rode up at first, on sharp but smooth ups and downs.

Exit the area via Horse Gulch Road. For an excellent option, instead of descending all the way to Horse Gulch, find the singletrack continuation of the Power Line Trail contouring west above Horse Gulch Road. Power Line becomes a widetrack that takes you around the southern side of The Ridge and beneath the power lines. Keep climbing the Power Line Trail until you find a sweet singletrack dropping steeply through the brush on your left. This favorite trail is called The Shocker, and it does a lot of damage. Enjoy a concentration of tight, steep switches and drop-offs. The trail spills out onto College Drive (6th Street), which takes you right back into town near Horse Gulch Road.

MilesDirections

0.0 START from the bottom of Horse Gulch Road, located at the dead-end of 3rd Street in southeast Durango. Climb up Horse Gulch Road , the fairly steep dirt road in front of you.

0.7 Hang a left onto the Ridge Trail angling up the hillside. *[FYI. The Telegraph Trail takes off to the right here, on the other side of Horse Gulch Road.]*

0.8 Switchback left.

0.9 Stay left as the Sport Loop (E.Z. Loop) joins from the right.

2.9 Take a sharp right onto a descending trail called Traverse Trail. *[Option. If you continue straight, you'll descend sharply to Horse Gulch Road.]*

3.8 Stay left on still-rockier widetrack, the Rocky Road.

4.1 Take a right onto the Sport Loop.

4.4 Take a left at the T-intersection, back onto the Ridge Trail. This is the same intersection you saw at mile 0.9. Descend.

4.6 Stay left, cutting down to Horse Gulch Road and back to the starting point (One branch of the Ridge Trail continues straight here, and becomes the Power Line Trail). *[Option. To end the ride with a memorable singletrack descent, contour around the ridge, then follow the power lines up, on the Power Line Trail. About 0.7 past the Driveway you'll find a killer trail called The Shocker winding down to College Drive.]*

5.3 End the ride at the bottom of Horse Gulch Road.

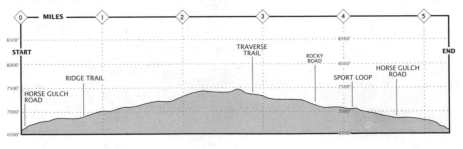

Ride Information

Trail Contacts:
Trails 2000, P.O. Box 3868, Durango, CO 81302, (970) 259-4682 or *www.trails 2000.com. Trails 2000 is a highly effective non-profit that builds and maintains trails around Durango.* **Bureau of Land Management,** Durango, CO (970) 247-4082

Schedule:
Try it any time of year, if you feel lucky. On the Ridge itself, there are almost enough rocks to pave the way over any mud, but Horse Gulch Road has no such protection.

Maps:
USGS maps: Durango East, CO

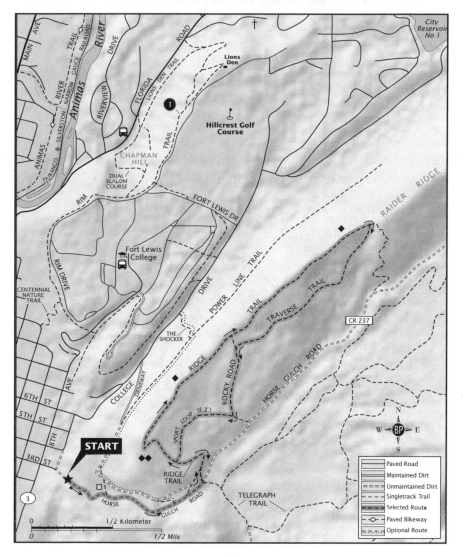

How to Resurrect Your Bike After a Big-Time Mud Attack: A Three-Step Program

Everyone knows that you should not ride on muddy trails. It trashes the singletrack. And in Durango the trails are a great source of civic pride, so riding them when they're wet is like going to Boston and burning down Fenway Park. The villagers will chase you with pitchforks. Even if you don't give a hoot about saving the trails, the Devil-possessed mud around here crushes your spirit, ruins your day, and tortures your equipment. Avoid it at all costs! But mud happens, and despite our best efforts, we could find ourselves hauling an 80-pound, seized-up ball of slop home from the trailhead. (The really unlucky ones never free themselves from the mud pits, and eventually turn to oil.)

Typically, after a harsh mud event cyclists will take their rigs to the car wash and hose them off. This traditional remedy is always problematic. It's sloppy and tends to damage bearings. Anyway, pressurized water is barely powerful enough to rinse Durango's super-sticky death glue from your machine, and you could find yourself dropping about $5 in quarters before giving up.

In the end, there is only one way to save your bike: LET IT DRY. Set your steed in a warm area, not outside or in a cold garage where the mud will stay soft (a kiln would be ideal). About eight hours of drying time should do the trick.

When the mud is good and hard, start chipping it away. With a little muscle, and maybe with the aid of a pedal wrench or some other tough implement, the hardened clay should break off in big, satisfying chunks. Be careful not to damage your paint job.

After the removal process has liberated all the moving parts, it's time to re-lubricate. Start with a solvent like WD-40, freely bathing everything but taking pains not to get any spray on the rims or brake pads (speaking of pads, you may

20

find that your pads need to be replaced after just a few of these episodes). After the solvent bath, start in with a good lubricant. Concentrate on the pivot points of your brakes, and the brake cables. Then hit the pedals, the derailleurs, and the chain, taking time to work each link so they all move freely. Wipe off the excess, and you're ready to rock. Just watch for villagers with pitchforks.

Telegraph–Carbon Junction Loop

Ride Specs

Start: From the bottom of Horse Gulch Road, located near the intersection of East 8th and 3rd Avenue

Length: 10.1-mile loop

Approximate Riding Time: 1–2.5 hours

Technical Difficulty: Moderate to Difficult: challenging singletrack just outside town

Physical Difficulty: Moderate: the climb on Telegraph Hill is kind of tough

Trail Surface: 70% singletrack, 7% 4WD road, and 23% paved road

Lay of the Land: Semi-arid meadows and piñon-juniper-ponderosa pine woodland

Elevation Gain: 1,961 feet

Land Status: BLM and La Plata County lands

Other Trail Users: Hikers and joggers—often with dogs

Getting There

In Durango: This ride starts at Horse Gulch Road, which can be found at the dead end of 3rd Street in southeast Durango. One good way to get there is to head east from Main Avenue (U.S. 550/U.S. 160) on College Drive (6th Street) to East 8th Avenue. Take a right on East 8th to 3rd Street, then a left on 3rd Street. The street dead-ends in one block, and there you will find the dirt Horse Gulch Road continuing east. Park here, if possible, or along one of the streets nearby. Better still, ride to the trailhead from anywhere in town.

Public Transportation: Take the Durango Lift's FLC south bus, which stops at the corner of 8th Avenue at 3rd Street, Monday to Saturday, at four minutes past the hour until 6:04 P.M. (5:04 P.M. on Saturdays).

A ll around Durango, there are trails. Steep trails, flat trails, wide trails, and skinny trails. Rocky and smooth, fast and slow. A vast array of singletracks to make your head and your legs spin. This is especially true on the east side of town, where there are so many trails snaking around that even the most fanatical riders are forced, for reasons of practicality, to ignore or forget about some of the coolest stuff—there's just too much to deal with. Obscure tracks encircle the campus of Fort Lewis College and reach onto the adventurous Raider Ridge and into the area of Telegraph Hill, culminating in a chaotic web of singletrack madness that has been known to swallow trail lovers for weeks at a time. Bleached skeletons scattered trailside, hanging with flaps of Lycra and busted Briko sunglasses, are sad reminders that some riders never make it out.

Manic trail builders have apparently been unloading their frustrations on these modest ridges, valleys, and mesas. The origin of new trails remains a mystery, although a few locals have reported seeing a naked, bearded figure with a pickaxe bounding like a mule deer between the ridges at dusk, giggling maniacally. Actually, we have Trails 2000 to thank for much of the trail work around Telegraph. Trails 2000 is a non-profit group that builds and maintains prime singletracks—and lots of 'em—in the Durango area. Help to keep the ball rolling by donating your time or money. (See *Ride Information*.)

Rather than just say *Hey, there are a ton of trails in this zone—go check 'em out!*, I have detailed a few routes that I hope will help you make some sense of the labyrinth and point you in the direction of the best stuff. This particular loop links a few prime trails to span the Telegraph Hill area, north to south, and is one of the longer natural routes available south of Horse Gulch Road. You could manufacture a longer—much longer—ride by linking all sorts of connectors, but this loop, when looking at the map, just seems to make sense. It's a beauty.

Horse Gulch Road gives the easiest access for this and many other rides in southeast Durango. The moderately rutted road is extremely popular with cyclists, runners, and happy dogs. You may also see some utility trucks up here. Mud on Horse Gulch is a terrible omen—*turn back while you still can!* The mud around here is an evil radioactive death-pudding that was conjured by serial killer clowns in the black pits below the dark sub-levels of Hell. The slippery, sticky atomic slop makes trails and roads impassable after rain and during periods of snowmelt. Even pushing your bike through it for a few seconds will cause the wheels to seize. You and your bike have no answer for this stuff.

Find Telegraph Trail about 0.7 mile up Horse Gulch Road, on the right—it should be obvious. (Don't be confused by the trails shooting off to the left of Horse Gulch Road. They lead north to Raider Ridge, which, by the way, is highly recommended if you enjoy this Telegraph-Carbon Junction ride.) The Telegraph Trail is the main artery south of Horse Gulch. When dry, Telegraph is generally smooth, but there are the occasional bumpy sections where the clay has hardened to the consistency of concrete, preserving all the footprints and tire tracks created during the mud phase. Also expect it to be dusty, slippery, and fast, with all kinds of tight turns. Fast and twisty are the dominant themes of most of the trails in the Telegraph area, but there are plenty of rough rock problems as well. Painful injuries could result if you try to ride faster than your abilities allow. For evidence of this phenomenon, check out the bloody, bruised, beaten-down bodies crossing the finish line at the Iron Horse, the famous mountain bike race which uses many of these trails. (In fact, the Iron Horse

Mountain Bike Classic is much more than a mountain bike race. An annual Memorial Day weekend tradition in Durango, the Iron Horse event also includes a prestigious Durango-Silverton road race, dual slalom, trials—you name it. The races tend to attract some of the world's top cyclists.)

Stay right on Telegraph as it twists across The Meadow (there are many connectors shooting to the left). Into the shadow of Telegraph Hill, you will notice the trail zigzagging somewhat ominously up the hillside next to a line of old telegraph poles. This section is a bit of a grunt but gains the saddle in a no-nonsense hurry. At the top, the Anasazi Descent cuts back down to the meadow, creating a hair-raising bailout possibility. Still rolling along the saddle, you'll also notice Crites Connect Trail headed down to the right. This optional shortcut will chop significant mileage off the loop and rejoin the route at mile 5.4.

The Telegraph Trail drops steeply off the back of Telegraph Hill and ends at a T-intersection with the Sidewinder Trail. Sidewinder is a quick, wide cruiser that won't contribute much in the way of technical challenges, though there may be some thrills derived from excessive speed.

MilesDirections

0.0 START from the bottom of Horse Gulch Road, located at the dead-end of 3rd Street in southeast Durango. Climb up a fairly steep dirt (shale) road.

0.7 Hang a right onto the obvious and well-signed Telegraph Trail. Thanks to the Trails 2000 organization, most of the trails in this area are well marked (and nicely maintained).

0.8 Stay right continuing on Telegraph Trail.

1.2 Stay right.

1.4 Stay right.

1.5 Stay right.

2.6 Stay right again! *[Option. You could take a left here, sacrificing the rest of the loop for a few minutes of ecstasy on the Anasazi Descent.]*

2.8 Pass the intersection with the Crites Connect Trail. *[Option. Crites is a fast twister short-cutting down to mile 5.4.]*

3.3 Turn right at the T-intersection with the Sidewinder Trail.

4.3 Stay right at the intersection with the Grandview Ridge Trail.

5.4 Veer left onto the Carbon Junction Trail. *[FYI. Crites Connect rejoins the trail here.]*

7.7 The singletrack ends, spilling out at an informal trailhead on CO 3. Turn right onto the highway, which leads directly back to town and becomes East 8th.

10.0 After passing the Sonic, turn right onto 3rd Street.

10.1 At the dead end of 3rd Street, Horse Gulch Road begins and this ride ends—unless you want to do it again.

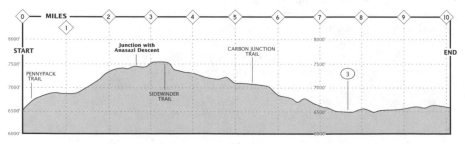

At mile 5.4 the Sidewinder Trail joins the Carbon Junction Trail, and the *real* fun begins. Often overlooked, Carbon Junction is a smooth twister and one of the best singletrack descents in the area. The trail winds directly past a strip-mining operation and eventually switches down to CO Route 3, spilling out at mile 7.7. Cruise the highway back to the starting point at Horse Gulch Road.

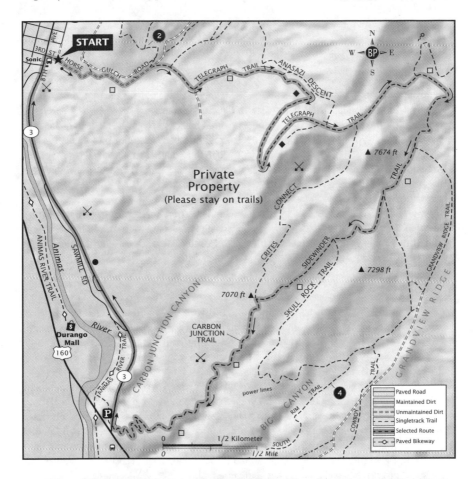

Ride Information

📞 Trail Contacts:

Trails 2000, P.O. Box 3868, Durango, CO 81302, (970) 259–4682 or *www.trails 2000.com. Trails 2000 is a highly effective non-profit that builds and maintains trails around Durango.* **Bureau of Land Management,** Durango, CO (970) 247-4082

🕐 Schedule:

May through October, approximately, due to mud problems

🅽 Maps:

USGS maps: Durango East, CO; Loma Linda, CO

Sale Barn–South Rim–Cowboy Loop

Ride Specs

Start: From the new Sale Barn trailhead south of town
Length: 7.0-mile loop
Approximate Riding Time: 1–2.5 hours
Technical Difficulty: Moderate: smooth singletrack, lots of turns
Physical Difficulty: Moderate: built for speed; some climbs
Trail Surface: 100% singletrack
Lay of the Land: Scrub oak, cactus, piñon, juniper, and ponderosa pine in the vicinity of Grandview Ridge south of town
Elevation Gain: 866 feet
Land Status: County and BLM lands
Other Trail Users: Hikers (often with dogs) and equestrians

Getting There

From Durango: Drive south on Main Avenue (U.S. 550/U.S. 160) for a few miles to Dominguez Drive, and take a left—there's a traffic light there. At a T-intersection one block from the highway, take a right onto a frontage road and drive south. Just before the frontage road reaches U.S. 550/160, turn left onto a dirt road that leads immediately to an informal parking area. This is the new Sale Barn trailhead.

Public Transportation: Take the Durango Lift's FLC South bus to Wal-Mart. Now on your bike, turn left at Dominguez Drive and cross U.S. 550.

T he Sale Barn and South Rim trails are both brand new strips of smooth singletrack southeast of Durango, built in the summer of 2000 by volunteers working with the Trails 2000 organization. Already these excellent tracks are showing signs of becoming local favorites.

This loop uses both trails in their entirety (and also some of the Cowboy Trail, another smooth, curvy strip of dirt in the Grandview Ridge area). Start the ride from the new Sale Barn trailhead off of U.S. Route 160, which at present is one of the ugliest and least obvious trailheads you're likely to see, with all kinds of dead dirt and industrial relics camouflaging the singletrack. If not for the small sign placed there by Trails 2000, it would be very difficult to recognize the start of this infant trail—a classic blessing in disguise.

The Sale Barn Trail is the kind of singletrack you'd like to keep secret, if that were somehow possible. No such luck: now it's in the guidebook.

Sale Barn gains quick altitude from road-level, switching nicely up a piñon-juniper slope and then angling into a brushy scrub oak cove. The kind, loving hand of the trail-builders is on clear display here. The track twists around, finds the easy route, and gently levitates through a bevy of switchback. The shale surface is cleared of rocks and groomed. Sloppy edges are reinforced with rock walls. The result is a thoroughly rideable, magic carpet climb. There is no doubt this one is completely accessible to intermediates. If anything, Sale Barn (along with the South Rim) is *too* tame and easy. The Trails 2000 army is heroic in its painstaking efforts, and I love the idea of longer trails with gentler grades, but personally I'd like to see more challeng-

ing, rocky sections interspersed with the fast and smooth. Rocks, by the way, have the added benefit of not being mud.

Sale Barn continues to the right at mile 1.4, but turn *left* here onto the South Rim Trail—you'll be coming back down that section of Sale Barn later on. South Rim, not to be confused with the Rim Trail that circles Fort Lewis College, is another brand-spankin' new ribbon that continues where Sale Barn leaves off, on the quick and smooth tip, except South Rim is even faster, smoother, and twistier. (The South Rim Trail is also being called Grandview Rim.) This is a truly fun trail, with countless round turns near the mesa's edge. This trail descends gradually at first, then makes up most of the altitude loss by the time it reaches its intersection with the Cowboy Trail. A genuine roller. In either direction, South Rim is a delight, and the trail-builders should be commended for creating an instant classic.

At mile 4.2, South Rim intersects with the Cowboy Trail. Turn right onto Cowboy and grind up a steep corkscrew section with some delicious, tight switchbacks. Cowboy tops out soon, then flirts with and crosses the dirt road on top of Grandview Ridge—very smooth and curvy. Around mile 5.1, a sharp right turn puts you back on the Sale Barn Trail, and the loop is completed after a quick twist through an open meadow. Turn left at the mile 5.6 intersection—this is the same intersection you saw at mile 1.4—and cruise back down Sale Barn to the trailhead. All singletrack, all the time.

Both Sale Barn and South Rim (along with the Cowboy) are technically part of the Telegraph Trail System. To many mountain biking veterans, the term *trail system* conjures unpleasant images of canned singletracks that are too convenient, too wide, and too close to civilization—not to mention, most of the trails don't really *go* anywhere, instead they just twist around at the whim of the builder. Telegraph is afflicted with just a hint of this disease, but as trail systems go, it's a great one. The construction of these new trails has greatly improved this already excellent, extensive network.

Getting lost, confused, turned around, and bedazzled by the quantity of trails is a way of life in a web like this. Options abound. Try turning left onto the Cowboy Trail from South Rim, instead of right, and climb to the Sidewinder Trail. Sidewinder connects with the Telegraph Trail, which could be looped up-and-over the "Suicide" climb into the vast web of singletracks north of Telegraph Hill.

Or drop *down* Sidewinder to the Carbon Junction Trail, descend—in grand style—to road-level, and pop out north of the new Sale Barn trailhead. It's hard to go wrong (unless the clay is wet, in which case you will die a mastodon's death in the tar pits). Crites Connect, the Anasazi Descent, and Skull Rock are all well within reach. Customize your ride according to ability and mood.

Ride Information

🕻 Trail Contacts:
Trails 2000, Durango, (970) 259–4682 or *www.trails2000.com. Trails 2000 is a highly effective non-profit that builds and maintains trails around Durango.* **Bureau of Land Management,** Durango, CO (970) 247–4082

🕘 Schedule:
May through October, due to weather

Ⓝ Maps:
USGS maps: Durango East, CO; Loma Linda, CO

MilesDirections

0.0 START riding south up a doubletrack from the new Sale Barn Trail trailhead. About a half block up this doubletrack, take a left onto the brand-new Sale Barn singletrack and begin a winding, gradual climb.

1.4 Take a left onto the South Rim Trail, also called the Grandview Rim Trail. Take a good look at this intersection—you will see it again at mile 5.6.

3.1 Pass the intersection with an inviting singletrack that leads to a gas well.

3.9 Pass the well-camouflaged intersection with the Skull Rock Trail on the left.

4.2 Take a sharp right at a major intersection, onto the Cowboy Trail. Begin a tough, steep, winding climb.

4.4 The trail comes very close to the road on Grandview Ridge—stay right on singletrack.

4.5 Turn right onto the road. About a half block down the road, turn left onto the singletrack again.

4.9 Pass the intersection with an un-mapped half-trail.

5.1 Curl to the right, onto the Sale Barn Trail. *[FYI. The Cowboy continues briefly from here, to a promontory.]*

5.5 Cross a dirt road/doubletrack.

5.6 Turn left at the intersection with the South Rim Trail. You were here at mile 1.4.

7.0 Drop back in on the Sale Barn trailhead.

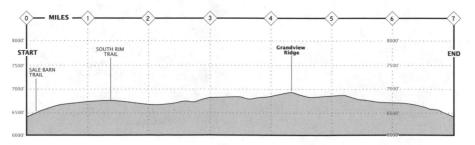

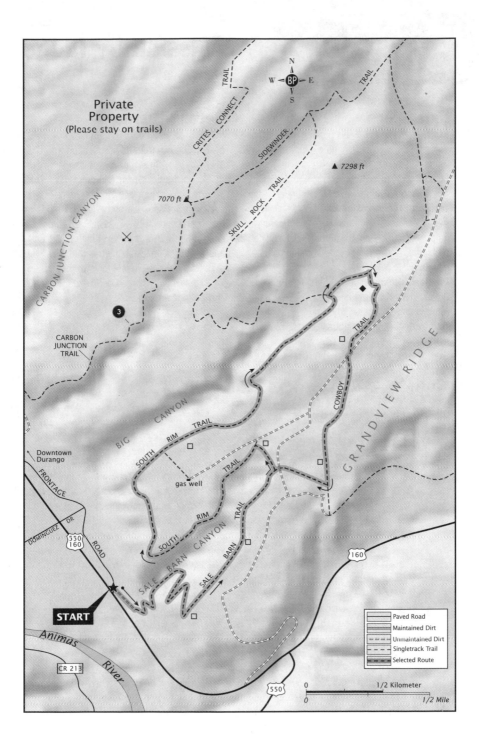

N W BP E S

Private
Property
(Please stay on trails)

▲ 7298 ft

CRITES CONNECT TRAIL

SIDEWINDER

7070 ft ▲

SKULL ROCK TRAIL

TRAIL

CARBON JUNCTION CANYON

❸

CARBON
JUNCTION
TRAIL

BIG CANYON

SOUTH RIM TRAIL

gas well

SOUTH RIM TRAIL

COWBOY TRAIL

GRANDVIEW RIDGE

Downtown
Durango

FRONTAGE

DR

DOMINGUEZ

550
160

ROAD

SALE BARN CANYON

SALE BARN TRAIL

SALE BARN TRAIL

160

550

★

START

Animus River

CR 213

550

	Paved Road
	Maintained Dirt
	Unmaintained Dirt
	Singletrack Trail
	Selected Route

0   1/2 Kilometer
0   1/2 Mile

5

Missionary Ridge

Ride Specs

Start: From the small dirt parking area at the end of FS 71, where a gate blocks further motorized travel

Length: 16.4-mile out-and-back

Approximate Riding Time: 2.5–5 hours

Technical Difficulty: Moderate to Difficult: a moderately rocky climb via jeep road leads to quick singletrack laced with difficult technical problems, and a bit of steep walking in the middle

Physical Difficulty: Moderate to Difficult: modest length saves this ride from a difficult rating, but be prepared to sweat

Trail Surface: 80% singletrack and 20% 4WD road

Lay of the Land: Aspen-themed ridge-top northeast of Durango

Elevation Gain: 3,890 feet

Land Status: National forest

Other Trail Users: Hikers and equestrians

Getting There

In Durango: Head north on Main Avenue (U.S. 550/U.S. 160) from its intersection with U.S. 160. At 15th Street, turn right and drive two blocks to the three-point intersection of 15th Street, 3rd Avenue, and Florida Road. Take a left onto Florida Road and drive 6.3 miles to the intersection with FS 71 (CR 249), on the left. Turn left onto the gravel FS 71 (CR 249) and climb 2.8 miles through a confusing web of residential roads—just look for the little FS 71 signs—until the road dead-ends at a gate and parking area.

This out-and-back mini-adventure opens with a two-mile grunt up moderately chunky jeep road. The initial climb hurts quite a bit less when you consider it's the quickest way to access the Missionary Ridge Trail, a loveable but demanding stretch of rustic singletrack waiting quietly for you on top of the ridge.

As the climbing jeep road approaches the ridgeline, it forks at a telephone pole. Go left at the fork and head up into the aspens. About 30 or so yards past the treeline, poke around for the start of the singletrack on your right. (Continuing on this road would take you to the top of the technical Haflin Canyon descent.) The Missionary Ridge singletrack is unmarked and fades out just before its intersection with the jeep road, but you can find it without too much trouble, and once you locate the trail it will be nearly impossible to lose.

Missionary Ridge is a joyous celebration of singletrack. The trail dips and dives along the bumpy ridgetop, spilling over the edges, carving through meadows and lush aspen groves. Breaking up the fast, smooth sections are water bars, rock gardens, a handful of mudbogs and fallen trees, and a few tight switchbacks, one of which is very difficult and claims its share of victims. Also, there are lots of moderate climbs that need to be reckoned with, in both directions all along the ridge. This isn't really a climber's trail, but you need to be in shape to stylishly conquer the waves. After about

3.5 miles of tight singletrack, there is a technical segment that includes a steep walk-down and some serious off-camber ledges.

At around mile 7.6, the trail levels and straightens as it joins an old roadbed. Check out the cross-valley views of the La Platas and Kennebec Pass as you speed along to the junction with the Stevens Creek Trail at mile 8.2. Turn around here for an action-packed 16.4 total miles (the route described below), or try one of the many options available from this junction. You could continue on the ridge as far as Lime Mesa, with epic possibilities. The singletrack Stevens Creek Trail drops off the ridge and meanders all the way down to the floor of the Animas Valley, with some excellent sections along the way. Or, you could use one of the trails plummeting from Missionary's southeastern flank (First Fork Trail or Red Creek Trail) as part of a cool loop—note that both these singletracks are far better suited for descending.

Ride Information

🕐 Trail Contacts:
San Juan National Forest, Supervisor's Office, Durango, CO (970) 247–4874

🕐 Schedule:
Late May through mid October, due to weather and snowmelt

Ⓝ Maps:
USGS maps: Durango East, CO; and Hermosa, CO • **USFS maps:** *San Juan National Forest Map*

MilesDirections

0.0 START from the parking area at the end of FS 71. Head up the hill, past the gate.

2.1 In a clearing, the road forks at a telephone pole. Take the left fork.

2.2 Enter the aspen trees. About 30 yards beyond the treeline, find the subtle and faded start of the Missionary Ridge Trail on the right. Then, ride that sucker. *[FYI. The doubletrack continues to a high point on the ridge, where a radio tower stands over the singletrack continuation of the Missionary Ridge Trail, and the legendary Haflin Canyon descent.]*

3.6 Pass the intersection with the First Fork Trail on the right.

5.6 Begin a tough technical section, with some steep walking and off-camber madness.

6.7 Pass the intersection with the Red Creek Trail dropping off the ridge on your right.

7.6 Pass the intersection with an overgrown jeep road coming in from above. Beware: On

the return trip, this road can look pretty inviting and may masquerade as the correct route.

8.2 Turn around at the intersection with the Stevens Creek Trail. *[Options. The Stevens Creek Trail descends for about eight miles to the Animas Valley, pops out about 10 miles north of Durango. The Missionary Ridge Trail continues to Lime Mesa.]*

14.1 Arrive back at the jeep road, take a left. *[Option. It's not too late to break away from the group and head to the nearby Haflin Canyon descent, which may be calling your name at this point. The start of the descent is located near the top of this jeep road –just take a right instead of a left here. At the radio tower clearing, look for the little singletrack angling to the left. A few blocks down this trail, you'll find the beginning of the Haflin Canyon Trail.]* The final descent on the road is probably the most dangerous part of the ride.

16.4 Arrive back at the parking area, with a slightly creaky headset.

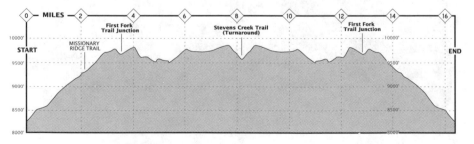

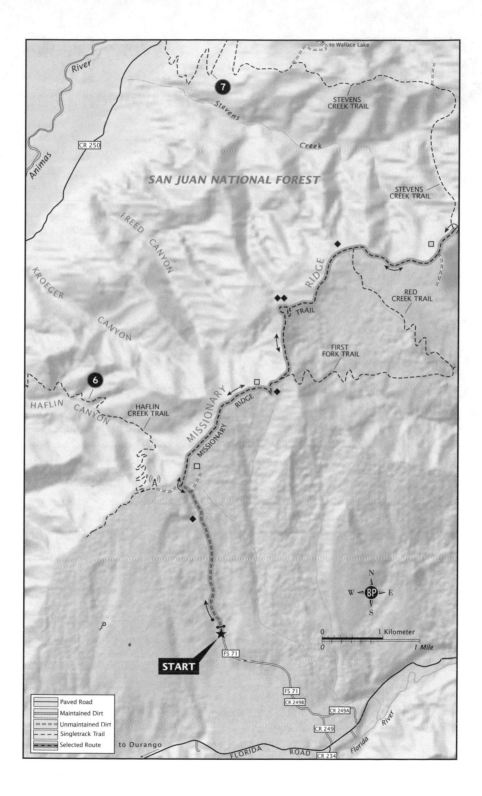

River

to Wallace Lake

⑦

Stevens

STEVENS
CREEK TRAIL

CR 250

Creek

STEVENS
CREEK TRAIL

Animas

SAN JUAN NATIONAL FOREST

FREED CANYON

RIDGE

RED
CREEK TRAIL

KROEGER CANYON

TRAIL

FIRST
FORK TRAIL

⑥

MISSIONARY

HAFLIN CANYON

HAFLIN
CREEK TRAIL

RIDGE

MISSIONARY

(A)

N
W   BP   E
S

START

FS 71

0   1 Kilometer
0   1 Mile

Paved Road
Maintained Dirt
Unmaintained Dirt
Singletrack Trail
Selected Route

FS 71
CR 249B
CR 249A
CR 249

to Durango

FLORIDA   ROAD
CR 234

Florida
River

Stevens Creek– Missionary Ridge– Haflin Canyon Loop

Ride Specs

Start: From the Haflin Creek Trail parking area

Length: 22.8-mile loop

Approximate Riding Time: 3.5–5.5 hours

Technical Difficulty: Difficult: action-packed singletrack and a legendary descent

Physical Difficulty: Difficult: opens with an eight-mile climb

Trail Surface: 75% singletrack, 10% doubletrack, and 15% paved road

Lay of the Land: A dry, scrub oak hillside; a lush, ridgetop forest; and finally a steep, red-walled canyon

Elevation Gain: 6,055 feet

Land Status: National forest

Other Trail Users: Hikers and equestrians

Getting There

In Durango: Drive (or ride) west on 32nd Street, from its intersection with Main Avenue (U.S. 550/U.S. 160), for 1.3 miles to a T-intersection with CR 251. Take a left and drive for 5.5 miles. CR 251 becomes CR 250. Park at the Haflin Creek Trail trailhead, which is located on the right (east) side of the road and marked with a small sign.

C onfident, aggressive riders who want to experience all the best that Durango has to offer should not miss this incredible loop into the rugged hills just northeast of town. This route, connecting three awesome singletracks, begins with a long, punishing climb onto Missionary Ridge, then dances along the beautiful ridge for six miles before diving into Haflin Canyon. The Haflin Creek Trail is one of the most combative trails you will ever ride, and one of the most memorable.

Since parking is generally scarce at the Stevens Creek trailhead, I suggest beginning this ride from the Haflin Creek trailhead, which lies four miles south, along the same road. Of course, given this route's close proximity to Durango, it would be easy to cycle out of town to the trailhead, dispensing with gas-guzzlers entirely. This would add about 13 miles of paved road to the total mileage. From the Haflin Creek trailhead—however you get there—cruise north on the rolling pavement of County Road 250 for four miles, then look for Stevens Creek Trail singletrack (unmarked) rising from the road on the right, next to a wooden fence. The trailhead can be hard to locate. If you arrive at the intersection with the dirt Missionary Ridge Road, you've gone about a half mile too far.

The Stevens Creek Trail is baby-smooth as it twists up into ponderosa pine and scrub oak, but it requires strenuous effort, as the incline approaches the threshold of unrideability several times. This section could have you wishing for a lesser gear. A 23x32 would be about right. As the smooth singletrack winds higher, becoming rockier as it goes, ignore the false trails, game trails, and unauthorized connectors that tend to shoot off at every switchback. Stay on the main vein.

Use this first challenging section as a barometer to measure your willingness and ability to complete the remainder of this loop, which continues to climb on and off for about 15 miles before becoming extremely technical. If you're struggling mightily down here, within a few miles from the road, then the chances that you'll be able to complete the entire loop safely are slim to none—ride for a while and then turn around, before it's too late, because there are no easy bailouts available from the ridge. If you're conquering the trail, congratulations. Keep on keepin' on.

After a few miles of heavy climbing on singletrack, the Stevens Creek Trail joins an old roadbed and climbs relatively easily for about two and a half miles on a nice mix of rocky doubletrack, widetrack, and singletrack. Cattle and horse damage is an occasional hassle along this stretch; any hoofprints in the spring mud will harden like concrete under a hot sun, giving the trail a painful, cobblestone-like texture. Also, keep an eye out for the tell-tales signs of heavy lion activity in this area: scat, tracks, and the bones of mule deer (*see "A Few Words on Pumas" on page 38*).

An open meadow on Missionary Ridge.

Slowly but surely, you approach the base of Missionary Ridge, its heavily forested spine in plain sight across the valley. Looming, you might say. Eventually you'll be up there, but first you'll have to conquer the lower slopes of the ridge itself. As the Stevens Trail curls to the south, expect some singletrack glides through the aspens, and a few rocky, straight-up grunts where walking may be required.

MilesDirections

0.0 START riding north up CR 250 from the Haflin Creek trailhead. Traffic is usually light, but CR 250 has its share of blind curves and speeding motorists.

4.0 Turn right onto the Stevens Creek Trail and begin a steep climb. The trail has been unsigned and may be hard to locate—look for the wooden fence that marks the trail. If you arrive at the intersection with the dirt Missionary Ridge Road, you've gone about a half mile too far.

6.5 Pass the intersection with the Stevens Connector on the left. Continue straight on Steven's Creek Trail. *[Option. The Connector cruises over to Missionary Ridge Road and provides a possible bailout—Missionary Ridge Road descends immediately to CR 250 north of the Stevens Creek trailhead.]*

8.7 Stay right at the intersection with the Wallace Lake Trail.

11.4 The Stevens Creek Trail climbs next to a livestock fence, then passes a doubletrack descending on the left.

11.9 Finally, you reach the Missionary Ridge Trail. Take a right.

12.5 Veer right, staying on singletrack, as a doubletrack shoots off to the left.

14.3 This is the steepest, most technical portion on the ridge.

16.5 Pass an intersection with the First Fork Trail leading off to the left.

17.8 The Missionary Ridge Trail spills out onto a 4WD road. Stay right, continuing uphill. *[Option. A left turn here leads down the backside of the ridge to FS 71, then to the paved Florida Road and ultimately back to Durango. This is a possible emergency alternative to the upcoming descent, for those with broken equipment or egos.]*

18.1 As the road arrives at the base of a serious-looking radio tower, rejoin the singletrack descending to the left. This is still the Missionary Ridge Trail.

18.6 Turn right onto the Haflin Creek Trail and hold on to your socks.

22.8 Arrive at the Haflin Creek trailhead, back on solid ground.

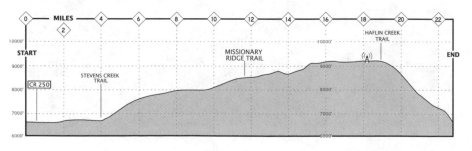

The Missionary Ridge Trail is a strip of dirt with a lot of character. This trail rider's delight starts off easy, fast, and straight on an overgrown roadbed, then antes up with semi-technical descending, some violent ups and downs, and interesting root and rock combos sprinkled along a fairly smooth surface. Expect a little of everything along this six-mile stretch of bumpy ridgeline, including several rocky walk-ups. (Unfortunately, you will probably be too tuckered out from the long clime to properly dominate the Missionary Ridge Trail. Check out Ride 5, which attacks the ridge from the southeast on a mere two-mile climb, leaving you much fresher for ridge-top

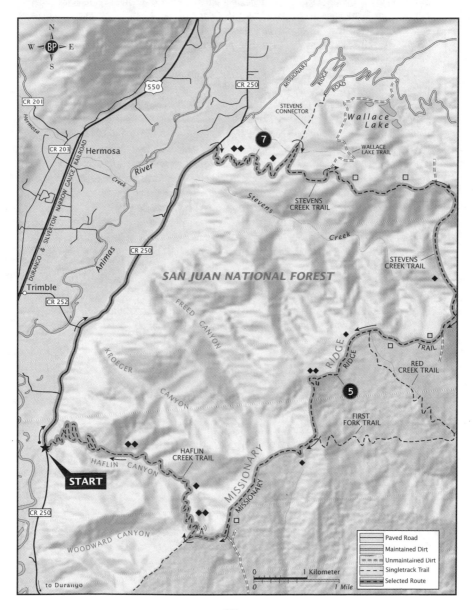

A Few Words on Pumas

As an off-road cyclist puttering around the foothills near Durango, it may trouble you to learn that these hills are crawling with mountain lions. But don't you worry your pretty little head. These big cats—pumas, as I like to call them—are at least as focused on avoiding human contact as they are concerned with tackling big game, mating, or anything else. Staying away from us has become a prime directive of cougar culture.

Even in areas where the signs of the puma lifestyle are ubiquitous and in plain sight, your chances of laying eyes on the actual beast are incredibly slim. You see fresh tracks in the mud, scat right out in the middle of the trail. On the outskirts of town, pets vanish under suspicious circumstances. But the lions remain unseen. This leads to an uneasy Puma Awareness: You can't see 'em, but you know they're out there, and sometimes you can feel 'em watching you.

It's no wonder that pumas avoid humans like the plague. Ever since we began filling the West with livestock, big cats and other predators have been regarded as a great enemy of commerce. It's true that pumas have enjoyed the easy opportunity provided by the lazy crowds of grazing horses, sheep, and cattle that were placed in their midst. As a result, our government promoted the destruction of the species. Between 1929 and 1965, the Colorado Division of Wildlife actually shelled out fifty bucks for each lion hunted, trapped, or poisoned. No comprehensive numbers were recorded, but based on the scant evidence at hand, it would be a conservative estimate to say this program accounted for a few thousand puma kills. Even with all the institutionalized killing and private hunts (often using packs of dogs to tree the lion), the too-smart pumas thrive today on the area's burgeoning deer population.

Pumas are very efficient killers of big game. About once each week, the average adult puma (about six feet long, 140 pounds) will ambush a suitably juicy-looking deer, typically leaping onto the prey's back from above and delivering a single fatal chomp to the neck. This is not the sustained, speedy chase of the cheetah, as seen on Mutual of Omaha's Wild Kingdom. With a body built for explosive power rather than sustained speed, the puma's modus operandi is close, quick combat. After the deed is done, the mountain lion drags its prey to a nice spot and hides it, then returns over the next week to feed on the aromatic corpse.

Pumas have been known to jump the occasional jogger, probably due to a jogger's tendency to mimic the prey behavior of a sick doe. Mountain bikers, with their strange machines, have been pretty much left alone by the lions. There is one confirmed attack by a puma on a cyclist, which occurred in California about ten years ago. Beyond that, I have heard only a few rumors. There is a Colorado man who claims that a puma jumped on his back momentarily while he was riding at White Ranch, a popular spot on the Front Range, but I don't think I believe him.

If you do happen to see a puma in the wild, consider yourself lucky to be in the presence of such greatness. Then, back away slowly. Do not run daintily away like a doe or jogger. Raise your arms over your head to make yourself look large and in charge. If a puma has in fact jumped on your back, there's not much advice I can give except scream like a little girl.

On Puma Tracks

Don't be surprised if you notice some puma tracks out on the trail. The cat tracks can be easily distinguished from the similar but far more common canine tracks: just remember that puma tracks almost never show claw marks, while those of dogs and coyotes do. Also, notice the large pad of the cat track, which is three-lobed and has a distinctive M-shape.

surfing.) The ridge trail provides intense bird's-eye views of the Animas Valley before spilling out onto a 4WD road at mile 17.8.

As fun as they were, the Stevens Creek and Missionary Ridge trails will be forgotten soon after you drop in on the incredible Haflin descent. Haflin Creek Trail is the most action-packed trail in the area, and probably the most dangerous as well. Elsewhere in this guide, I discuss the hazardous descents on Dutch Creek (see Ride 22) and the sleeping dragon section of Colorado Trail below Gudy's Rest (see Ride 9), but Haflin is the reigning undertaker of all Durango singletracks. Years ago, when Durango was the undisputed mountain bike capital of the universe, few riders attempted Haflin Canyon. And if they did, they were so beaten up by it that they seldom went back for seconds. The cliff-climbing trail was the exclusive domain of adventurous day hikers.

Today, however, young riders at the vanguard of their sport use Haflin as a rite of passage, and it's not unusual to find a sizable group of precocious teenagers gathered at the bottom, discussing the spills and chills of the previous four miles. It's a little alarming to see what the kids are riding these days.

The Haflin descent can be divided into three parts. The first is probably the toughest and most dangerous: a very steep and unforgiving switchbacked drop through scrub oak and ponderosa pine. The trail here seems to be composed entirely of loose, rolling, babyhead rocks. If you survive that, the next section is somewhat easier and very enjoyable, tucked into the dark of the canyon, a roller coaster with tight turns, numerous sharp dips and dives, and a gauntlet of technical challenges. Gradually the slope of the canyon falls away on your left and the trail becomes more exposed, leading to the third and most famous section of the descent. Here the red-colored trail clings, decidedly off-camber, to what could almost be called a cliff, with a load of hardcore steps and ledges along the way. This section is pretty much rideable until your inner alarm goes off, that voice in your head that says *Whoa! You are going to fall a thousand feet and land on some rocks!* Remember, on off-camber sections like these, leaning into the hill will only make things worse; instead, keep both feet on the pedals, your ass off the seat slightly, and your eyes up the trail. Relax.

Easier said than done.

Ride Information

🖋 Trail Contacts:
San Juan National Forest, Supervisor's Office, Durango, CO (970) 247–4874

🕐 Schedule:
Late May through October, due to weather

📍 Maps:
USGS maps: Durango East, CO; and Hermosa, CO • **USFS maps:** *San Juan National Forest Map*

Stevens Creek Mini-Loop

Ride Specs

Start: From the bottom of Missionary Ridge Road

Length: 7.2-mile loop

Approximate Riding Time: 45 minutes–1.5 hours

Technical Difficulty: Moderate to Difficult: singletrack descent with rocks and steeps

Physical Difficulty: Moderate: short, with one decent-sized climb

Trail Surface: 50% dirt road, 45% singletrack, and 5% paved road

Lay of the Land: A steep scrub oak-ponderosa pine hillside on the east side of the Animas River Valley

Elevation Gain: 1,911 feet

Land Status: National forest

Other Trail Users: Motorists (on Missionary Ridge Road) and hikers and equestrians (on the singletrack)

Getting There

From Durango: Drive eight miles north out of Durango on U.S. 550, then turn right (east) onto CR 252, which is located across from the Trimble Hot Springs, and drive for one mile until the road runs into a T-intersection. Take a left at the T-intersection, onto CR 250, and drive for about three miles until the overtly signed, graded dirt Missionary Ridge Road forks off to the right. Park at the beginning of Missionary Ridge Road.

Sadly, even with hundreds of billions of miles of prime dirt snaking away from your back door, there are days when all you have time for is a short ride. An hour, maybe two, then it's back to the mundane responsibilities of everyday life—so I've been told anyway. That's where the Stevens Creek Mini Loop comes in. Fit this little loop into your after-dinner plans, and it will put a smile on your face before the sun has a chance to set behind the La Plata foothills.

This loop is short, but it's not necessarily easy. The ride begins with nearly four miles of steady climbing on Missionary Ridge Road. This climb will seem somewhat relentless to some, but it is in no way technical. The extremely wide and smooth road ascends the eastern wall of the Animas Valley, and the cross-valley northwesterly views, as well as the look straight down into the valley floor, are pretty excellent, especially as the sun sets.

At mile 3.8, at an elbow in the road, find an obvious turn onto an apparent 4WD road. The non-road is blocked immediately by large rocks, beyond which a nice singletrack heads off into the woods. (With a few spaces to park, this is another possible starting point for this loop; however, I prefer to start with the climb, rather than end with it.) This workmanlike trail—a legal and authorized connector—contours across

Missionary Ridge Road, wide and smooth.

the hillside, gently gaining altitude. After just 0.6 mile, the trail ends at its intersection with the Stevens Creek Trail.

The segment of the Stevens Creek Trail used by this loop is entirely downhill. Confident riders who are tuned in to the force of gravity, and other uncompromising mountain spirits, will shine on this quick, challenging descent; timid, inexperienced downhillers will not. The top of this descent is scattered with all kinds of loose, tire-tossing rocks. The incline here is extremely mellow but soon shows signs of dropping more seriously. There are a few spots where you may need to schlep your rig over some big, chunky obstacles.

As the trail drops over the edge into steep corkscrew turns, the rockiness steadily fades away. The last half mile of twisty, gray shale is free of obstruction, a thrilling, stomach-in-your-throat dive to the road. Like a hawk, you make a swift, silent attack on the trailhead.

If this short but sweet loop has left you somewhat unsatisfied, there is an easy solution. Do it again.

Ride Information

Trail Contacts:
San Juan National Forest, Supervisor's Office, Durango, CO (970) 247–4874

Schedule:
June through October, due to weather

Maps:
USGS maps: Durango East, CO; and Hermosa, CO • USFS maps: San Juan National Forest Map

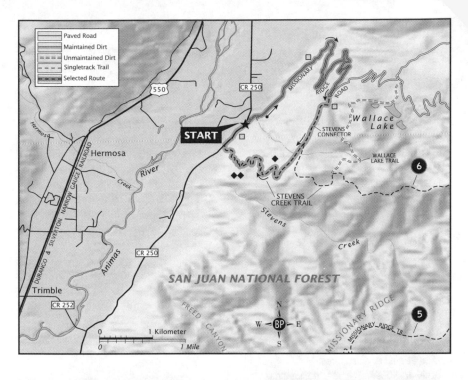

MilesDirections

0.0 START riding north up the dirt Missionary Ridge Road.

3.8 At a left-turning switchback, turn right off of Missionary Ridge Road onto what looks like a Forest Service road. The "road," in fact, narrows into a trail after about 15 yards, and a line of boulders halts motor travel. This is the trailhead for the Stevens Connector. *[Option. This is a possible start point, but keep in mind that instead of starting with a climb, you'd end with one.]*

4.4 Turn right onto the Stevens Creek Trail, headed slightly downhill. The trail gets steeper and smoother as it descends.

6.8 Take a right onto the paved CR 250.

7.2 Arrive back at the starting point.

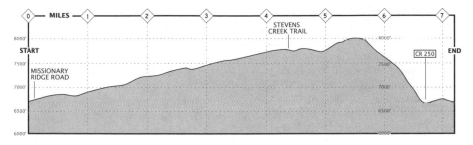

Log Chutes

Ride Specs

Start: From the parking area at the Log Chutes trailhead on Junction Creek Road (CR 204)

Length: 6.6-mile loop

Approximate Riding Time: 1–2.5 hours

Technical Difficulty: Moderate: lots of different stuff to deal with, in small doses

Physical Difficulty: Moderate: climbing, but short overall length

Trail Surface: 50% singletrack and 50% abandoned roads

Lay of the Land: Thick brush and pine trees in the dusty foothills over Durango; one shady aspen grove

Elevation Gain: 1,210 feet

Land Status: National forest

Other Trail Users: Hikers and equestrians

Getting There

In Durango: From the intersection of Main Avenue (U.S. 550/U.S. 160) and 25th Street, go west on 25th Street (which becomes Junction Creek Road, a.k.a. CR 204) for 6.1 miles to the well-signed Log Chutes trailhead. The trailhead is located 2.2 miles after the pavement ends on Junction Creek Road (CR 204).

With a total length under seven miles, and a trailhead located close to town, the Log Chutes loop is a popular and attractive outing for Duranguys and Durangals who are pressed for time or simply want a less taxing ride. There are actually two similar loops available from the same starting point; each is fun but this is the longer of the two. The area is crisscrossed with partially overgrown roads, doubletrack, and false trails, but this particular route is easy to follow due to the thorough signage and obvious bike tracks at every turn. Here, the adventure is user-friendly, and is served in bite-size morsels.

The main Log Chutes loop is a fairly even mixture of quick old logging roads and singletrack. The trail sections are pretty juicy, especially the twisting climb through the aspens after about mile 4.0 (this section provides a few thrilling minutes of tight downhilling if you ride the loop in the other direction). Most of the counter-clockwise route's excitement is provided by a serious, bombs-away descent on the far side of Junction Creek Road. This descent, on a steep, eroded widetrack with lots of big jump opportunities, was used years ago as a downhill racecourse, and there must have been some intense wrecks. You could film a seriously irresponsible video on this downhill. At reserved speeds, the descent is pretty safe, although your brake-grabbing muscles will probably be hurtin' near the bottom.

The route described here begins at the actual Log Chutes trailhead. Given this loop's lack of length, some riders may consider starting from the Colorado Trail trail-

44

head (located 2.2 miles down Junction Creek Road from the Log Chutes trailhead), or all the way from town. The moderate climb up Junction Creek Road makes a nice addition to the loop. Another good way to add mileage to your Log Chutes experience: go back and ride the Short Loop, too (see mile 1.9 below).

Haze from the Las Animas, New Mexico fire, 2000.

MilesDirections

0.0 START riding up the abandoned Log Chutes Road from the parking area at the Log Chutes trailhead, on Junction Creek Road.

1.3 Veer left at the fork; it is possible this road will be gated.

1.9 Pass a well-marked singletrack on the left. *[Option. This is the turnoff for the short loop.]* About a half block beyond this first trail, turn left onto the second well-marked singletrack. This main Log Chutes trail climbs moderately for more than a mile before the terrain starts rollin'.

3.7 Continue left and down here, where remnants of an old road can be seen.

3.8 Take a right onto singletrack (the tracks are pretty obvious).

4.3 Cross Junction Creek Road. *[Bailout. Turn left and cruise down Junction Creek Road back to the trailhead, if you've had enough of the trails.]*

4.4 Head left, going pretty much straight down.

5.9 Pass an old corral on the right. *[FYI. The short loop's singletrack swoops in from the left.]*

6.0 Take a right onto singletrack.

6.5 Meet Junction Creek Road again; turn right down the road. It's a short distance to the parking area from here.

6.6 Arrive back at the trailhead.

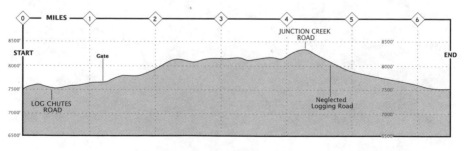

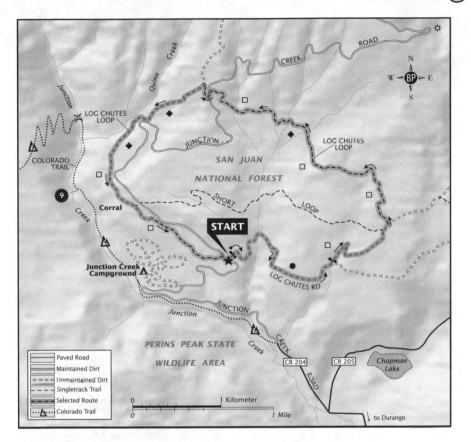

Ride Information

📞 Trail Contacts:
San Juan National Forest, Supervisor's Office, Durango, CO (970) 247–4874 • **Trails 2000,** P. O. Box 3868, Durango, CO 81302, (970) 259–4682 or *www.trails 2000.com. Trails 2000 is a highly effective non-profit that builds and maintains trails around Durango.*

🕐 Schedule:
May through October, due to muddy off-season conditions

Ⓝ Maps:
USGS maps: Durango West, CO • **USFS maps:** *San Juan National Forest*

Colorado Trail– Dry Fork– Hoffheins Loop

Ride Specs

Start: From either of the small dirt parking areas near the Colorado Trail trailhead on Junction Creek Road (CR 204)

Length: 16.0-mile loop

Approximate Riding Time: 2–4 hours

Technical Difficulty: Moderate to Difficult: lots of rocks and difficult challenges, especially in the first and last four miles

Physical Difficulty: Moderate to Difficult: tough climbs but nothing too evil

Trail Surface: 100% well-used singletrack (less than a mile of rocky widetrack, hardly worth mentioning)

Lay of the Land: This ride sports many different looks in a relatively small area—steep spruce-fir canyon, aspen groves, and dry ponderosa pine-scrub oak hillsides

Elevation Gain: 3,170 feet

Land Status: National forest

Other Trail Users: Hikers, joggers, and equestrians—and snakes

Getting There

In Durango: Head north on Main Avenue (U.S. 550/U.S. 160), from its intersection with Camino del Rio (U.S. 160/550), to 25th Street and take a left. Follow 25th Street (which becomes Junction Creek Road, a.k.a. CR 204) for 3.9 miles to the Colorado Trail trailhead. The trailhead is located at the point where the pavement ends on Junction Creek Road (CR 204).

Putting things into perspective at Gudy's Rest.

The lower portion of the Colorado Trail is dang crowded by Durango standards. Even on weekdays you're likely to find several cars in the parking area, with a scattering of friendly joggers, hikers, and picnickers (not to mention cyclists) getting ready to head up the canyon. Not to worry—the congestion may be getting worse but it's still a long way from wrecking your trail riding experience. The singletrack is too wonderfully curvy, the climbs and descents too challenging, the views too nice. Before long, you forget all about the other trail users, and, for that matter, all other annoyances of your everyday life as the singletrack takes over. This sensation has been called *Trail Trance*.

Around Durango, when folks talk about a trail being *too crowded*, you have to take it with a grain of salt. Take it from a guy who has been immersed in the ant-farm open-space experience of Colorado's Front Range—where on any given day, you could find more vehicles in the parking lot of one of those Front Range McTrail systems than you would in front of Durango's Super Wal-Mart. Despite all the understandable concern that crowds could ruin mountain biking in this area, Durango is still a good destination for cyclists who crave a little loneliness in their riding experience.

Dry Fork.

The opening miles of this all-singletrack route bristle with sharp rocks that are likely to challenge your skills. When a succession of short, sharp climbs is added to the technical mix soon after the start, beginners and pathetic hangover victims will be pushing (or bailing out onto Junction Creek Road via an escape chute at mile 1.2). After a few miles worth of stair-step climbs, the trail cruises back down to river level and crosses Junction Creek on a luxurious bridge at mile 2.7. From this point, enjoy countless switchbacks (almost all are imminently rideable) as the trail climbs moderately up the thickly wooded canyonside toward Gudy's Rest, a simple wooden bench placed on a slab of exposed rock near the top of the hill. The spot is named for Gudy Gaskill, who was the prime mover behind the entire Colorado Trail project. As most Colorado mountain bikers know, the Colorado Trail winds from Junction Creek Road all the way to Waterton Canyon, south of Denver, and provides in many sections

MilesDirections

0.0 START from the parking area at the Colorado Trail trailhead, on Junction Creek Road.

1.2 [*Bailout. While climbing away from Junction Creek on some fairly steep and technical terrain, pass an intersection with a side trail that leads about a half block to Junction Creek Road.*]

2.3 Begin descending back down to the river.

2.6 Tackle a technical crossing of Quinn Creek, usually a dry creek bed, occasionally a raging tributary in the Spring.

2.7 Cross a Bridge over Junction Creek and begin the switchback ascent up the opposite slope.

4.3 Enjoy a well-earned breather at Gudy's Rest.

4.5 After a too-short section of fast rollers, intersect with the Hoffheins Connection Trail coming up from the left. Continue straight on the Colorado Trail, more climbing.

6.1 The singletrack finally tops out, begins to roll quickly, then descends moderately toward the Dry Fork trail.

7.2 Take a sharp left onto the Dry Fork Trail. The trail will descend on an old, rocky wide-track for a bit. [*FYI. The wide Colorado Trail continues north from here on an old road.*]

8.0 The route becomes sweet, curvy single-track, and stays that way for the next 2.6 miles.

10.6 Take a left onto the well-designed Hoffheins Connection Trail, headed up.

11.4 Back at the junction with the Colorado Trail. Take a right, back down where you came from.

16.0 If you survive the rocky descent, arrive back at the trailhead.

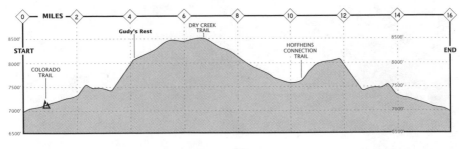

along the route some of the finest trail riding in the entire world. Gaskill has done more for mountain bikers in this state than just about anyone I can think of.

After gandering good and long at the view, and giving thanks to the Great Gaskill, continue down smooth rollers for a few blocks to the intersection with the Hoffheins Connection Trail and the start of the upper loop. This nice singletrack loop, made up of pieces of the Colorado, Dry Fork, and Hoffheins trails, is seven miles long and can be ridden in either direction. I particularly enjoy the winding 2.6-mile descent offered by the counter-clockwise loop.

On the way back down to the trailhead, pay particular attention to the rocky, tricky, some would say treacherous descent down the Colorado Trail. Any loss of control will be painfully rewarded, as there are no soft landings available along this 4.5-mile section, which has bloodied several of my riding buddies. One quick note: The nearest emergency room is located in town at 375 East Park Avenue, and they have a nice waiting area.

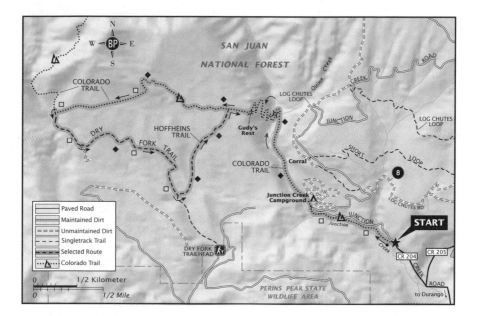

Ride Information

🕐 Trail Contacts:
San Juan National Forest, Supervisor's Office, Durango, CO (970) 247-4874 • **Trails 2000**, P.O. Box 3868, Durango, CO 81302, (970) 259-4682 or *www.trails 2000.com. Trails 2000 is a highly effective non-profit that builds and maintains trails around Durango*

🕐 Schedule:
May through October, due to muddy off-season conditions

Ⓝ Maps:
USGS maps: Durango East, CO; Hermosa, CO • **USFS maps:** *San Juan National Forest*

Hidden Valley ("Church Camp") Loop

Ride Specs

Start: From the City Market at 32nd Street and Main Avenue (U.S. 550/U.S. 160)

Length: 15.0-mile loop

Approximate Riding Time: 2–4 hours

Technical Difficulty: Moderate to Difficult: paved roads lead to twisty trails, some steep walking, rocks on the outbound descent

Physical Difficulty: Moderate: lots of pavement, but the trails are moderately challenging

Trail Surface: 67% paved roads, 3% dirt road, and 30% singletrack/widetrack

Lay of the Land: A grassy valley just outside town, and an adjacent ridge encrusted with rocks and scrub oak

Elevation Gain: 1,644 feet

Land Status: National forest

Other Trail Users: Equestrians, hikers, and lost souls

Getting There

In Durango: The ride begins from the City Market at 32nd Street and Main Avenue (U.S. 550/U.S. 160), on the north end of town.

L ocals love this foray into the gorgeous and history-charged hidden valley northwest of Durango. The views on this loop are quite nice, but the real attraction here is the cache of twisty singletrack that rolls all over and around the modest ridge that forms the valley's eastern rim.

The north City Market is a convenient starting point for this one, but certainly not the only one. Carefully cross the Main drag and cruise south on an established bike route, quickly reaching 25th Street. This road becomes Junction Creek Road and ushers you nicely into the suburban foothills. At mile 3.8, still in the suburbs, take a right onto Falls Creek Road. Both Junction Creek Road and Falls Creek Road sport a multitude of moderate climbs, elevating heart rates to respectable levels long before the first dirt is seen.

Falls Creek Road meanders past Chapman Lake, on the right, and past more ruralistic suburbia; then, near mile 6.0, it finally enters the hidden valley. With a flat, wet floor of waving green grass and striking sandstone cliffwork around the rim, the valley hosts homesites on both ends, and a chunk of trailed-up national forest in the middle. Someday, when I make a million bucks from writing guidebooks, I'd like to get a little place here, too.

Dropping anchor in Hidden Valley is not a new idea. In 1934, amateur archaeologists Zeke Flora and Helen Sloan Daniels began pulling the remains of 44 humans, in widely varying stages of decay, from crevasses below the cliffs on the northwest end

of the hidden valley, in Falls Creek Canyon. (The two amateurs were later joined by sympathetic pro Earl Morris, of the University of Colorado.) Along with the human remains, they uncovered yucca sandals, beads, bags, robes, bows and arrows, axes, various stone tools, and necklaces of shell and stone. These were still-pungent leftovers from the so-called Basketmaker II civilization that inhabited the valley around 50 AD, give or take a few hundred years. The two enthusiastic amateurs displayed a considerable lack of common sense when handling the freakishly well-preserved artifacts—Flora took a garden hose and a scrub brush to the mummified body of a 22-year-old female, who he named Esther—but their discovery painted a vivid picture of prehistoric life in the area, and trained scientists reluctantly acknowledged the find as the most significant in the rich Animas district.

In the Durango hills during the 1930s and 1940s, trained scientists were vastly outnumbered by amateur pot hunters and grave robbers who found a modest market for the region's abundant dirt-encrusted artifacts. Flora and Daniels grew out of this environment of amateur enthusiasm, a minor southwestern tradition that flared up after the fantastic accidental discoveries at Mesa Verde. Daniels tended to emulate the university purists, while Flora struck fear into their hearts with his maverick indiscretions. More prolific and unrepentant than any grave robber, and perhaps more passionate about digging than any of the university-trained archaeologists, Flora was a royal terror who became a symbolic nemesis to the scientific community. Modern scientists cringe at the thought of Flora scouring the Animas Valley and leaving no stone unturned—they cringe at his reckless methods, but maybe they cringe a little harder at having their thunder stolen by this one-man archaeological firestorm.

Even though he left earthen carnage in his wake, and notebooks filled with unintelligible scratchings, not even the most staunch and jealous academic could deny

On the Domes.

MilesDirections

0.0 START from the parking lot of the north City Market. Cross Main Avenue (U.S. 550/U.S. 160) and head west on 32nd Street.

0.1 Hang a left onto West 2nd Avenue.

0.4 Take a left onto 29th Street then, real quick-like, a right into the alley. This alley is an established bike route.

0.8 Turn right onto 25th Street, which will become Junction Creek Road.

3.8 Turn right onto Falls Creek Road. You'll soon pass Chapman Lake on your right and head up some moderate climbs.

5.9 Still cruising on Falls Creek Road, enter the Hidden Valley proper.

6.1 Falls Creek Road sheds its pavement. Enter the national forest.

6.4 Unable to contain yourself, turn right off the road onto a singletrack that cuts a diagonal across the valley floor. *[FYI. You might need to walk some of this section due to its inherent muddiness.]*

7.2 Turn right at an intersection with another trail.

7.3 Take a right onto the Ridge Trail, headed back south, with some steep climbing.

8.0 Enjoy the minor summit composed of white slickrock, then head back down.

8.8 Cross the singletrack you came in on.

8.9 Take a right (goin' east now) at a four-way trail intersection.

9.0 Veer left at the fork. Are there a lot of trails around here or what? *[Option. Take a right here onto this extremely fun and somewhat challenging singletrack, which will twist down and rejoin the route at mile 10.4. Realize, however, that by doing so you will bypass the side-trip to the waterfall at mile 10.0.]*

9.5 Pass a singletrack coming down on your left.

9.6 Pass another well-camouflaged singletrack coming off the steep slope on your left.

9.7 Stay right here, ignoring the little wooden bridge to your left. Your trail swoops down and crosses Falls Creek on another bridge, then, headed briefly to the west, climbs out of the minor gully.

9.8 Curve all the way back to the right, joining the Falls Creek Trail, a flat singletrack that parallels Falls Creek, headed east (this trail will soon become a rocky, dangerous widetrack). Pass an intersection with the Church Camp singletrack that continues north on the ridge.

10.0 *[Side-trip. Pause for a moment or two and enjoy a side-trip down behind the waterfall.]*

10.3 Cross the creek.

10.4 Pass a little singletrack swooping down on the trail from the right. *[FYI. This is the same trail you passed at mile 9.0.]*

10.6 The trail spills out onto the groomed pavement of Animas View Drive. Take a right.

13.0 Cross over U.S. 550 on Animas View Drive. Continue south.

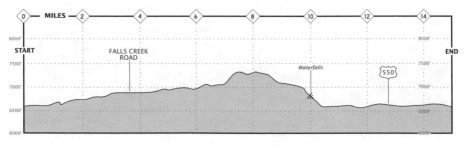

14.6 Animas View Drive ends. Cruise the final stretch on the Main drag (carefully—two thirds of these people are drunk), perhaps stopping to pick up some serious Texas barbecue.

15.0 Finish the loop at the City Market.

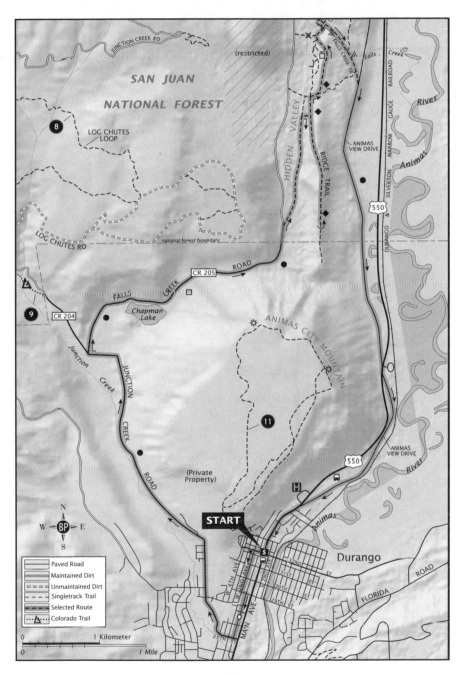

55

the importance of Flora's many discoveries. After Falls Creek (the most important Basketmaker II site), Flora claimed to locate 1,500 or so other sites and amassed a collection of about 60 skulls, 500 pots, and countless other items. Most of his treasures were sold for a Depression-era pittance and ended up in museums, though some of it—including the entire skull collection—was lost, stolen, or possibly tossed into a dumpster after he shipped it off to professional researchers. (The disappearance of the skull collection is suspicious considering the universities' pattern of antagonism toward Flora.) The preserved body of "Esther" was displayed at the Mesa Verde visitor center for seasonal parades of sickly white mobile home jockeys from South Dakota, until offended Native Americans pressured her removal to a back room. Current protocol dictates that her closest ancestral tribal group should be determined—although it is difficult to imagine exactly how this could be done, as many different groups are now claiming that association—and that these relatives will decide where she'll end up. Smart money says she'll be tucked back into that cave above Falls Creek at some point, to continue her 2,022-year-old journey from dust to dust.

Without Zeke Flora and Helen Sloan Daniels, it's unlikely the universities would ever have laid eyes on the prime pithouses and burial grounds of the Durango area. They have been less than thankful. Professionals viewed these successful do-it-your-

Hidden Valley.

selfers as a threat to scientific integrity, and, getting right to the point, their livelihood. This thinly-veiled paranoia and antagonism was apparent from the beginning, as Flora and Daniels were repeatedly snubbed when seeking professional aid and opinions (Earl Morris was the exception). Scientists and university officials then worked behind the scenes to keep word of Flora's achievements out of the popular press! As a final insult, the archaeologists who proudly displayed Esther and the artifacts from Falls Creek gave credit for the blockbuster finds not to Flora, not to Helen Sloan Daniels, but to Earl Morris, the professor from the University of Colorado who came on the scene *after* the initial discoveries were made. It's rotten, I tell ya.

The Basketmakers and their pottery-mongering descendants vanished from Falls Creek and the hidden valley by around 800 AD. If only they had mountain bikes, they would have stayed. In 1993, the Forest Service turned the area surrounding the cluster of Falls Creek sites into the Falls Creek Archaeological Area, and public access to the area is now outlawed completely. No climbing on the rocks over there, and no digging. The pot-hunting party is over. If you'd like to read more about Zeke Flora and the prehistoric inhabitants of the Durango area, check out Florence Lister's *Prehistory in Peril* and Philip Duke and Gary Matlock's *Points, Pithouses, and Pioneers*.

Back to the ride: At about mile 6.4, turn right onto a trail that cuts a diagonal across the green valley toward the ridge. (Farther up Falls Creek Road are a few other obvious singletracks cutting across the expanse.) Any trails on the valley floor could be boggy and unrideable. The trail heads to an intersection at a low-point on the ridge, where you'll find a thin track twisting up (back southward) through the scrub oak. The knowledge that this valley was filled with "cave men," as Flora called them, could lend a pleasant eeriness to the ride. Ponder the possibility that this ridgetop singletrack is 2,000 or more years old, stamped in by the sandaled feet of the Basketmakers on their way up for some good old-fashioned sun worship. The ancient track, moderately rocky but quick, offers brief opportunities for showing off before slamming into a few ultra-steep chutes that will make pedestrians out of the best pedalers.

So why should you tackle these steep walk-ups when there's so much nice-looking, fast singletrack headed the other way? Your reward, after about three tiers of southbound hiking, is an excellent mini-summit composed of round domes of smooth rock, falling into minor cliffs on three sides. The white slickrock summit is made even more excellent by the preceding hike, because, like a moat around the castle, it keeps most folks away. The pinnacle is a memorable lunch spot for sun lovers. Although the stubborn trail persists southward just below the slickrock domes, there's no better spot from which to view this valley, and perhaps no better valley view anywhere. Over to the east, in the Valley of El Rio de las Animas Perdidas (the aptly-named River of Lost Souls, commonly known as the Animas River), a single engine Cessna hauls gliders continuously into the heights over Missionary Ridge and Haflin Canyon, providing a constant drone.

Attempting to ride back down the chutes can get you into trouble, but it can also be a heckuva lot of fun. Try not to tear the trail up with a locked rear wheel. Continue past your original point of entry onto the ridge. The trails continue north from here, on top of the ridge as well as on its flank, in awesome tight turns. Great stuff. There are enough sweet tracks in this general area to keep you smiling for some time. (The route described here is just one of several possibilities at "Church Camp," as this extensive trail network is known to locals. The name "Church Camp" comes from the Whispering Pines Bible Camp located at the network's north end.) Exit the valley to the east, on the rocky, dangerous trail that follows Falls Creek steeply into the Animas Valley. The trail runs into the flat roads that lead perfectly back to town.

Bonus suburban waterfall: As you begin the easterly descent down the rocky wide-track next to Falls Creek, the sound of a waterfall competes with the drone of the tow-plane (mile 10.0). Find a spur leading down to, and actually *behind*, the falls. Another excellent spot to hang, but keep an eye out because this is also where local endurance pro Steve Fassbinder was attacked ruthlessly by a swarm of bees.

Ride Information

Trail Contacts:
San Juan National Forest, Supervisor's Office, Durango, CO (970) 247–4874

Schedule:
June through October, due to weather, and possibly during off-season droughts

 Maps:
USGS maps: Durango East, CO; Durango West, CO • USFS maps: *San Juan National Forest*

Animas City Mountain

Ride Specs

Start: From the Animas City Mountain trailhead at the northern dead-end of West 4th Avenue

Length: 5.7-mile loop

Approximate Riding Time: 1–2 hours

Technical Difficulty: Difficult: notably rocky single and widetrack

Physical Difficulty: Difficult: tough climbing, very steep at first

Trail Surface: 100% singletrack/widetrack

Lay of the Land: Sloping, forested mesa-top just northwest of Durango

Elevation Gain: 1,575 feet

Land Status: City and BLM land

Other Trail Users: Hikers (There are actually two separate trails along most of this loop, one designated for hikers and the other for bikes, which eliminates many conflicts.)

Getting There

In Durango: Drive west on 32nd Street until it ends at West 4th Avenue, then take a right on West 4th Avenue for a block, where, in the midst of houses and an electrical substation, you'll find a small parking area. The trailhead is just up the hill from this parking area.

This is a short ride that nonetheless dishes out the physical punishment. Most of the pain comes as a result of the first few hills, which rise from the trailhead at a startling angle, completely ransacked with babyhead rocks. Conquering these first few pitches of pure brutality without pushing your bike requires a superhuman effort. While locked in mortal combat with this little hill, it becomes apparent why Durango produces some the strongest climbers in the sport of cycling. Most of us will be off and pushing almost immediately, even before gaining the first saddle, up near the green water tank. (At this point, ignore the nice-looking singletracks crisscrossing the saddle and heading west, as most of these mavericks will lead down into private property.) North from the tank, the route climbs up another harsh pitch or two of chunky widetrack, then eases up where another bike route, a singletrack marked with blue arrows, splits to the right just above the hiking trail. Take a right here to begin a counter-clockwise loop.

You're on the mesa now. (Actually, since the sandstone mesa top is set at a bit of an angle, the formation would more properly be called a *cuesta*.) The angle of the *cuesta* keeps you climbing, although at a much gentler rate than before. The enjoyable trail meanders near the eastern edge of the mountain. The technical difficulty relaxes just a hair, but the trail remains rocky for the most part and pointy chunks are a major theme. All in all, the climbing continues for a solid three miles from the trail-

head, making this a great training hill. (The clockwise loop, by the way, has a steeper, harder, but shorter climb.)

There are a few points on the way up where you can look over the eastern edge onto the glistening curves and oxbow lakes of the Animas River, but these overlooks take a backseat to the vantage point reached at about mile 3.0, near the top of the climb, where the trail edges right up to the end of the sandstone slab. From here, continuing along the counter-clockwise loop, the hiking and biking trails, formerly separated, now join as one; the route runs up and over a steep little knob, then begins a long, barreling downhill all the way home.

The unique signature of Animas City Mountain is the separation of hikers and cyclists on different trails. Nowhere else in the region have the land managers separated the two contentious user groups like they have here, and by all accounts, it's a success. (Although the creation of dueling trails would obviously be impractical in many other areas.) In Durango, where cyclists own the trails, it's nice for hikers to have some place to get away. This separation does not carry the rule of law, and the most enforcement you are likely to encounter if you ride the hikers' trail is the raised

From Animas City Mountain, looking down at the town.

eyebrow of one of the hikers. Some riders have made a habit of using the hikers' trail to bypass the hard climb at the bottom of the bike route, but I won't recommend it.

Animas City Mountain is named for Animas City, the forgotten development on the Animas River. In 1880, the mining supply town of Animas City had about 450 inhabitants and threatened to grow into a significant point on the map when the Denver & Rio Grande Railroad started placing rails up the valley toward Silverton. Unfortunately for the citizens of Animas City, who saw dollar signs with the coming rail line, the D&RG built their station a few miles down river. The planned, corporate development called Durango sprang up around the railroad buildings. It didn't take long for the railroad town to dwarf, then finally absorb, its poor neighbor to the north, and Animas City faded into oblivion.

MilesDirections

START from the Animas City Mountain trailhead, which is just up the hill from the parking area. Behind the big sign, take a left and head up steeply, following the trail marked with blue arrows. *[Note. Follow the BLUE ARROWS all the way. The trail marked with white arrows is for hikers, and this trail will intersect the bike trail several times before the two trails finally join near the top, at mile 2.4.]*

0.3 Reach a saddle just below the green water tank. Ignore the pretty little singletracks crossing the saddle. *[Note. These unauthorized ribbons will put you on heavily patrolled private property in a hurry. Still, don't be surprised to see a local or two ripping westward toward Junction Creek, smiling.]* Take a right (north), continuing up a steep, rocky widetrack.

0.5 The hikers' trail, marked with white arrows, branches off to the right.

0.6 Take a right where the bike route splits to begin a counter-clockwise loop (blue arrows).

The incline mellows significantly, but the climbing continues.

2.4 After several well-marked intersections and crossings, the hiking and biking trails converge into a single route, so expect hikers on the trail after this point.

3.2 The trail turns to the southwest and down. The singletrack morphs into widetrack and pseudo-double due to the erosional stress on the straightforward descent.

5.1 Back at the start of the loop, continue straight and retrace your path down to the trailhead.

5.7 End the ride at the trailhead and parking area.

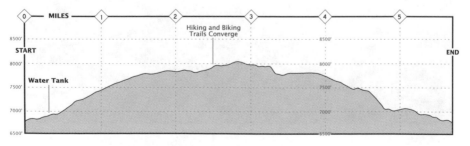

Ride Information

Trail Contacts:

Trails 2000, P.O. Box 3868, Durango, CO 81302, (970) 259–4682 or *www.trails 2000.com—Trails 2000 is a highly effective non-profit that builds and maintains trails around Durango.* **Bureau of Land Management,** Durango, (970) 247–4082

Schedule:

May to October. You may be tempted to try this one in the off-season, but you'll likely encounter deal-breaking mud after snowmelt. Also, the Division of Wildlife reserves the right to close this area from December 1 to April 15 depending on the circumstances from year to year.

Maps:

USGS maps: Durango East, CO; and Durango West, CO

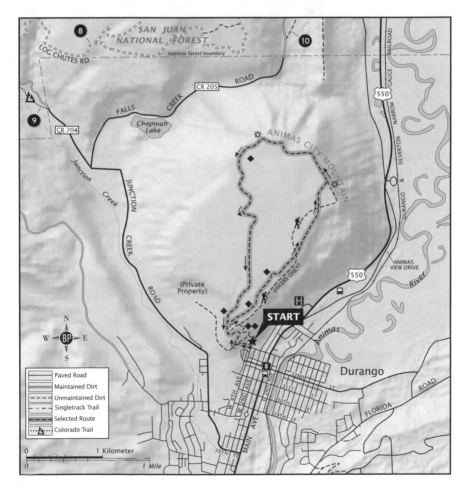

Test Track– Perins Peak Loop

Ride Specs
Start: From the north City Market at 32nd and Main Avenue (U.S. 550/U.S. 160)
Length: 6.5-mile loop
Approximate Riding Time: 1–2 hours
Technical Difficulty: Moderate to Difficult: generally smooth trails on steep hillsides
Physical Difficulty: Moderate to Difficult: a quick workout
Trail Surface: 45% singletrack/widetrack and 55% paved roads
Lay of the Land: Dry, semi-forested, shale hills, and arroyos
Elevation Gain: 1,248 feet
Land Status: State wildlife area, and city park
Other Trail Users: Hikers, joggers, and walkers (often with dogs)

Getting There
In Durango: The ride begins from the City Market at 32nd Street and Main Avenue (U.S. 550/U.S. 160), on the north end of town. The dirt portion begins at the dead-end of Montview Parkway in western Durango.

Note
Keep in mind that the upper portion of this ride passes through the Perins Peak State Wildlife Area, and will be off-limits from December 1 through August 1. Those dying for a Test Track ride during this time should simply confine themselves to the lower, unaffected trails. The Trans-Test Track Loop (Ride 13) is an example of a route that does not enter the restricted zone.

This ride is just one of the routes available in Durango Mountain Park, the city-annexed chunk of land located roughly west of the Crestview subdivision, in the shadow of Perins Peak. Criss-crossed with quality singletrack, this area is known informally as the Test Track, a casual name that could give would-be riders the wrong impression. This brief but exciting lariat loop—a loop with a tail on it, giving it the general appearance of a rope lasso on the map—is not regarded as a great ride…by Durango's standards, that is. In any other town, it would be. With its steep climb and smooth, swooping descent, this is actually one of my favorite short trail rides.

Lack of parking at the trailhead means you'll have to find a remote location to stage this one. This particular ride begins from the north City Market. Due to the close proximity of the trails, it could easily begin from any joint, crib, hole, or spiritual center in town. (Keeping in mind that the mileage cues below use the supermarket as the start/finish.) The choice of the corporate mega-mart is based on two primary assumptions: (1) It's hard to miss, and (2) it has a big parking lot. There is, of course, the easy access to Clif Bars.

There are about 14,000 points of entry to the Test Track in western Durango. Perhaps the most convenient is reached by simply taking 22nd Street west. This res-

idential street leads up a steep hill and becomes Montview Parkway. Montview Parkway dead-ends at a signed trailhead.

About 10 yards up this trail you'll find a T-intersection with a flat widetrack that is one of the main arteries in the Test Track. For this ride, take a left. The widetrack passes connectors on the right and left, then splits briefly into parallel tracks that rejoin before crossing a bridge. Beyond this bridge, the track thins and winds around a bit. Within minutes from the trailhead—within minutes from anywhere in town—you're on thin, twisting singletrack that mimics a real mountain trail. Because this singletrack crosses two sturdy bridges, we'll label it the "Bridges Trail." The well-designed track finds its way onto the steep slope of a minor gulch, then climbs acutely to a thin saddle of crumbling gray shale, with sparse vegetation, at the base of stately-looking Perins Peak. Durango veterans know that the shale makes an impossible, unrideable slop when wet.

The backside of the loop consists of tall, sharp rollers along the peaks of the eroded ridges, Fruita-style. Some of the short, steep hills will have to be walked. Then the trail drops back into the dark of the canyon on a tight, swooping roller coaster. Excellent. The small (1.5-miles) but exhilarating loop should be ridden several times, don't you think?

Perkins Peak, just a big ol' chunk of rock.

63

If you're all about the short but sweet thrills offered by the Test Track, you won't want to miss Church Camp (Ride 10), the Ridge (Ride 2), or the Telegraph Hill network (Rides 3 and 4). The Stevens Creek Mini-loop (Ride 7), using the lower portion of the Stevens Creek Trail and a connector to Missionary Ridge Road, is another short thriller near town.

MilesDirections

0.0 START from the parking lot of the north City Market. Cross Main Avenue (U.S. 550/U.S. 160) and head west on 32nd Street.

0.1 Hang a left onto West 2nd Avenue, ride about one half block, then take a left into a one-lane alley that provides immediate access to the alley running between 2nd and Main Avenue. *[FYI. The idea behind the alley route is to ride south from the City Market to 22nd Street without using Main Avenue, a bad road for cycling. But the alley does not connect directly to 32nd —and West 2nd does not go all the way through to 22nd.]*

0.8 Take a right onto 25th Street, then a quick left onto West 2nd to continue south (the alley dead-ends ahead).

1.1 Turn right onto 22nd Street and follow it up a steep hill, where it becomes Montview Parkway.

1.7 Montview Parkway dead-ends at the trailhead. Ride up a short, steep slope, then turn left onto a widetrack. Stay on the main track as a trail heads up the slope on your right, and an access trail heads to Leyden Street on your left. The main widetrack also splits into two parallel trails briefly—don't be alarmed.

1.9 Cross a bridge, and pass a steep trail coming down the slope on your left.

2.1 Pass another trail cutting in from the left.

2.3 Pass a trail cutting in from the right.

2.5 Take a left at another fork and immediately cross a bridge.

3.0 Turn right at a high point and roll down and up the saddle. *[Note. Here is where you enter the restricted Perins Peak State Wildlife Area, so if it's not August, September, October, or November, you must turn back here.]*

3.3 Turn right at a T-intersection.

3.8 You probably won't notice, but your trail veers right and joins the Riverbed Trail in here somewhere, at the bottom of a steep descent.

4.0 Cross a ditch, then swoop down onto the Bridges Trail. Veer left. This is the same intersection you saw at mile 2.5.

4.6 Back over the first bridge.

4.8 Turn right off the widetrack, and spill out onto Montview Parkway.

6.5 End the ride at el supermercado.

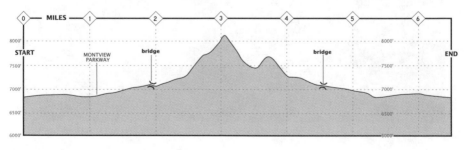

Ride Information

🕐 Trail Contacts:
Trails 2000, P.O. Box 3868, Durango, CO 81302, (970) 259–4682 or *www.trails 2000.com—Trails 2000 is a highly effective non-profit that builds and maintains trails around Durango* • **Colorado Division of Wildlife,** Durango, CO (970) 247–0855 • **Bureau of Land Management,** Durango, CO (970) 247–4082

🕐 Schedule:
August 1 through November 30 due to seasonal closure of the Perins Peak State Wildlife Area

Ⓝ Maps:
USGS maps: Durango West, CO; and Durango East, CO

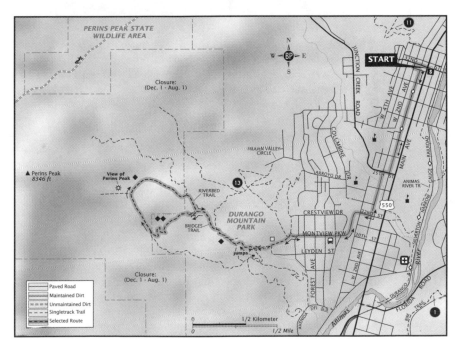

Trans–Test Track Loop

Ride Specs

Start: From the City Market at 32nd Street and Main Avenue (U.S. 550/U.S. 160)
Length: 6.4-mile loop
Approximate Riding Time: 1–2 hours
Technical Difficulty: Difficult: steep climbs and fast descents
Physical Difficulty: Moderate to Difficult: a few straight-up climbs that may require walking
Trail Surface: 70% paved roads and 30% singletrack
Lay of the Land: Scrub oak, ponderosa pine, juniper, and occasional spruce trees on steep shale slopes, in the shadow of Perins Peak
Elevation Gain: 876 feet
Land Status: City park
Other Trail Users: Hikers, joggers, and walkers (often with dogs)

Getting There

In Durango: The ride begins from the City Market at 32nd Street and Main Avenue (U.S. 550/U.S. 160), on the north end of town. The dirt portion begins a few blocks up Hidden Valley Circle in western Durango.

I mmediately west of Durango lies Durango Mountain Park, known to local fat tire fanatics as the Test Track. The trail network in the Test Track area has never been adequately mapped, and one doubts if it ever could be. Too many pseudo-trails and connectors. Flying over the site in a helicopter could be helpful, although I imagine the trails, seen from above, would look something like a clump of hair in the shower.

The other Test Track ride in this book (Ride 12) runs right up the guts of the area on a main track, and is therefore pretty easy to follow. This ride, on the other hand, spans the zone from north to south and crosses a load of intersections with other tracks along the way. It is admittedly a tall order to guide folks through this confusing network, without actually holding their hand. But this ride sports so much excellent singletrack surfing that it's worth a try.

Due to a lack of sanctioned parking where the dirt portion of this ride begins—there is, in fact, no real trailhead there at all—it is necessary to begin from some point in town. The route described here begins from the north City Market (32nd Street and Main Avenue), one of many convenient base camps available in north Durango, and winds through quiet neighborhoods to the Test Track's northern edge.

The trails along this particular route alternate between straight, steep climbs and winding descents—ride the loop in the other direction and you'll find smooth, twisting climbs with laundry chute descents. Your first taste of the singletrack here is one

Perins Peak and its eroded abyss.

MilesDirections

0.0 START from the parking lot of the north City Market. Cross Main Avenue (U.S. 550/U.S. 160) and head west on 32nd Street.

0.1 Hang a left onto West 2nd Avenue, ride about one half block, then take a left into a one-lane alley that provides immediate access to the alley running between 2nd and Main Avenue. *[**FYI.** The idea behind the alley route is to ride south from the City Market to 22nd Street without using Main Avenue, a bad road for cycling. But the alley does not connect directly to 32nd —and West 2nd does not go all the way through to 24th.]*

0.9 Take a right on 24th Street.

1.0 Turn left on West 3rd Avenue. Travel for a half block, then right onto Weston Drive.

1.2 Turn right onto Columbine, ride for another half block, then take a left onto Arroyo Drive. *[**FYI.** You have just ridden around the elementary school.]*

1.5 Pass a small trailer park, then take a left onto Hidden Valley Circle.

1.7 Hit the dirt! Turn left onto an eroded track angling steeply up the hillside. Veer left at an intersection about 0.06 miles up from the pavement.

2.2 Top out and find yourself in the midst of a confusing cluster of trails. For this ride, head straight across and find a flat track that seems to be aimed directly at Perins Peak. This trail should begin to curve right (to the northwest).

2.3 After winding pleasantly through the woods for a short time, turn left, dropping in on a singletrack twisting down a dry gulch.

2.7 Take a left at a significant intersection, onto the Bridges Trail.

2.8 Stay left as a trail climbs steeply to your right.

3.0 Veer right from the Bridges Trail onto another trail, and begin a straight, steep climb onto the ridge. *[**Note.** If you reach the bridge, you've gone too far. Bailout. Continue straight here and exit the Durango Mountain Park without any additional climbing.]*

3.1 Topping out momentarily, arrive at an intersection where two trails come in from above (on your right), and another descends to your left. Take a right onto the right-most trail and climb gently. *[**Option.** Play around on the man-made jumps along this section.]*

3.2 Turn left across the shale onto a descending track.

3.7 Pop out onto pavement. Take a right, then a quick left onto Avenida del Sol. Descend.

3.9 Take a left onto Forest Avenue.

4.8 Take a right on Arroyo Drive and retrace your path back to City Market.

6.4 Arrive back at the parking lot.

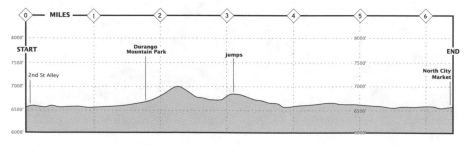

of the aforementioned straight-up pitches, and this one will certainly seem like a hassle if you're looking for a pain-free day. You'll probably need to walk a substantial piece of this half-mile climb.

At the top of this initial ascent, you find yourself at the center of a shocking jumble of trails. This is the most confusing part of the ride. Basically, head straight through this multi-point intersection, on the same vector you were on previously. Ignore the steep connectors on your right and the inviting widetracks heading off to your left. If all goes well, you should be heading straight at Perins Peak momentarily on a gentle, winding path. This trail tends to the right and up, but before it heads steeply up the side of a crumbling shale ridge, find a sweet-looking singletrack snaking down a dry arroyo on your left. Here begins a swooping downhill into the heart of Durango Mountain Park. Soft landing areas and a notable lack of other users invite riders to really open it up along this sweet stretch.

Mile 2.7 effectively ends the first descent, as you join the Bridges Trail, the most well-traveled, popular trail in the park, and are forced to reign in your gravity-aided antics. Descend gradually (and slowly) through a few more intersections, then angle south on a side trail to climb another straight, steep one. This climb brings you up onto another gray ridge, where you can gaze down on the tranquil suburban cul-de-

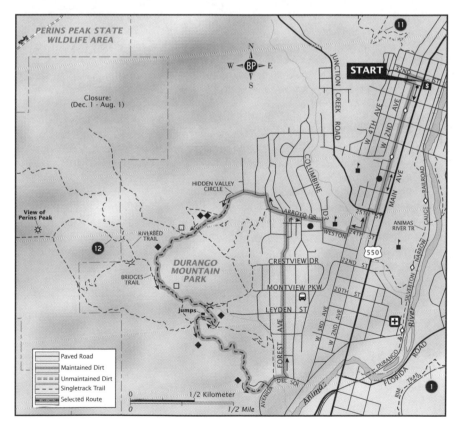

sac of Leyden Street. (The last time I was on this trail, I saw a woman on the roof of a house down there, talking on her cell phone—trying to get some privacy, I guess.)

This ridge holds some nice surprises for aggressive riders. At the topside three-point intersection, with two trails high and one trail low, climb the rightmost of the two parallel trails going up. As you spin up this open ridgetop section you'll notice that many small but powerful kicker jumps, including some doubles, have been constructed. You may want to spend some time up here *airing it out* before continuing with the loop. This handcrafted playground is another example of the Durango crowd's devotion to mountain biking in all its forms.

When you're done catching air and snapping collarbones on the ridge, meander down the dry slope on a nice, smooth, curvaceous singletrack, with poetic views of the old garbage dump and Greenmount Cemetery. The downhill lasts long enough to make the preceding climb worthwhile, then spills out onto pavement, leaving you to find your way back to the home base.

Mancos Shale (Just Add Water)

Durango may be a cyclists' paradise, but it isn't because of the Mancos Shale. This dreaded geologic formation was laid down in the Cretaceous Period (66.4 to 144 million years ago), by a huge finger of an ocean that stretched from the Gulf of Mexico to present-day Alaska. Continuous fluctuations in the level of this ocean, over millions of years, left several thousand feet of tidal mud and organic material behind. This Mancos Mud was quickly buried deep under a variety of sandstones and other sedimentary materials, but time has since stripped the top layers away and, today, the Dark Monster has become unburied.

The Mancos Shale, about 3,000 frustrating feet thick in the vicinity of Durango, makes for a decent trail as long as it remains dry. Just add water, however, and the crumbling shale morphs into an all-powerful super-slop that will execute a shocking deathgrip on your cycle's vital organ systems. Unlike lesser brands of mud that are messy but remain rideable, the Duranglue will stop you cold. So what gives the Mancos Shale its evil powers? Geologist Donald Baars, who has exhaustively studied this and other geologic formations of the Four Corners region, points to the presence of bentonite—"a clay with a high shrink-swell capacity, formed from...volcanic ash"—as the likely culprit.

Baars sounds like a man who knows too much when he writes of the shale's mastery over 4WD vehicles: "Unpaved roads entrap vehicles as if in wet glue after a rain...Dirt roads built on the Mancos Shale are truly treacherous when wet!" One-wheel-drives like your mountain bike will be even more stymied by patches of rain-soaked, bentonite-rich Mancos Muck.

In Durango, if you go for a trail ride in the rain, or in the snowmelt season, getting wet will be the least of your problems. You will have to Pay the Clay.

This ride will give you a good gulp or two of Test Track, although it leaves many nice trails untouched. The route does not enter private property or the Perins Peak State Wildlife Area, and there are no closures of any kind to worry about. The off-season mud, however, is a deal-breaker.

Ride Information

🕭 Trail Contacts:
Trails 2000, P.O. Box 3868, Durango, CO 81302, (970) 259–4682 or *www.trails 2000.com—Trails 2000 is a highly effective non-profit that builds and maintains trails around Durango*

🕒 Schedule:
May through October, due to mud. Durango Mountain Park is great for a winter ride, as long as the temperature stays below about 30°F, but very few people other than myself would consider this to be a fun time.

Ⓝ Maps:
USGS maps: Durango West, CO; and Durango East, CO

14

The Big Loop (La Plata Canyon–Kennebec Pass–Colorado Trail)

Ride Specs

Start: From where U.S. 160 splits off from Camino del Rio (U.S. 550/U.S. 160) in south Durango
Length: 50.7-mile loop
Approximate Riding Time: 6–9 hours
Technical Difficulty: Difficult: hours of challenging singletrack
Physical Difficulty: Very Difficult: a climber's loop with serious length and elevation gain—bring a water filter, iodine pills, and a huge pile of food
Trail Surface: 45% singletrack, 30% paved roads, and 25% dirt roads/4WD roads
Lay of the Land: This ride climbs through the zones, from the foothills to alpine boulder fields, and back
Elevation Gain: 9,071 feet
Land Status: National forest
Other Trail Users: Hikers, motorists (4WDs on La Plata Canyon Road), equestrians (on the upper section of the Colorado Trail), and walkers (on the lower trail)

Getting There

In Durango: Begin where U.S. 160 splits off from Camino del Rio (U.S. 550/U.S. 160) in south Durango, and end at the intersection of 25th Street and Main Avenue (U.S. 550/U.S. 160). (Note, however, this ride could begin anywhere in Durango.)

"Flipping channels" while sitting on the chair.

T here are several variations on this powerful loop, but this is the town favorite. The route climbs to Kennebec Pass (about 11,700 feet above sea level) on a tough dirt/4WD road. On the way back to town, it's twisty, groomed singletrack the whole way. With towering peaks all around and thoughts of smooth backcountry rollers filling their heads, riders will be nicely distracted from the unrelenting 25-mile ascent which is this loop's first half.

Harsh Hidden Climb Alert! Before embarking on the singletrack second half of this ride, you should be aware that after its initial five-mile descent from Kennebec, this trail climbs about 1,000 feet out of the Junction Creek drainage, twisting skyward for a buzz-killing 4.5 miles. By itself, this climb isn't too much to handle, but there will be hell in the backcountry for long-loopers who have failed to haul enough food along. (When I did this loop, I started on a full stomach, then along the way I ate three sandwiches, three energy bars, a few pieces of fruit, some jerky, and I was still a bit shaky.) This baby nails the coffin shut on those who had trouble just getting over the pass, and there are no possible bailouts once you've committed by descending to the creek. An option exists to turn your back on the singletrack climb by sneaking

onto Junction Creek Road (via an unnamed side road) a few miles below the pass, but even this route involves a gentle three-mile climb that cannot be avoided. Big climbs are always a theme of rides in the mountains above Durango, and this ride has some of the biggest.

The Big Loop requires no automotive support, which is a beautiful thing. Unfortunately, looping straight from town means you'll be riding the highway for the first 10 miles and gaining significant altitude in the process. Think of it as a warm-up. The shoulder is wide and smooth, and the paved climb could help you locate a smooth rhythm. (A popular option is to shuttle to the start of the dirt at Mayday. Drive up La Plata Canyon Road as far as your conscience allows, to any one of a number of suitable turn-offs. Leave another car anywhere in town, or perhaps at the Colorado Trail trailhead on Junction Creek Road.)

After turning north off U.S. Route 160 onto County Road 124 at Hesperus, ride pavement through the hamlet of Mayday (mile 15.0). The road continues as pleasant, smooth gravel up the La Plata River canyon, but steadily deteriorates and gets a little steeper with each mile. By the time it reaches the gorgeous Cumberland Basin just under the Kennebec Pass summit, you're on a rough jeep route and possibly grunting like a sick pig. This is a tough pass, but it's not as difficult as the other passes in this guide—Engineer (Ride 34) and Imogene (Ride 29).

The road to the Notch.

MilesDirections

0.0 START from anywhere in town, but reset your odometer at the intersection of U.S. 160 and Camino del Rio (U.S. 160/U.S. 550), and head west up U.S. 160, toward Mancos.

10.4 Turn right onto La Plata Canyon Road (CR 124).

15.0 The road passes through Mayday and then turns to gravel. *[Option. To avoid U.S. 160, shuttle to the start of the dirt at Mayday. Leave a second vehicle anywhere in town or at the Colorado Trail trailhead just outside town on Junction Creek Road.]*

16.5 Kroeger Campground is on the left.

19.6 Pass the turnoff to Eagle Pass on the right (FS 60). *[Side-trip. Turn here to see the Gold King Mill.]*

22.5 Veer left at the fork. *[FYI. The right-hand road leads to the Columbus Mine.]*

24.7 Top out where a singletrack Colorado Trail comes in from the left. Ignore it, continuing about a half block down the road. Turn left onto another singletrack, headed east. This is the continuation of the Colorado Trail route. *[Side-trip. The road persists to The Notch, and through it.]*

25.4 Kennebec Pass summit! The trail has become two-track.

25.5 Veer left from the doubletrack onto singletrack. You're still following the route of the Colorado Trail but this section is known as the Sliderock Trail. The talus trail is moderately technical and scary for a while, but recently it was tamed considerably by volunteers working with the Colorado Trail Association (thanks?).

27.3 Cross this road to continue on the Colorado Trail. *[Option. If you're looking for a bailout, head left down this road to meet Junction Creek Road.]*

30.7 Creek crossing.

32.1 Cross Junction Creek on a bridge. A long climb begins.

36.6 Finally reach the top of the climb and join a widetrack.

39.8 Pass through a livestock gate.

40.1 Junction with the Dry Fork trail. Either way gets you home, but I like going left and staying on the Colorado Trail to prolong the singletrack. It's smooth here, but there is rough descending ahead, made rougher by your fatigue at this point. *[Option. Stay right and descend on the excellent Dry Fork Trail, which soon leaves the old road and dives into beautiful, tight turns; pass the intersection with the Hoffheins Trail, and twist down a smooth tooshort single' to the Dry Fork trailhead. Cruise down Dry Fork Road to Lightner Creek Road, left on Lightner Creek to U.S. 160, left on U.S. 160 back to town.]*

42.8 Pass the intersection with the Hoffheins Trail on your right, then, not long after, pass Gudy's Rest. *[FYI. This is a popular rest -stop, where a bench sits on a slab of rock high over Junction Creek.]* The descent gets serious from here.

44.4 Cross a bridge over Junction Creek.

47.1 Turn right onto Junction Creek Road.

50.7 After cruising through a residential zone, reach Main Avenue in Durango. Seek Mexican food.

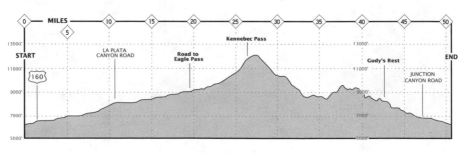

For the past 100 years, the La Plata Canyon has been all about mining, a fact that becomes immediately obvious if you head up any of the side-canyons along the way. Each of the steep spurs leads to a mining complex of some sort, a few of which are still operational. For a quick side-trip to the towering ruins of an old mill, head up Forest Service Road 60 toward Eagle Pass—the turnoff is almost five miles above Mayday—then take a quick right across the river to the Gold King Mill. The impressive structure looks as if it could topple at any second, and it probably could, so be careful. That sucker will make a big crash when it comes down.

If old ruins were the only physical legacy of the area's mining operations, the canyon would be better off. For a disturbing lesson about the effects of mining on local ecology, check out Bedrock Creek. (Bedrock is the second drainage up from Kroeger Campground; a jeep road ascends to the Allard Mine). A quick examina-

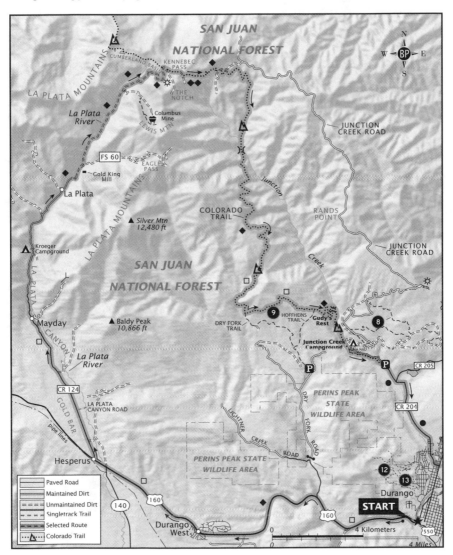

tion of the creek reveals that it is void of any kind of flora or fauna—completely dead. Compare it to other creeks in the area for a frightening contrast. The water of Bedrock Creek is clear and cold, but I wouldn't recommend drinking from this stream even with a filter and a magic chant. To my paranoid mind, the condition of Bedrock calls into question the quality of the water in the other streams of La Plata Canyon, not to mention the other area drainages affected by mining, which is basically all of them.

Finally, don't let all this negative talk—the highway, the climbs, the dead creek—give you the wrong impression. If you are fit, prepared, and accustomed to spending all day in the saddle, this could be your new favorite ride. The views alone make the ascent to Kennebec Pass worthwhile, and the following half day of singletrack cruising is a dream come true.

Waterfall in La Plata Canyon.

Acute Mountain Sickness (AMS)

It is estimated that 75 percent of those traveling higher than 10,000 feet above sea level experience at least some of the symptoms associated with Acute Mountain Sickness (AMS), also known as Altitude Sickness. At high altitudes, a lack of air pressure in the lungs leads to a decrease in the body's oxygen supply. Those not fully accustomed to this decrease in oxygen will suffer some combination of headaches, nausea, fatigue, and a general sense of feeling like dung.

To minimize the shock of decreased oxygen and the uncomfortable symptoms of AMS, those arriving in this area from sea level may want to simply relax for a few days before attempting any high-altitude rides, giving their bodies a chance to adjust. Once minimally acclimatized, it is extremely helpful to remain hyper-hydrated, and to just plain take it easy while exercising in the thin air.

Above all, pay attention to your symptoms. Altitude Sickness is usually more of a nuisance than a real danger, but it should not be taken too lightly. If the warning signs are ignored for an extended period, fluid will begin leaking into the lungs and brain (High Altitude Edema), and, eventually, death will result. (This would totally ruin your ride.) Difficulty with balance and coordination is an ominous sign that the condition has advanced to this life-threatening stage.

Fortunately, there is one surefire cure for AMS: descend. A retreat of just 1,500 feet or so is usually sufficient to cause dramatic and immediate relief.

Ride Information

📞 Trail Contacts:

San Juan National Forest, Supervisor's Office, Durango, CO (970) 247–4874 • **Trails 2000,** P.O. Box 3868, Durango, CO 81302, (970) 259–4682 or *www.trails 2000.com—Trails 2000 is a highly effective non-profit that builds and maintains trails around Durango*

🕐 Schedule:

June through mid October, due to snow at high altitude. Your window of opportunity will vary wildly from year to year.

Ⓝ Maps:

USGS maps: Durango West, CO; Hesperus, CO; La Plata, CO; and Monument Hill, CO • **USFS maps:** *San Juan National Forest*

Smelter Hillclimb

Ride Specs

Start: From the parking area at the bottom end of CR 211

Length: 7.6-mile out-and-back

Approximate Riding Time: 1–2 hours

Technical Difficulty: Easy: this wide dirt road, rutted deeply in spots, could be considered technically moderate under the right (wrong) conditions

Physical Difficulty: Moderate: sustained but gradual climbing, for the most part

Trail Surface: 40% wide, graded dirt road and 60% slightly rougher dirt road

Lay of the Land: Sparse piñon-juniper forest

Elevation Gain: 1,271 feet

Land Status: State wildlife area (stay on the road)

Other Trail Users: Motorists (trucks), joggers, and drunken high schoolers

Getting There

From Durango: Head south on Camino del Rio/U.S. 160. Pass Santa Rita Park, on your right, then turn right off the highway onto Frontage Road, at the light. After about one block, take a right onto CR 211 (dirt). There is a parking area located about 75 yards up this road on the right.

S melter Mountain. Sounds appetizing, don't it?

True to its name, Smelter Mountain is covered with all sorts of industrial detritus, like power stations, uranium tailings, and radio and television towers. With all the man-made goodies around, it's a strange place for a protected wildlife area. (The roads described here pass through the Bodo State Wildlife Area, a protected zone for deer and elk in the winter. Sounds great, until you realize that the only reason the land was set aside for wildlife is because it's unlivable for humans.) The immediate environs are not the most striking and beautiful around, and some may find the straightforward climb positively boring, but there are plenty of locals who love and appreciate this route for its convenience, and for the nice views from the lonely summit.

If time is an issue, Smelter will give you a good workout in the blink of an eye. The wide dirt road climbs gradually at first, then flattens for a moment before climbing in earnest. When the big power station comes into view (after mile 1.0), you're in the middle of a long, tough stretch leading to the intersection with County Road 212, located at the top of the hill just beyond the power station. A right turn on County Road 212 leads to slightly more technical surface that ascends gently for a short time, then winds left and skyward, granny-gear style. Areas of interest along this climb include a giant pile of uranium tailings covered in rocks, over to your right, looking like the backside of a dam.

The steep pitch abates before too long, but expect a few more toughies before the summit at mile 3.8. Even the *ubermensch* with bionic lungs could find himself panting and sweating while standing among the radio towers, staring out at the impressive panoramic view of ridges and ranges, pondering the colorful, urban-inspired graffiti on the many service shacks.

This is one of those roads that becomes impassable when wet, due to the freakish and evil nature of the fine shale. Don't let its south-facing orientation fool you.

Looking up the road at the top of Smelter Mountain.

MilesDirections

0.0 START from the parking area near the bottom of CR 211.

1.7 After passing a power station, take a right onto the dirt road at the top of the hill. This is CR 212—it looks tame from the bottom but will degenerate as you climb, and is often deeply rutted.

2.8 Pass a gated doubletrack on your left. This track is closed to the public.

3.8 You have conquered Smelter Mountain.

5.9 Back at the intersection, make sure you take a left.

7.6 That's all she wrote.

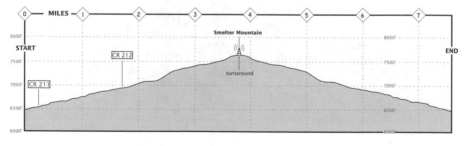

Ride Information

Trail Contacts:
Colorado Division of Wildlife, Durango, CO (970) 247-0855

Schedule:
May through October, due to weather. Mud is a crucial factor.

Maps:
USGS maps: Durango West, CO; Basin Mountain, CO

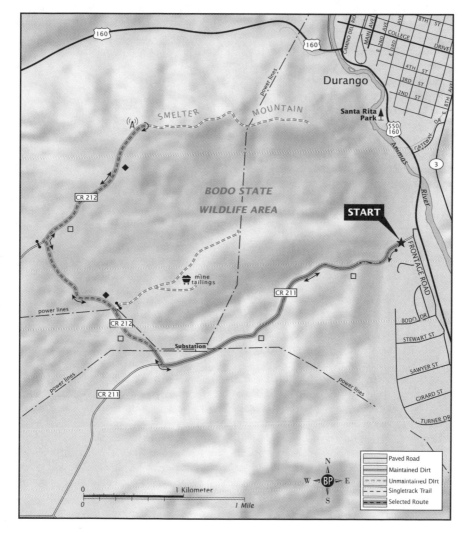

16

Old Railroad Grade

Ride Specs

Start: From the intersection of the Old Railroad Grade (FS 568) and Madden Peak Road (FS 316), about 20 miles west of Durango off U.S. 160

Length: 13.0-miles out-and-back

Approximate Riding Time: 1–3 hours

Technical Difficulty: Easy: wide, flat dirt road (with an option for some moderate double-track and singletrack)

Physical Difficulty: Easy: cruisin', on a Sunday afternoon

Trail Surface: 100% dirt road (with an option for rustic doubletrack and brief singletrack)

Lay of the Land: The semi-arid foothills west of Durango, in the transitional zone between deserts and mountains

Elevation Gain: 1,558 feet

Land Status: National forest

Other Trail Users: Motorists (cars and trucks), hikers, and equestrians

Getting There

From Durango: Drive west on U.S. 160 for about 20 miles. At the top of a hill, before the town of Mancos but beyond the Target Tree Campground, find FS 316 (Madden Peak Road) on the north side of the road—FS 316 is usually not marked. Follow FS 316 as it winds (briefly to the east) for almost a mile to the intersection of the Old Railroad Grade, also known as FS 568. There is parking available there, all around the intersection.

What's this? An easy ride on dirt in the vicinity of Durango? HOW CAN THIS BE?!!! It is not known who first hatched the idea of clearing this old rail route and thus giving local cyclists a chance to cruise on flat terrain, but it is said the poor bastard was dragged to the town square by an angry mob and beaten with an old pair of Rock Shox.

Seriously—Southwesterners are happy to have this pleasant and relaxing ride in their midst. The cruising takes place on the grade of the old Rio Grande Southern (RGS) railroad. Born in 1890, during the hot years of mining, the RGS operated on a route connecting Ridgway, Placerville, Telluride, Rico, Dolores, Mancos, and finally Durango, where it connected with the tracks of the Denver & Rio Grande. The RGS was a *narrow-gauge* line, its rails placed a mere three feet apart as an adaptation to the sharp turns and tight spaces of the rugged mountains.

After the last rails were spiked into Durango, in 1891, the line had one highly profitable year hauling ore to Durango's big smelter. Then the Sherman Silver Purchase Act (mandating the government's purchase of 4.5 million ounces of silver each year) was repealed in 1893, leading to the *Silver Panic*, and the air was let out of the balloon. Along with much of Colorado's mining industry, the RGS went bust,

then into receivership, but somehow managed to survive until 1951 as a hauler of agricultural products.

The iron between Mancos and Durango was the last to be laid down on the RGS line, and it was the last of the entire system to be abandoned and ripped up. In 1951, the rails of the RGS were sold as scrap for $409,000 to a Chicago company. The land and timber were sold off to various interests. Somewhere along the line, the section in question here was obtained by the Forest Service, cleared of brush, and transformed into Forest Service Road 568. (Nobody was beaten or even probed with Rock Shox as a result.)

The RGS was one of the briefly shining achievements of Otto Mears. Mears also developed 450 miles of toll roads in the region and sprouted three other narrow-gauge outfits into the impossible heights above Silverton, earning him the title *Pathfinder of the San Juans*. Mears managed to connect almost all but the tiniest mining hamlets of southwestern Colorado; however; considering that the actual routes were laid out by engineers like Charles Gibbs, and that most of the routes they appropriated were the time-honored paths of Utes, trappers, miners, and big game, Mears should be remembered less as pathfinder than fundraiser, motivator, and capitalist bulldog. Mears' fund-raising talents were mysterious and legendary. It's said that he went back East on one of his visits with potential investors and came home with $4 million—not a bad score for the 1800s. All of Mears' projects were completed with other people's money, although Mears himself was a frequent presence at the various job sites, sternly bossing the proceedings. His vision profoundly altered the landscape and the experience of living in the mining camps, making it both more comfortable and more expensive. Imagine trekking across a remote mountain pass in the late 1800s, and coming across a *tollbooth* of all things, like some kind of Monty Python skit. Such was the weirdness perpetrated on travelers through Otto Mears country. Mears' tolls were expensive, forcing low-wage miners to find alternate routes between towns.

The transportation legacy of Otto Mears alters our reality even today, especially as mountain bikers. The Old Railroad Grade is far from the only example of an archa-

ic Mears transportation project being put to use by post-modern recreationalists. Others include Engineer Pass (Ride 34), Cinnamon Pass, and all of the 4WD roads of the Alpine Loop, and most of the 4WD roads branching out from Silverton; the now-paved *Million Dollar Highway* that connects Silverton and Ouray, over Red Mountain Pass; and, near Telluride, South Fork Road and the excellent Galloping Goose singletrack (Ride 30), also on the RGS cut.

IF YOU THINK I'M THROUGH TALKING ABOUT OTTO MEARS, YOU'RE CRAZY. Mears mastered many more areas of life than can be hinted at with his web of roads and rail lines. Part and parcel of his ravenous capitalist fervor, Mears was deeply involved in the process of removing the Ute Indians from the San Juans, and thus removing another perceived obstacle to commerce and development. Mears, the orphaned son of a Russian mother and an English father, born in Russia, eased into the role of principal negotiator with the Utes. His method was successful but controversial. In the end, what finally induced Chief Ouray's Utes to agree to relocation was Mears' offer of $1,000, out of his own pocket, for every adult member of the tribe. The offer looked quite good to the Utes against a backdrop of bunk treaties and other government-sponsored fakery. Although a few members of congress protested that the mass bribe was an affront to morality as well as government protocol, the feds were ultimately not too proud to give the deal their official stamp of approval. Mears' cash was later reimbursed by the government. (The town of Ouray was named for the chief when the latter was good 'n' gone.)

After the tribe was marched to Utah, with U.S. soldiers prodding the refugees and lining the route with guns leveled, Mears learned that some of the Utes were plotting to kill him, and he immediately abandoned his self-appointed position as Indian liaison.

There's not much I can say about the physical features of the Old Railroad Grade. The accommodating dirt strip contours across the foothills, not exactly flat but almost, through scrub oak, ponderosa pine, and occasional aspen. The area—in fact,

MilesDirections

0.0 START from the intersection of the Old Railroad Grade (FS 568) and Madden Peak Road (FS 316). Head east on FS 568.

4.8 Tackle the only technical section along the way, the usually-dry crossing of Starvation Creek.

6.5 Turn around where the grade intersects FS 320, which drops steeply to the highway. *[Option. If you keep going on the railroad grade (staying right at the fork at mile 6.7), you'll find an increasingly technical surface leading to a fun singletrack. The track fades out about one mile after it starts.]*

13.0 Arrive back at your vehicle.

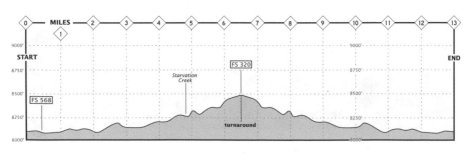

Ride Information

🕭 Trail Contacts:
San Juan National Forest, Supervisor's
Office, Durango, CO (970) 247–4874

🕙 Schedule:
Try it any time of year, but wait for several sunny days after any wet storms—the
mud will ruin you.

🅝 Maps:
USGS maps: Thompson Park, CO; and
Hesperus, CO • **USFS maps:** *San Juan
National Forest*

the entire zone between Durango and Mancos—is impressive during the fall color
change, and just a pleasant place to be any time of the year. Due to the low altitude,
this route could be clear even in deep, dark winter.

Except for occasional potholes and some very minor chunks, the grade is smooth
until it crosses Starvation Creek at mile 4.8. Poor Starvation Creek is often dry as a
bone. This crossing is only about 10 or 15 feet wide, is easily walked, and therefore
will not jeopardize this ride's "easy" rating.

At mile 6.5 you'll find a natural turnaround spot at the intersection with Forest
Service Road 320, beyond which the railbed quickly degenerates into rustic doubletrack.
The unimproved route from here becomes quite wavy and much rockier, eventually
morphing into a singletrack that provides some surprisingly good surfing along the old
rail grade. This could be just what you're looking for. Don't get too attached, however,
as the trail bogs out and loses itself after about a mile, then hits private property.

Even without the optional extension, this ride provides a significant chunk of mileage
for beginners. If 13 miles is too much—you know the drill—just turn around earlier.

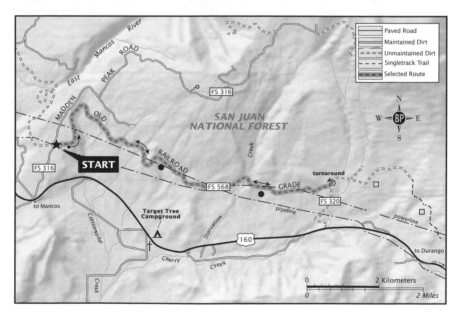

17

Purgatory 1990 World Championship Course Sampler

Ride Specs

Start: From the main parking lot at the Purgatory Ski Area
Length: 6.3-mile loop
Approximate Riding Time: 1 hour
Technical Difficulty: Moderate: primarily dirt road, doubletrack, and 4WD road
Physical Difficulty: Moderate to Difficult: a small loop with many short, steep climbs
Trail Surface: 80% 4WD road, 10% dirt road, 5% singletrack, and 5% paved path
Lay of the Land: The steep hillside of the Purgatory Ski Area
Elevation Gain: 1,448 feet
Land Status: National forest and ski area land
Other Trail Users: Hikers

Getting There

From Durango: Drive north on U.S. 550 for about 25 miles to the Purgatory Ski Area. Take a left into the ski area and park in the main parking lot.

Durango legend, Juli Furtado, bustin' a move.

I n 1990, not that long ago really, American racers were on top of the mountain biking world, and the capital city of that world was Durango. That was the year the first-ever UCI-sanctioned Mountain Bike World Championships were held at the Purgatory Ski Area north of town, and the cross-country races were won by two great Durango legends, Ned Overend and Juli Furtado (who is one of the most successful bike racers of all time, mountain or road, male or female).

Foreshadowing the soon-to-come dominance of Europeans in an American-made sport, Overend found himself battling an unknown Swiss, Thomas Frischknecht, for the top podium spot. The 19-year-old crushed the field and forced Overend into one of the most inhuman performances of his career. These days, you're likely to see Frischknecht's name near the top of the mens' World Cup standings, along with a whole bunch of Euros, Australians, and Canadians, but you'll be lucky to find a single American in the top 50. If you care about this sort of thing, you'll be pleased to know that several American juniors have been faring extremely well in international competition lately, so the situation is due to change.

This short loop doesn't follow the course entirely but it will give you a taste of what the racers had to deal with on that hot August day, when, ironically, the Euros were complaining that the course was too hard and set at too high of an altitude. (Purgatory isn't really very high, but compared to France it's in the stratosphere.)

Start at the ski area parking lot and head north to the adjacent dirt road. Climb up this road (Forest Service Road 578) for almost three miles, then turn left onto Elbert Creek Road. Soon after the turnoff, you'll find the right turn onto singletrack and the racecourse. Unless vandals have been at work, the course and its many turns will be marked clearly with signs.

Looking up one of the resort's lifts.

Generally, the racecourse is composed of brief strips of singletrack linking painfully steep doubletracks and 4WD roads. If you're like me, you'll probably find this, like many mountain bike racecourses, gratuitously steep and difficult. Recent construction has eclipsed the southern section of the Worlds loop, but there's still plenty of remaining terrain to help you imagine how it must have felt to chase Overend (a.k.a. The Lung) up an endless series of sharp climbs.

Personally, there are other things I would prefer to do with my Sunday afternoon, like go for a mountain bike ride and sit in the woods. Which is what I suggest you do as well, even after you've sampled your share of the old Worlds course. Purgatory—not a smart name from a marketing standpoint, you wouldn't think—is a great launching pad for a number of first-rate loops. The nearby Forest Service Road 578 leads west all the way to Bolam Pass or Hotel Draw and high adventure on the Colorado Trail, or, a little closer, the northern trailhead of the Hermosa Trail, which can be looped back down to the highway and back to the ski area. Or try the rest of Elbert Creek Road. About five miles on Elbert Creek Road leads either to the Elbert Creek singletrack, which winds down to the highway, or to the Dutch Creek Trail, which drops into Hermosa Canyon. The Dutch Creek Trail also has a connection across a rough ridge to the Jones Creek Trail, descending to Hermosa. Across the highway you'll find the famous, relaxing cruise on Old Lime Creek Road. Additionally, there are more options contained within the ski area itself. The Harris Park loop is one of these: a nice, mellow ride using gentle doubletracks that were ignored by the designers of the Worlds course.

MilesDirections

0.0 START riding north from the parking lot up the adjacent dirt road (FS 578).

2.9 Take a left onto Elbert Creek Road.

3.1 Turn right onto singletrack and the Worlds course. Usually, there are signs.

3.3 Turn left onto doubletrack.

3.9 Stay left at the fork.

4.5 Cross the road and bomb down a short section of singletrack.

5.9 Back at the base, take a left on the paved track that leads north to the parking area. *[Option. Construction has recently closed much of the course from this point to the south, but it may be worth a shot to poke around over there and see what's up. This was originally a 12-mile loop.]*

6.3 End the ride, back at the parking zone.

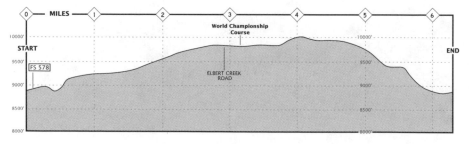

Ride Information

Trail Contacts:
San Juan National Forest, Supervisor's
Office, Durango, CO (970) 247-4874

Schedule:
June through mid October, due to weather

Maps:
USGS maps: Engineer Mountain, CO; and
Electra Lake, CO • **USFS maps:** *San
Juan National Forest*

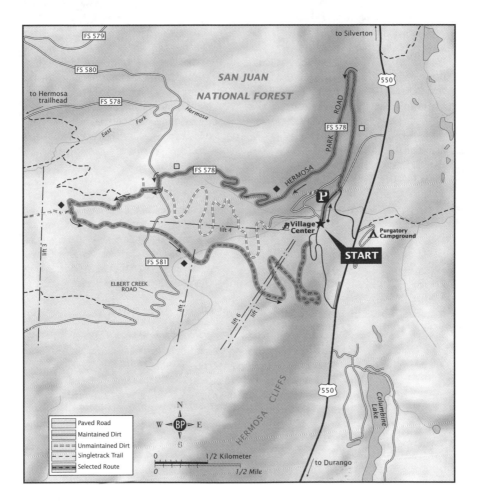

Old Lime Creek Road

Ride Specs

Start: From the northern intersection of Old Lime Creek Road and U.S. 550, about 30 miles north of Durango
Length: 11.4-mile point-to-point
Approximate Riding Time: 1–2 hours
Technical Difficulty: Easy to Moderate: dirt road with some notable rockiness
Physical Difficulty: Moderate: this road ain't flat
Trail Surface: 100% dirt road
Lay of the Land: Heavily forested corridor of Lime Creek, and its steep canyonside. Aspens are a major theme.
Elevation Gain: 1,720 feet
Land Status: National forest
Other Trail Users: Motorists (cars and trucks) and equestrians

China Wall at dusk.

Getting There

With Shuttle

From Durango: Drive north on U.S. 550 about 27 miles to the southern terminus of Lime Creek Road. There is parking available at this intersection, located on the right side of U.S. 550, just after the highway makes a sharp right-hand turn a few miles beyond the Purgatory Ski Area. Leave one vehicle here. Drive a second vehicle to Lime Creek Road's northern intersection with U.S. 550, located about 8.5 miles north of the southern intersection, at the low point between Coal Bank and Molas passes. Parking is readily available on the dirt around this intersection, on the right side of the highway.

Without Shuttle

From Durango: Drive north on U.S. 550 about 35.5 miles to Lime Creek Road's northern intersection with U.S. 550, at the low point between Coal Bank and Molas passes. Parking is readily available on the dirt around this intersection, on the right side of the highway.

L ime Creek Road is best ridden as a shuttle. That's a little hard for me to admit, because I've never been a huge fan of shuttles. You know: shuttles double the driving, the gas, the pollution, and all the other sniveling car-related hassles. But this pleasant ride along a surviving portion of the old Durango-Silverton stage road really lends itself to the shuttle approach, especially for beginning riders. The length of the road, 11.4 miles one way, is plenty for most folks. Also consider that riding Lime Creek Road both ways, in the out-and-back format, *triples* the total elevation gain.

The one-way shuttle is mostly downhill, but it's not necessarily easy, as some recent guidebooks have suggested. There is a significant climb from around mile 5.9 to mile 7.6, gaining 500-plus feet. It's not a killer, but you are guaranteed to feel this climb.

Old Lime Creek Road takes off from U.S. Route 550 in the sublime environs between Coal Bank Hill and Molas Pass, at the low point between the two lumps.

The road meanders southward for a few miles, then twists down to the valley floor, where it hugs Lime Creek for a mile or so. Your biggest danger on this bumpy but non-technical road is getting run down by a speeding SUV on a blind corner. Please be aware.

Lime Creek starts each spring with a lively flow, then diminishes to a meager trickle by summer's end. Those wishing to loiter by the creek and splash through the water (if there is any) should grab the opportunity before the road climbs back up onto the western slope. Those not wishing to loiter creekside should perhaps be placed in some sort of program, eh?

The road climbs moderately from the creek, narrowing and chunking-up a bit as it makes its way up the side of the canyon. As the road clings to a shelf perched high above the river, riders looking back north are treated to the best views of the day. Lots of folks take one look at this canyon and assume they're upstream on the Animas. In reality, the Animas River is over to the east, on the other side of the West Needles, carving a far more severe gorge. Lime Creek's canyon is subtler and more shallow, but it's still impressive.

Along the shelf-road section, an old castle-style stone wall, just a few feet high, separates travelers from the modest abyss. This is known as the China Wall (or Chinese Wall). The history of this structure has been somewhat clouded. It's been written that the wall was built in the late 1800s, and it's also been written that the

Civilian Conservation Corps built the wall in the 1930s as part of the Depression-era WPA program. Even the research department at the Durango Public Library has been somewhat stumped by the China Wall's past. I'd be willing to bet that some combination of the two explanations is correct.

After topping out, the road cruises quickly down to the highway, passing a boggy, beaver-built wetland on the left, and, on the right, the Potato Lake Trail, a mile-long hiking trail that leads to Potato Lake, on Potato Hill.

To explore the *upper* reaches of Lime Creek, where the creek is in its crystal clear infancy, try the Molas Pass to Coal Bank ride (Ride 19), a moderately strenuous, high-altitude singletrack shuttle that's accessible to enthusiastic novices and intermediates, but nonetheless requires thorough preparation.

Ride Information

Trail Contacts:
San Juan National Forest, Supervisor's Office, Durango, CO (970) 247–4874

Schedule:
June to October, due to snow and ice at moderately high altitude

Maps:
USGS maps: Engineer Mountain, CO; and Snowdon Peak, CO • **USFS maps:** *San Juan National Forest*

MilesDirections

0.0 START from the informal parking area near the northern intersection of U.S. 550 and Lime Creek Road, located at the low point between Coal Bank Hill and Molas Pass.

4.7 The road arrives at water level near Lime Creek.

5.9 The road starts up a long, sustained climb.

7.6 The grade flattens, and the route is basically downhill from here to the finish.

11.4 Lime Creek Road spills out onto U.S. 550, where your second vehicle is waiting. *[Options. Those without a second car can turn back here for a 22.8-mile out-and-back, or use U.S. 550 to loop it (19.9 miles).]*

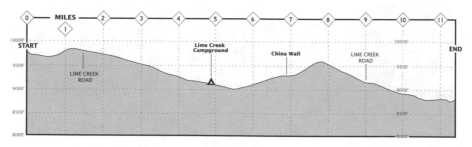

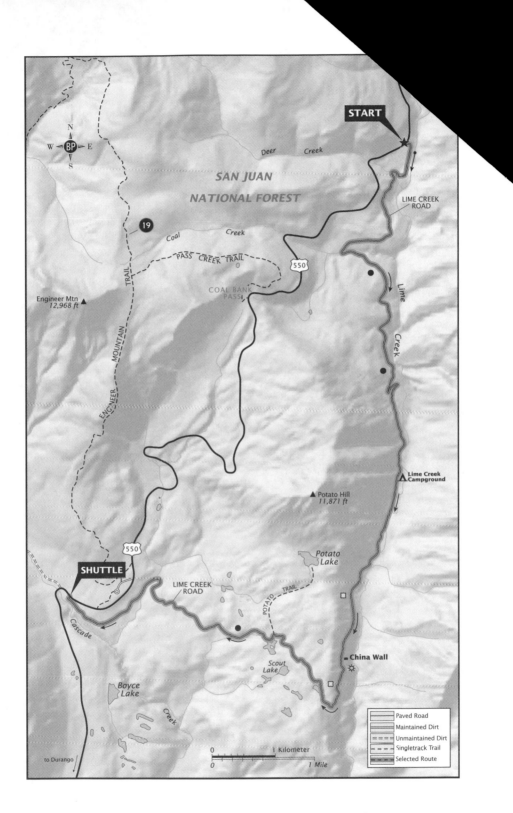

START

LIME CREEK
ROAD

Deer   Creek

SAN JUAN
NATIONAL FOREST

19

Coal   Creek

PASS CREEK TRAIL

550

COAL BANK
PASS

Engineer Mtn ▲
12,968 ft

Lime

Creek

ENGINEER   MOUNTAIN   TRAIL

▲Lime Creek
△Campground

▲ Potato Hill
11,871 ft

550

SHUTTLE

Potato
Lake

LIME CREEK
ROAD

POTATO   TRAIL

Cascade

□

□

Scout
Lake

☼ China Wall
☼

Boyce
Lake

Creek

to Durango

	Paved Road
	Maintained Dirt
	Unmaintained Dirt
	Singletrack Trail
	Selected Route

0   1 Kilometer
0   1 Mile

Molas Pass to Coal Bank Pass

to Silverton

...mmit.

...

Approximate ....–5 hours
Technical Difficulty: Moderate to Difficult: you don't have to be Hans Rey
Physical Difficulty: Difficult: a serious, high altitude ride
Trail Surface: 100% singletrack
Lay of the Land: Wide open meadows and sparse forests near timberline, with peaks all around
Elevation Gain: 3,670 feet
Land Status: National forest
Other Trail Users: Hikers and equestrians

Getting There

With Shuttle

From Durango: Drive two vehicles north from Durango on U.S. 550, 32 miles to the summit of Coal Bank Pass. Just on the other side of the pass, on the left, find the dirt parking area for the Pass Creek trailhead. Leave one vehicle here. Drive north another eight miles on U.S. 550 to the Molas Pass summit. Park near the top of the pass on either side. The start of the Colorado Trail is located about a half block down the other side, on the left (west) side of the highway.

Without Shuttle

From Durango: Drive north from Durango on U.S. 550, 40 miles to the Molas Pass summit. Park near the top of the pass on either side. The start of the Colorado Trail is located about a half block down the other side, on the left (west) side of the highway. *[Option. This ride also works great as a full loop from either pass summit (25.7 miles total, including eight miles on the paved highway).]*

G reat, incredible, sweet, fantastic. Trying to describe Durango's prime trail rides, I've used up all the words. I'm starting to sound like a talking head from the chamber of commerce. But that's just the way it is around here. And this ride, this elegant arc through the high hills, using prime bits of the Colorado, Engineer Mountain, and Pass Creek trails, could very well be the finest of them all.

Although this is indeed an adventurous ride, the adventure is derived primarily from the altitude and the quasi-backcountry setting. This is different from many other famous Durango-area rides—like Missionary Ridge, Haflin Canyon, and Dutch Creek—which remain at relatively low altitudes but are adventurous because of their challenging terrain and technical trail surfaces.

The high elevation on this loop (hovering around 12,000 feet) could cause a few problems for you. At best, you'll feel slightly short of breath. A small percentage of flatlanders will become nauseous just hanging out at the trailhead. The only cure for this potentially debilitating illness, officially called Acute Mountain Sickness, is to

retreat to lower altitudes. (Those arriving in the foothills from the lowlands should hang out a few days before attempting anything as high as this ride; during this period of acclimatization, pay attention to any symptoms of AMS, especially nausea and headaches, which would indicate that a trip to the high(er) mountains is inadvisable.) Another reality of big altitude is unpredictable and ever-changing weather, with generally much colder temperatures and stronger winds than those found below 7,000 feet in Durango. Prevent a weather-related disaster by packing a massive amount of "polypro" (a synthetic wicking fiber that works particularly well in under-layers), a waterproof shell, long fingered gloves, and a warm hat. You might also appreciate wool-blend socks and a thermal layer of wool or fleece.

This singletrack is largely smooth, with an assortment of interesting technical problems necessitating a dismount here and there. The general technical attitude of the trail is moderate, although there are lengthy sections on or near the Engineer Mountain Trail that are extremely boggy or dug into the tundra so deep and narrow that they have become impossible to pedal through. Much of the route has an eerie, Disneyland feel, as if the rock obstacles had been fabricated in Taiwan and placed at strategic intervals on an otherwise smooth singletrack. Sort of a computer-generated sensation. (The cool white steps at mile 1.1 are a good example. The hidden smooth line on these steps is all the way right, then all the way left.) As such, this route is accessible to strong-willed intermediate riders, and possibly newcomers to the sport,

The view from the Colorado Trail. This area was cleared by fire.

provided they are plenty enthusiastic and in good shape. For those strong roadies who have been wondering what all the fat-tired fuss is about, this ride will show them what's up.

The opening miles (using one of the finest lengths of the Colorado Trail) are through a popular camping zone, and there are usually a lot of hikers around. The consistent friendliness of the pedestrians around these parts is a happy indication that local mountain bikers have been doing a satisfactory job—so far—of getting along with other trail users. I know this sounds like something the hippy teacher from *Beavis and Butthead* would say, but this condition is like a fragile seedling that needs to be carefully nurtured. Do your part by slowing to a walking pace around hikers, maybe smiling a bit, saying *howdy*, and *thanks, by the way, for scrambling off the trail, even though everyone knows that bikes are supposed to yield to hikers.* (The reality is that hikers almost always jump off the trail to let mountain bikes pass, and are happy to do it, as long as they get some kind of thank you. That's all it takes. You

MilesDirections

0.0 START riding up the Colorado Trail from its trailhead at the Molas Pass summit.

0.8 Stay left as the Colorado Trail heads straight for Little Molas Lake.

1.0 Cross a dirt road at a camping zone. Begin a steady climb.

3.0 Take a left at the T-intersection, to remain on the Colorado Trail route. *[FYI. The right-hand fork looks like it might be a climber, but it descends to U.S. 550.]*

10.7 Turn left onto the Engineer Mountain Trail (Trail 507).

11.6 Enjoy some technical downhill switchbacks.

12.0 Pass the intersection with the White Creek Trail.

15.0 Take a left onto the Pass Creek Trail, and descend all the way home *[Option. For an alternate ending to this ride, continue straight here on the Engineer Mountain Trail. This will take you up onto the base of Engineer Mountain, then down the long slope to U.S. 550, dropping you on pavement about six miles south of Coal Bank Hill. If you choose this option, you may want your shuttle car located downhill at the Durango Mountain (Purgatory) Resort, or near Cascade Creek, where it crosses U.S. 550 just a few miles south of the Engineer Mountain Trail's end.]*

16.4 The trail swoops down to a pond.

17.7 Pop out at the Pass Creek trailhead near Coal Bank Pass *[Option. If you have only one vehicle to work with, or someone has stolen your shuttle car, use the highway to complete the loop: ride north on U.S. 550, down Coal Bank Hill and back up Molas Pass, for an additional eight miles of pavement.]*

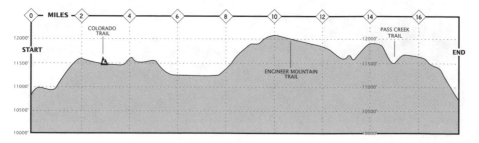

could really make a positive impression by (gasp) actually stopping for a few seconds to chat with a couple of hikers. Imagine—50 people a day stopping to chat with hikers. They'd call it a Movement.

After the camping zone at Little Molas Lake, the trail climbs steadily for a few miles to a T-intersection with a contouring singletrack. Turn left onto this smooth strand—still the Colorado Trail—and begin a rolling cruise that persists for an unbelievable five miles before arriving at the bottom of the next sustained climb. It would be difficult to overstate the excellence of this section, meandering through the glacier-scoured wetlands, around a handful of modest, rounded peaks. The alarmed chirping of pikas and marmots greets you at every turn. Among the singletrack's many modest climbs and occasional weird rock problems, what you will most likely remember is the large percentage of quick and smooth. I'm sure you'll agree that this is one of the finest trail sections anywhere.

With a wide perma-grin firmly planted on your face, the trail contours across the base of the 13,432-foot Twin Sisters formation and then begins a sobering climb, and generally becomes more challenging for a few miles prior to its T-intersection with the Engineer Mountain Trail (Trail 507). Up here, near the high point of the ride, the scene is even more otherworldly, giving the impression that you're trekking across Antarctica, or Ron Howard's vision of Antarctica. The Engineer Mountain Trail

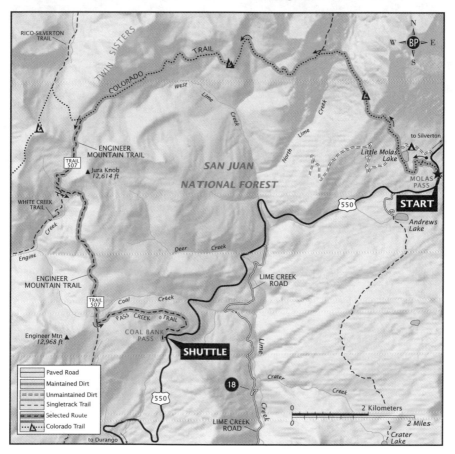

climbs briefly from the T-intersection, then drops off the back of Jura Knob (12,614 feet), on a series of rough switchbacks, into the Engine Creek drainage. Back into the timber, then comes the most serious climbing of the day (from mile 12.0 to 13.0) as the trail remounts the golden ridge. Much of the Engineer Mountain Trail has been made more difficult due to its having sunk deep into the spongy tundra, forming a narrow trough in places.

Proud-looking Engineer Mountain (12,968 feet), perhaps casting a massive shadow across the lumpy tundra, is viewed from a few impressive angles during the latter

Dressing for Colorado's Unpredictable Weather

*In the Northwestern states they talk about rain. In the South they talk about heat and humidity. The major theme of Colorado's weather is volatility. As the saying goes, "If you don't like the weather in Colorado, wait five minutes." Where else can you experience pounding rain, heavy snow, and blazing sunlight—not just on the same day but **at the same time**? Adding high elevation to the mix makes for even more explosive atmospheric conditions.*

*Those who know it well would not trade Colorado's alpine weather for anything, but it can cause serious problems for the unsuspecting cyclist who starts his ride under a clear blue sky, clad in a single confident layer of lycra, only to encounter whiteout conditions a few hours and several thousand feet up the mountain. Our poorly dressed cyclist—now soaked, chilled, and possibly bonking—could easily develop **hypothermia** in these circumstances.*

Riders who carry the proper gear will forever avoid such weather-related crises. Even on the nicest summer days, it's unwise to embark on a long, high altitude ride without a water- and windproof shell, polypropylene layers top and bottom, long-fingered gloves, and warm hat. Wool socks and weatherproof pants are also nice. Many riders will not like the extra weight, but it's best to bite the bullet and prepare for the worst.

Obviously, for short rides near town, one's meteorological paranoia can be left at the trailhead along with the extra gear. But longer rides carry the weight of many dangerous possibilities. Even if the weather stays clear all day, there is always a chance you will destroy a wheel or some other crucial piece of equipment (a leg perhaps), or you could simply become very lost. There are many ways to become stranded in the San Juans overnight, when summertime temperatures routinely dip below 30°F. Are you prepared?

portions of this ride. Don't confuse this Engineer Mountain with the Engineer Mountain up north, near Engineer Pass (Ride 34), or any of the many other Engineer mountains in the general vicinity. The Engineer Mountain Trail, pointed directly at its namesake, drops from the wide ridge and intersects with the Pass Creek Trail at mile 15.0, on the other side of a clearing. This intersection has been unmarked, but it's fairly obvious. This Pass Creek singletrack provides a quick, efficient escape from the dreamy sub-alpine zone, so maybe you'd prefer to loiter around up there for a while before returning to the pavement zone.

Ride Information

🕐 Trail Contacts:
San Juan National Forest, Durango, CO
(970) 247–4874

🕐 Schedule:
Mid June through September, due to weather and snowmelt. Expect winter conditions year round on this ride, and pack accordingly.

Ⓝ Maps:
USGS maps: Snowdon Peak, CO; Silverton, CO; Ophir, CO; and Engineer Mountain, CO • **USFS maps:** *San Juan National Forest*

The trail heads toward Engineer Mountain.

Hermosa Creek Shuttle (from the Top)

Start: The upper (north) Hermosa Creek trailhead, located about nine miles west of Purgatory, on FS 578

Length: 19.5-mile point-to-point

Approximate Riding Time: 2–5 hours

Technical Difficulty: Moderate to Difficult: there are some big, pointy rocks from the outset

Physical Difficulty: Moderate: mostly cruising

Trail Surface: 100% singletrack/widetrack

Lay of the Land: Up close and personal with Hermosa Creek and the green northern slope of Hermosa Canyon

Elevation Gain: 3,554 feet

Land Status: National forest

Other Trail Users: Hikers, equestrians, and motorcyclists

Getting There

With Shuttle

From Durango: Drive two vehicles north on U.S. 550 about eight miles to Hermosa. Take a left onto CR 203, then, almost immediately, a right onto CR 201. You could park here in the makeshift parking area by the railroad tracks, or drive another four miles on CR 201 until the road dead-ends at the Hermosa Creek trailhead. Leave one vehicle here. In a second vehicle, drive 18 miles north from Hermosa on U.S. 550. Just past the Purgatory Ski Area (recently renamed Durango Mountain Resort), take a left onto FS 578. Signs point the way to the Hermosa trailhead. Drive almost nine miles on FS 578 until the Hermosa Creek trailhead parking area comes into view on the left. Take a left onto the access road that crosses the East Fork of Hermosa Creek and leads directly to the parking area.

Without Shuttle

From Durango: Drive north on U.S. 550 about 26 miles. Just past the Purgatory Ski Area (recently renamed Durango Mountain Resort), take a left onto FS 578. Signs point the way to the Hermosa trailhead. Drive almost nine miles on FS 578 until the Hermosa Creek trailhead parking area comes into view on the left. Take a left onto the access road that crosses the East Fork of Hermosa Creek and leads directly to the parking area.

This famous one-way cruise down the well-named Hermosa Canyon (*hermosa* means beautiful) provides an extended dose of thrilling singletrack without much pain, and gives enthusiastic novices an unbelievable introduction to the joys of real trail riding. Personally, I prefer the non-shuttle approach to this trail (see Ride 21)—and most other trails, for that matter. But this time-honored, gravity-assisted shuttle—a Durango tradition—is better for beginners and intermediates than the more serious out-and-back.

The opening five miles of this predominantly downhill route are on a rocky, riverside widetrack. The trail is just barely wide enough to be labeled a widetrack—it's as wide as any little singletrack ribbon would eventually become if it were used as much as this one has been. Mountain bikes are probably not the worst trail abusers here. This dirt is punished regularly by cyclists, hikers, fishermen, picnickers, gawkers, strollers, the Whassup Guys, motorcycles, cows, and horses. Toddlers may dance

The north trailhead. Expect all kinds of trail user types here.

101

across your path. You could be stopped by a tail-swishing wall of horse in the narrows of the canyon. I've even seen Forest Service people out here on four-wheelers. The result of all the access-induced traffic is a chunky trail with lots of available lines. If taken slowly, it's a little rough but pretty easy. If you're going fast down the slight but invitingly straight descent, there could be danger, or at least pinch flats, among the sharp rocks. (Actually, pinch flats themselves can be quite dangerous. If a pinch flat causes a slow leak in the front tube—not uncommon—the rider will continue on his way, unknowing, and the deflating tire could eventually cause a bad, wheel-twisting wreck.)

The density of other trail users falls dramatically as the trail thins, smooths out, and switches to the south side of the creek via a cushy new bridge at mile 5.0, then hangs over the creek for a mile before recrossing on another bridge. These crossings, not long ago, were bridge-less and terribly adventurous during the spring run-off; today their most adventurous aspect is the looming possibility of sunburn.

Below the bridges, the trail passes the confluence with Salt Creek at mile 6.8, and enters a new phase. The trail leaves the valley floor and gently contours onto the

MilesDirections

0.0 START from the upper (north) Hermosa Creek trailhead.

3.2 Pass the intersection with the Corral Draw Trail.

5.0 Cross a bridge over Hermosa Creek. The trail is really starting to thin out.

6.0 Cross back over on another bridge.

6.8 Pass the intersection with the Salt Creek Trail. Get ready for the best section of the Hermosa Trail, dead ahead.

14.7 Cross Dutch Creek. Another bridge for the new millennium.

15.6 Pass the junction with the Dutch Creek Trail.

19.4 Stay left as one or two trails branch off to the right. Climb a short, steep hill.

19.5 The trail pops out on CR 201. *[Options. Riders with just one vehicle can turn back here to make a very long, excellent out-and-back. Also, several very long loop options are possible, but each is arduous and should be attempted only by very fit riders. An example: descend on the Hermosa Trail to the Dutch Creek turnoff and take a left (mile 15.6). Climb roughly up the Dutch Creek single-track—here's where that fitness comes in handy—until its intersection with the Pinkerton-Flagstaff Trail, then take another left, continuing the climb. Pop out onto Elbert Creek Road (FS 581), which winds north across the mountain and eventually descends through the ski area to FS 578. Take a left onto FS 578 and cruise back to the upper Hermosa Creek trailhead. That's in the neighborhood of 45 miles.]*

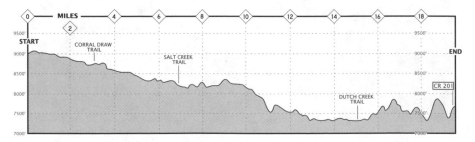

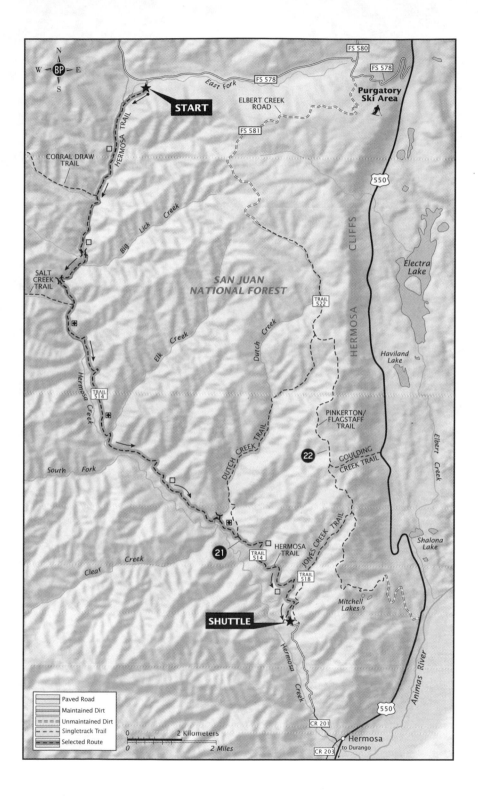

N
W—BP—E
S

START

Purgatory
Ski Area

FS 580

FS 578

FS 578

ELBERT CREEK
ROAD

FS 581

CORRAL DRAW
TRAIL

HERMOSA TRAIL

Big Lick Creek

US 550

CLIFFS

Electra
Lake

SAN JUAN
NATIONAL FOREST

TRAIL
522

SALT
CREEK
TRAIL

Elk Creek

Dutch Creek

HERMOSA

Haviland
Lake

Hermosa Creek

TRAIL
514

PINKERTON/
FLAGSTAFF
TRAIL

22

GOULDING
CREEK TRAIL

South Fork

Elbert Creek

Shalona
Lake

DUTCH CREEK TRAIL

JONES CREEK TRAIL

21

TRAIL
514

HERMOSA
TRAIL

Clear Creek

TRAIL
518

Mitchell
Lakes

SHUTTLE

Hermosa Creek

Animas River

US 550

Paved Road
Maintained Dirt
Unmaintained Dirt
Singletrack Trail
Selected Route

0   2 Kilometers

0   2 Miles

CR 201

CR 203

Hermosa
to Durango

slope of the canyon, and soon it is far above the creek, winding from side-drainage to mini-drainage in sublime, round turns. Expect occasional rock obstacles, roots, big mama pinecones, and assorted detritus from an impressive crop of evergreens. Here is a trail that rewards the subtle, relaxed moves of an experienced trail rider—feathering the brakes, constantly shifting body weight and gears—and can be ridden quite thrillingly. Without any significant, sustained climbs, the physical and technical levels rarely approach the red zone, although the trail gives you a little something to think about at every turn. This section, roughly between Salt Creek and Dutch Creek, is the soul of Hermosa Canyon and a must-do for any mountain biker passing within 300 light years.

After Dutch Creek, the trail climbs for a few miles. Shuttlehounds tend to worry about this pitch, a 500-footer, but many advanced riders see this section for what it is: a gentle ramp leading to the finishing rollers.

Ride Information

Trail Contacts:

San Juan National Forest, Supervisor's Office, Durango, CO (970) 247–4874

Schedule:

Mid May through mid October, due to weather

Maps:

USGS maps: Hermosa, CO; Monument Hill, CO; Elk Creek, CO; and Hermosa Peak, CO • **USFS maps:** *San Juan National Forest*

Hermosa Creek Out-and-Back (from the Bottom)

Ride Specs

Start: From the lower (south) Hermosa Creek trailhead, located at the dead end of CR 201, about four miles west of Hermosa
Length: 25.4-mile out-and-back
Approximate Riding Time: 3.5–7 hours
Technical Difficulty: Moderate: this trail alternates between sections of fast cruising and rougher patches of roots and rocks of all sizes. Lots of gear shifts.
Physical Difficulty: Moderate to Difficult: although the ride's many climbs ascend relatively gently, the overall length and consistent up-and-down make for an unavoidable workout
Trail Surface: 100% singletrack
Lay of the Land: Gorgeous, lush forest of tall trees in a long, deep canyon, accompanied by Hermosa Creek and its many tributaries
Elevation Gain: 3,420 feet
Land Status: National forest
Other Trail Users: Hikers, equestrians, motorcyclists, and Ned Overend

Getting There

From Durango: Drive north on U.S. 550 for eight miles to Hermosa. Take a left onto CR 203, then, almost immediately, a right onto CR 201. Drive four miles on CR 201 until the road dead-ends at the Hermosa Creek trailhead.

I t has become somewhat of a tradition to experience the ethereal Hermosa Creek singletrack by shuttling to the trail's northern trailhead, west of the Purgatory Ski Area (see Ride 20). From the north end, a five-mile runway of rocky, riverside widetrack leads to the curvy singletrack, which thereafter loses about 1,000 feet of elevation (with a few significant climbs thrown in) on the way to its southern terminus near the village of Hermosa. This popular one-way route allows intermediate and novice riders to enjoy the entire length of trail without killing themselves. In my humble opinion, however, a better time can be had with an out-and-back from the southern trailhead. This makes for a longer and more adventurous ride, and, as such, riders will probably need a pile of food as well as water filters or iodine pills. Still, the simple out-and-back eliminates the shuttle-induced hassle of extra vehicles and extra driving, allows for customizable ride length, and, most importantly, provides even more trail surfing opportunities.

Those who are addicted to the shuttle approach may not realize that the Hermosa Trail is fast from the bottom, too. This trail invites speed right out of the gate, even though you're gaining altitude for the first several miles (before a significant, rock-strewn descent into the Dutch Creek drainage). After crossing Dutch Creek on a luxurious bridge, there is plenty more climbing, but hardly any could be classified as steep

by mountain bikers' standards, and around every third corner or so there seems to be a nice section of smooth downhill to fuel your momentum. Along the 12.7-mile stretch of winding singletrack (25.4 miles roundtrip, with an option for much more), enjoy all the usual suspects: roots, rocks, brook crossings, downed timber in the spring, and a variety of other trail users who deserve your respectful consideration. There are spots where the trail seems somewhat precariously perched on the side of the canyon. But the overall feel of this trail is quick. This is trail riding at its finest. Few will experience these sweet curves without falling in love.

Adding to the moderately adventurous feel of this ride is the canyon topography, which prevents riders from seeing what storms are bearing down on them. Expect an afternoon thunderstorm, and haul the proper gear so you don't have to worry about it.

At some point, after carving a half million turns along the winding singletrack, simply turn around and head back. I like Salt Creek for a turnaround (mile 12.7),

Riding along Hermosa Trail during the fall color change.

where the trail drops to the wet valley floor. The trail hugs the river from here to the northern trailhead (another seven miles) and soon morphs into a rocky widetrack. Many riders will decide to turn back before Salt Creek, and others, no doubt, would feel strong enough to continue all the way to the northern trailhead before turning back (training for the Olympics or something). Such is the beauty of the out-and-back format, allowing for fully adjustable riding distance. On the return trip, the Hermosa Trail reinvents itself, and rewards your effort with more down than up.

This route plunges into the heart of an impressive fir and spruce forest. Like much of the San Juan forests (surrounded all around by arid and semi-arid lands), the Hermosa Canyon is surprisingly lush and the trees are impressively tall. Near Dutch Creek the trail passes through a stand of gigantic aspen, then dives into a creekside area where the towering Douglas firs are covered with hanging moss. It's not the kind of scene normally associated with Colorado, but that's the paradox of the San Juans. A wide variety of furry and feathered creatures flourish in this watery environment. Don't take it too personally, but the many coyote and puma scats left right out in the middle of the singletrack are a kind of symbolic protest against the humans hogging their trail.

MilesDirections

0.0 START from the lower (south) Hermosa Creek Trail trailhead.

3.9 Pass the Dutch Creek Trail turnoff on the right. *[Option. This trail climbs over a little hump then cruises into the Dutch Creek drainage, where it climbs roughly for several miles. From the top side, there are options to Elbert Creek Road and the Elbert Creek Trail, or, to the south, the ragged Pinkerton-Flagstaff Trail drops down to Mitchell Lakes or the*

Jones Creek Trail. (See Ride 22 for a description of a counter-clockwise loop featuring the Jones Creek, Pinkerton-Flagstaff, Dutch Creek, and Hermosa Trails.)]

4.8 Cross the bridge over Dutch Creek.

12.7 Enter a clearing as the trail nears Hermosa Creek. There is a sign pointing out the Salt Creek Trail. Turn around here. (Or keep going. It's basically still a free country, at the time of this writing.)

25.4 Arrive back at the trailhead.

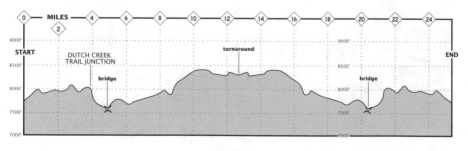

Ride Information

☏ Trail Contacts:
San Juan National Forest, Supervisor's Office, Durango, CO (970) 247–4874

⏱ Schedule:
May through October, due to weather

Ⓝ Maps:
USGS maps: Hermosa, CO; Monument Hill, CO; Elk Creek, CO • **USFS maps:** *San Juan National Forest*

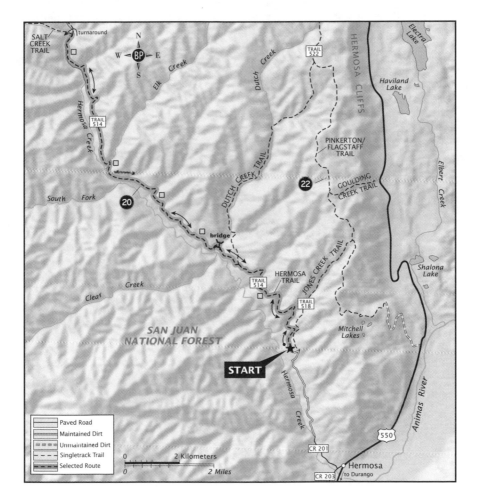

Jones Creek–
Dutch Creek Loop

Ride Specs

Start: From the Hermosa Creek/Jones Creek trailhead near Hermosa
Length: 19.5-mile loop
Approximate Riding Time: 3.5–6 hours
Technical Difficulty: Difficult: dicey trails may cause you to eat some dirt
Physical Difficulty: Difficult: many steep walking sections make this a strenuous adventure
Trail Surface: 100% singletrack
Lay of the Land: Pleasant, cow-trampled meadows and aspen forests on fairly steep slopes, with occasional views of the jagged northern peaks
Elevation Gain: 4,730 feet
Land Status: National forest
Other Trail Users: Hikers, equestrians, motorcyclists, and cows

Getting There

From Durango: Drive north on U.S. 550 for eight miles to Hermosa. Take a left onto CR 203, then, almost immediately, a right onto CR 201. Drive four miles on CR 201 until the road dead-ends at the Hermosa Creek trailhead. The start of the Jones Creek Trail is about a block back down this road, on the north side. Essentially, both trails share the same trailhead.

Jones Creek, Dutch Creek, Hermosa. Just mentioning the names gets the juice flowing. Using the inhospitable Pinkerton-Flagstaff Trail as a connector, this loop connects all three classic, Durango-area trails into a challenging mini-epic. Feint-hearted souls should save themselves the trouble of even embarking on this quite difficult but rewarding singletrack adventure through the foothills of the La Plata Mountains.

Enjoy the first leg of this route, on a trail that's often mentioned as a favorite among two-wheeled townies. The Jones Creek Trail often gives the impression that it was designed for cycling (which it was not). The general feel of Jones Creek is moderate, steady climbing on smooth trail, although there are more than a few steeps and techno root problems along the way. The four-mile stretch is bound to beat you down to some degree. My advice is to take it easy on Jones Creek, save your energy for the somewhat harsh Pinkerton-Flagstaff connector.

At mile 4.3, the trail ushers you into a sizable cow-sponsored meadow, one of many along this route. The huge plops of dung are provided free of charge for your enjoyment. Also in this meadow, there *would* be a T-intersection with the Pinkerton-Flagstaff Trail, if both trails weren't faded out. Take a left onto the ghostly traces of the Pinkerton-Flagstaff Trail, and find the well-defined cut as it twists out of the meadow and into the aspens. Here begins a long grunt that will make you appreciate the thoughtful construction of the Jones Creek ascent—a mere memory—as Pinkerton-Flagstaff gains altitude with little or no subtlety, dispensing with switch-

backs on its straight and painful climb to the ridge. Much of the Pinkerton-Flagstaff climb is unrideable due to major inclines, even with a good-sized downhill section in the middle.

It's difficult to say when the trail actually mounts the ridge—I'd guess about mile 7.4 or so—because the ridge itself is hilly and there are some minor walk-ups all the way until about mile 8.6, when you begin the final roll down to the intersection with the Dutch Creek Trail. Along the ridge, expect not only steep climbs but very difficult, rocky descents among the occasional rollers. Pinkerton-Flagstaff can be an ordeal for cyclists, but it functions nicely as a connector between two classic moun-

tain bike trails. Like an obnoxious relative, we tolerate it. You should allow several hours to conquer this section, which is just over five miles long.

The Dutch Creek Trail is the third leg of our journey. This exciting ribbon descends rapidly and somewhat dangerously next to Dutch Creek for about five miles (with a half-mile climb near the bottom). If you don't already know what you're doing on the descents, you will by the time you reach bottom on this one, or you'll be injured. With an endless series of rock gardens, drop-offs, and speedy off-camber sections hanging just barely onto menacing slopes over the creek, you could say this section is a face plant waiting to happen. (Interestingly enough, when I was up here checking mileage for this guide, I avoided the Dutch Creek face plant but ate some dirt on the Pinkerton-Flagstaff ridge section, augering hard on one of those root-mangled rock slides. Several years had gone by since I experienced such a dramatic wreck.) Don't let me scare you away with my warnings. Though Dutch Creek is dangerous, it's also excellent and fun, with enough twists and turns to keep the inclines manageable, and there are even smooth sections. Ironically, it is probably the occa-

MilesDirections

0.0 START riding up the Jones Creek Trail from its trailhead on CR 201. The trail climbs on a cycling-conducive route for over four miles, with a few downhill breaks along the way, and a few steeps.

4.3 Arrive at the lower end of a decent-sized sub-alpine cow pasture. As the trail approaches the top end of this meadow, it completely fades out. Look for a well-defined trail headed up into the aspens on your left. Begin the strenuous climb up this, the Pinkerton-Flagstaff Trail. The next ten miles of singletrack are full of technical difficulties.

5.2 No, you are not hallucinating. You are actually going downhill. There is plenty more climbing ahead, followed by rocky descents, and more climbing.

7.6 I ate some trail around here somewhere. Not on purpose.

8.6 Climb off and on until this point, where the trail starts rolling quickly.

9.3 Turn left onto the Dutch Creek Trail and descend. The next several miles demand your full concentration.

12.1 Cross a cattle guard.

14.7 Begin a tough, 0.4-mile climb as the trail leaves the Dutch Creek drainage.

15.6 Turn left onto the Hermosa Creek Trail. The trail is headed slightly uphill here, but the next four miles are predominantly downhill.

19.4 Stay left here. Climb a short, steep one.

19.5 The Hermosa Trail spills out onto CR 201. Ride over.

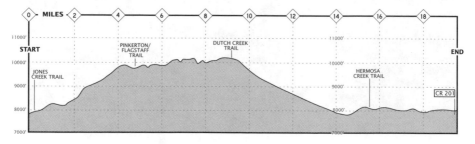

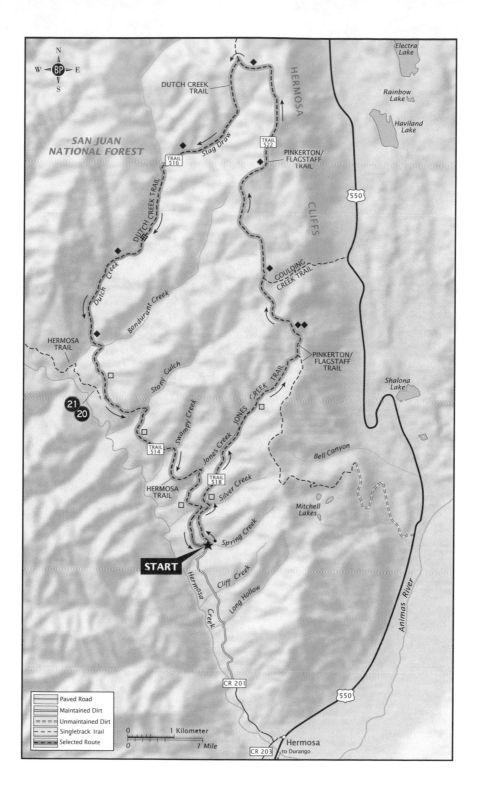

N
W ⊕ E
S
BP

DUTCH CREEK TRAIL

HERMOSA

Electra Lake

Rainbow Lake

Haviland Lake

SAN JUAN NATIONAL FOREST

Stag Draw

TRAIL 516

TRAIL 522

PINKERTON/ FLAGSTAFF TRAIL

DUTCH CREEK TRAIL

550

CLIFFS

Dutch Creek

Bondurant Creek

GOULDING CREEK TRAIL

HERMOSA TRAIL

Stony Gulch

PINKERTON/ FLAGSTAFF TRAIL

Shalona Lake

21
20

Swampy Creek

JONES CREEK TRAIL

Bell Canyon

TRAIL 514

Jones Creek

TRAIL 518

Silver Creek

Mitchell Lakes

HERMOSA TRAIL

Spring Creek

START

Hermosa Creek

Cliff Creek

Long Hollow

Animas River

CR 201

550

Paved Road
Maintained Dirt
Unmaintained Dirt
Singletrack Trail
Selected Route

0   1 Kilometer
0   1 Mile

Hermosa
to Durango

CR 203

Skull and trail sign near the intersection of Jones Creek and Pinkerton-Flagstaff.

...us, as riders are seduced into trav-
...eeling into the creek bed!
...uch safer and flattens into quick
...ng for you: a half-mile climb that
...y out of place, but it's not wicked

...rail deposits you on the Hermosa
...n this final stretch is another five
...d section has become a bit too
...e Hermosa Creek valley back to
...e steep hike-a-bikes which were
...rs, motos, and horses along this
...pular tracks in these hills. If this
...aydreaming about getting back

Ride Information

Trail Contacts:
San Juan National Forest, Durango, CO
(970) 747-4874

Schedules:
June through October, due to weather.

Maps:
USGS maps: Hermosa, CO; Electra Lake, CO; Elk Creek, CO; and Monument Hill, CO • **USFS maps:** *San Juan National Forest*

Devil Mountain

Ride Specs

Start: From the bottom of Devil Mountain Road (FS 626), located on U.S. 160

Length: 23.2 miles out-and-back

Approximate Riding Time: 2–4 hours

Technical Difficulty: Easy to Moderate: this route is located entirely on a wide dirt road, but it could not be classified as smooth

Physical Difficulty: Moderate to Difficult: strong riders will never have to use the little ring on this long, gradual climb

Trail Surface: Moderately rocky dirt road

Lay of the Land: Forested foothills of the San Juans, with powerful views of Chimney Rock to the south and high mountains to the north

Elevation Gain: 4,233 feet

Land Status: National forest

Other Trail Users: Motorists (occasionally), equestrians, and mountain lions

Getting There

From Durango: Drive east approximately 38 miles on U.S. 160 to Devil Mountain Road (FS 626), on the left. The turn-off is well marked with a big sign. The land at the very bottom of Devil Mountain Road is owned by the Southern Utes, and signs indicate parking there is not allowed; so, drive up Devil Mountain Road into the national forest, one half mile north of U.S. 160, where several nice pull-offs are available. *[Note. The mileage cues below assume this parking spot, not the intersection with U.S. 160, as the starting point.]*

Chimney Rock

The ascent up Devil Mountain is a straightforward but enjoyable climb on a moderately rocky dirt road. The big climb—gaining 3,000 feet in just over 12 miles—is softened by forgiving, middle-ring grades and rewarding vistas.

As you wind your way up the southern face of the mountain, a mere molehill in comparison to the jagged peaks of the San Juans, it won't be long before Chimney Rock is revealed to the south. The twin towers are actually Chimney Rock (on the left) and Companion Rock (on the right). Its impressive stature notwithstanding, Chimney Rock is known primarily for the mysterious ruins located high up on the spine of the formation.

The ruins at Chimney Rock are the remains of an outpost of the Chaco Canyon civilization, which thrived a millennium ago about 100 miles southwest of here. Perhaps the greatest known achievement of the Chacoans was their engineering of a grand network of straight roads emanating in all directions from the Chaco Canyon hub; Chimney Rock was the extreme northeast settlement, or *outlier*, at the end of the Chacoan roads. But why did they build it? The location of this site, placed directly on solid rock and far above any arable land (just to the west of Companion Rock), suggests either a ceremonial or defensive purpose. Professor Kim Malville of the

University of Colorado has the scientific community pretty much convinced that the 35-room compound was in fact ceremonial, built to observe the moon rising between the spires. Using tree-ring dating of timbers found in the ruin, Malville has shown that the two primary periods of the site's construction, in October 1075 and June 1094, correspond very nearly to the 19-year lunar cycle; on these approximate dates, for about thirty days at a time, an observer at the ruin would have seen the moon rise dramatically between Companion Rock and Chimney Rock. Interesting coincidence or hard scientific evidence—*you make the call.*

If you finish your ride in time, drive over and check out this and more than 100 other ruins at the Chimney Rock Archaeological Area. The area is open May 15 to September 30, from 9:00 A.M. to 4:30 P.M. It's suggested that you hike up onto the ridge and consider the precise stonework of the Chacoan builders.

Wildflowers.

Like many of the rides in this volume, the Devil Mountain route begins at a relatively low altitude, in a dry zone dominated by ponderosa pine, then climbs into a green forest of aspen, Engelmann spruce, and Douglas fir. When the road becomes solid rock, near mile 11.3, you know you're close to the top. A left at the fork there loops you around to the other side of the mountain, where there is a first class panoramic view of the tall mountains of the Weminuche Wilderness.

Contrary to popular opinion, the Devil does not own Devil Mountain. Rather, the mountain is ruled over by a large puma. This mountain lion's existence is betrayed by several healthy-looking lion turds dropped in the road (primarily along the middle third of the ride, from about mile 3.5 to mile 8.0) and by the accompanying cat tracks, which at the time of this writing are about four inches wide. The size of the tracks indicates a healthy, dominant beast. Cyclists shouldn't be worried. There is only one known incident of a mountain lion attacking a mountain biker, and that occurred in California, where the mountain bikers are tastier and even more annoying than they are here.

MilesDirections

0.0 START riding up Devil Mountain Road (FS 626) from the parking spot .5 miles north of U.S. 160.

3.9 At the fork, take a right.

11.3 The road surface turns to solid rock; go left at the fork, around to the other side of the mountain.

11.6 The site of the rustic lookout tower is a good turnaround point.

23.2 After cruising safely down the hill, arrive back at the starting point.

Ride Information

Trail Contacts:
San Juan National Forest, Supervisor's Office, Durango, CO (970) 247–4874

Local Events/Attractions:
Chimney Rock Archaeological Area: (970) 883–5359 or *www.chimney rockco.org*

Maps:
USGS maps: Devil Mountain, CO • **USFS maps:** *San Juan National Forest*

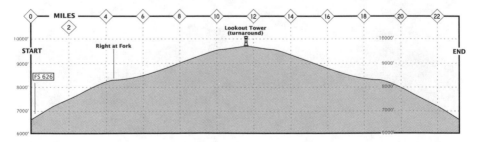

118

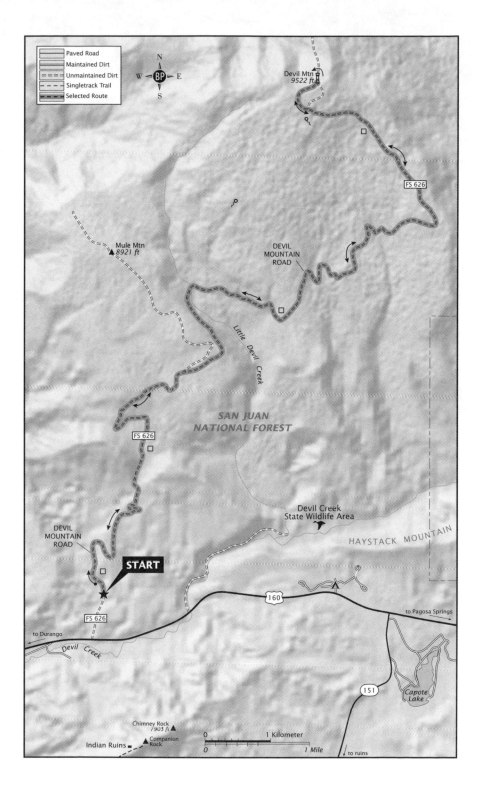

Paved Road
Maintained Dirt
Unmaintained Dirt
Singletrack Trail
Selected Route

N
W E
S
BP

Devil Mtn
9522 ft

FS 626

Mule Mtn
8921 ft

DEVIL
MOUNTAIN
ROAD

Little Devil Creek

SAN JUAN
NATIONAL FOREST

FS 626

Devil Creek
State Wildlife Area

HAYSTACK MOUNTAIN

DEVIL
MOUNTAIN
ROAD

START

FS 626

to Pagosa Springs

160

to Durango

Devil Creek

151

Capote
Lake

Chimney Rock
7903 ft

Indian Ruins   Companion
Rock

0   1 Kilometer
0   1 Mile

to ruins

Windy Pass Loop

Ride Specs

Start: From the Windy Pass trailhead on U.S. 160

Length: 20.1-mile loop

Approximate Riding Time: 3.5–5.5 hours

Technical Difficulty: Difficult: very technical climbing to Windy Pass, cruising thereafter

Physical Difficulty: Difficult: exercise your pushing muscles

Trail Surface: 45% singletrack, 30% dirt road, and 25% highway

Lay of the Land: Singletrack tours the primitive backcountry southeast of Wolf Creek Pass, then drops into the mellow valley of the East Fork of the San Juan River

Elevation Gain: 3,144 feet

Land Status: National forest

Other Trail Users: Motorists (occasionally), hikers, and the occasional stray bullets

Getting There

From Pagosa Springs: Drive east on U.S. 160 for 13.5 miles to the base of Wolf Creek Pass. Look for the obvious sign that indicates the start of the Windy Pass Trail. There is parking available on the left side of the highway. (Pagosa Springs is about 60 miles east of Durango on U.S. 160.)

Top of Windy Pass—go straight—the left track fades out after a tough climb.

This challenging loop—on singletrack, dirt road, and highway east of Pagosa Springs—rewards hard work, then keeps on rewarding. By "hard work" I mean a terribly difficult climb to Windy Pass. This three-mile ascent is ultra-technical and largely unrideable for the average cyclist. After summiting the modest pass, however, you'll find shockingly smooth singletrack descending pleasantly for more than five miles to the East Fork of the San Juan River. In the end, the surprising cruise down the back side of Windy Pass more than makes up for the hardship of the ascent.

Windy Pass is only three miles above the highway, but these are some of the longest, slowest miles you're likely to tackle on a bike. On a thin, loamy trail, riders face an endless lineup of gnarled root beds, with tall, slick, root-topped ledges. Imposing upon the remaining available surface area are fixed rocks and loose chunks churned out of the black earth by struggling horses. Roots and Rocks. These are the same obstacles you would find on any trail around these parts, but the overwhelming concentration of technical flak on this one is frustrating.

Combined with the relentless uphill grade, the frequent obstacles force a comical dance of clip-out, hop-off, straddle, waddle, and kick. The constant metallic *clank!* of popping cleats resonates through the dark forest, scaring the crap out of mule deer and elk. During huntin' season, a single mountain biker can sound like an army of locked-and-loaded, pissed-off cowboys ascending the mountain. The most you can hope for here is 20, maybe 30, consecutive seconds of clipped-in riding between over-

bearing root problems. You get the front tire up on the first ledge of the series, but then the rear spins out and *clank!* Straddle, push, and do it again. Experienced trail riders are quite familiar with this exhausting trail dance. Some of us never get into it on purpose, and some of us bask in the glory, happily immersed in any damn thing the mountain can throw down. *Bring it on, Mountain!*

Just before the top, the incline eases a bit, and the technical problems begin to thin out as well, foreshadowing your immediate trail-surfing future. At mile 3.2, the low saddle is achieved—surprisingly quick for these parts. Here is one of the finest lunching spots you're likely to find. Camera-happy tourists will be snapping shots back down toward Pagosa and the Bootjack, a powerful rock formation which guards the southeastern side of the San Juan River Valley, then across the same valley at the first wall of peaks of the Weminuche Wilderness Area. Turning 180 degrees, the rocky Thirteeners of the Continental Divide—Long Trek Mountain, Montezuma Peak, and Summit Peak, from north to south—also demand to be photographed. Lingering on the saddle is advised.

On top of Windy Pass, you'll find a tempting singletrack forking left from the main trail. This is not the Treasure Mountain Trail, it's a maverick unnamed track that climbs roughly onto a steep hillside and disappears. Ignore the left fork and drop off the back of the saddle through a steep cow pasture. The trail, you'll surely notice, is rutted but otherwise smooth. After just a few clicks, the white-knuckle descending abates and the trail winds through meadows and aspens on incredible, shallow rollers. The roots are still present, but compared to the pre-Pass chaos, this track seems smoother than Forsberg on a power play. If you're a cynical realist who suspects— quite naturally—that your ride will re-chunk and degenerate into root-infested anar-

Dropping off the back of Windy Pass.

chy at any time, you'll be blown away by this track's undying devotion to smooth, rolling terrain. Whooping with joy has the added benefit of scaring bears and mountain cats off the trail, by the way.

The Windy Pass Trail, having completely redeemed itself, ends at a T-intersection with the Treasure Mountain Trail at mile 4.5. Turn right to continue the gentle descent. A sign here indicates "3 miles to East Fork of San Juan River," referring to the next segment of the Treasure Mountain Trail, but the strip of singletrack descending to the river is actually 4.1 miles long—and a wonderful 4.1 miles they are. (The *left* (uphill) fork of the Treasure Mountain Trail climbs steadily to Treasure Pass, then descends to Wolf Creek Road, which pops out onto U.S. Route 160 just west of Wolf Creek Pass—another loop option rears up.) The Treasure Mountain ribbon carries on where the Windy Pass Trail left off, with quick descending on gently flowing terrain, on a narrow but smooth backcountry trail. In the fall, the singletrack is paved with golden aspen leaves, hiding occasional imperfections and covering the hoof-packed bumpiness that's present on a few sun-hardened sections. It's an exquisitely rare situation that such a fast and fun trail, without serious technicality or climbing in either direction, would see so few mountain bikers. The Treasure Mountain Trail by itself makes a great ride, as an out-and-back from the trailhead on East Fork Road (Ride 25). This back door out-and-back gives riders of almost all abilities a taste of lonely,

MilesDirections

0.0 START riding up the Windy Pass Trail from its trailhead on U.S. 160. Please be careful crossing the highway.

3.2 Reach the top of the Pass. Ignoring the left-forking singletrack, drop down the back side of the pass on steep singletrack which quickly levels.

4.4 The trail may be pretty faded through here. Don't get discouraged.

4.5 Arrive at the T-intersection with the Treasure Mountain Trail. Take a right and continue cruising. *[Option. The left fork climbs to Treasure Pass then drops onto U.S. 160 below the Wolf Creek Pass summit.]*

7.5 Pass through a cow fence that marks the San Juan National Forest boundary. Here the trail enters private property. Please stay on the trail to help ensure that it will remain open.

8.6 The singletrack ends at FS 667, in the East Fork valley. Take a right.

15.6 Take a right onto U.S. 160.

20.1 End the ride, back at the parking zone.

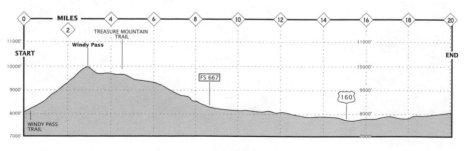

Ride Information

Trail Contacts:
San Juan National Forest, Durango, CO
(970) 247–4874

Schedule:
June through mid October, due to weather

Maps:
USGS maps: Saddle Mountain, CO; Wolf
Creek Pass, CO; and Jackson Mountain,
CO • **USFS maps:** *San Juan National
Forest*

skinny, backcountry ribbon without any of the typical brutality. (The climb up Windy Pass is a fine example of "the typical brutality.")

The singletrack spills out onto dirt Forest Service Road 667 (East Fork Road) at mile 8.6 and follows the East Fork of the San Juan River for seven miles to the wide-shouldered U.S. Route 160, and the San Juan itself. The final section on the highway is 4.5 miles of slightly uphill spinning to the base of Wolf Creek Pass. This loop could be nicely conquered in the other direction, using the highway and the dirt road as a long warm-up. This would give the loop a completely different feel, climbing to Windy Pass on gentle trail and ending with a hardcore descent. My suggestion is to ride it both ways.

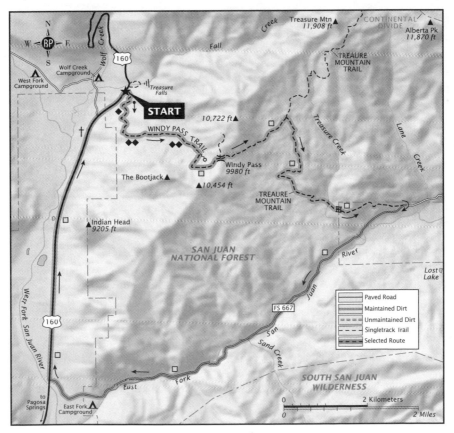

Waiting for the *Next* Last Grizzly in Colorado

Until characters arrived on the scene with repeating rifles, the grizzlies around here did as they pleased. Then, within 100 years, man wiped out 99 percent of the grizzlies in the lower forty-eight. Steadily the shy, golden-haired giants were pushed out of their preferred high plains habitat and into a few secluded alpine areas where man and his livestock feared to tread. You may know about the federally protected grizzly zones around Glacier and Yellowstone; it is also likely that a score of secretive survivors continues to hold out in the wilderness of southwestern Colorado, entirely behind enemy lines.

All grizzlies were proudly declared erased from Colorado long before 1952, when a rogue survivor was killed in the present-day Weminuche Wilderness. This was the last of eight grizzlies to be destroyed by a tough, bear-killing freak named Lloyd Anderson. In addition to his grizzly kills, the government-assisted, rancher-sponsored Anderson took out eighty or so black bears and continued to kill blackies long after his "Last Grizzly" had been immortalized in schoolbooks and popular fairy tales.

Anderson's Last Grizzly kept its title for a generation. Locals in the south San Juans, however, continued to insist that the grizzlies were still around. In 1971, the Division of Wildlife baited likely grizzly areas with dead horses, and rigged cameras with motion sensors in an effort to catch some grizzlies on film. The cameras malfunctioned, but at least one of the 1300-pound horse carcasses was dragged many hundreds of yards and devoured. Such was the work of the grizzly—or perhaps aliens. But under the heading of absolute "proof" only one bit of evidence would do.

In 1979 there was proof, twenty-seven years after the previous Last Grizzly. So the story goes: outfitter Ed Wiseman and his client, Mike Niederee, were bowhunting elk near Pagosa Springs when Niederee spied a huge bear lounging in its daybed. The bear caught the offending scent and bolted from the client, only to jump Wiseman coming the other direction. Wiseman was losing the ensuing battle in a big way, the griz on top of him tearing him to pieces, when he got miraculously lucky with the business end of a broken arrow that happened to be lying next to his head. Wiseman jammed the arrow into the bear's jugular.

Even after winning the battle of his life that September afternoon, Ed Wiseman was quite literally not out of the woods yet. He had to survive the cold night while his young greenhorn client went back across the jagged divide to retrieve help. Niederee lost his way and was slow to locate the cabin where his father (a surgeon) and one of Wiseman's hired hands were waiting. As the rescuers were coming back over the divide, a horse packed with medical supplies slipped off a cliff and disappeared. It was dawn when they finally located the hypothermic and near-dead Wiseman. A rescue helicopter came in to scoop him up, and one of the EMT's on board vomited at the sight of Wiseman's wounds...It didn't look good for Ed Wiseman at any time during his ordeal, but he made it, and to this day continues to guide hunting parties through the same wilderness where the attack took place. Try telling him there are no more grizzlies left in there and, well, you can imagine what he might say.

If the big griz had won that fight, or simply had escaped past Wiseman into the woods, wildlife officials no doubt would have pinned the encounter on a freakishly large and strong black bear, as usual. As it turned out, the so-called "Wiseman Bear" gave irrefutable proof that wildlife management agencies had been dead wrong about grizzlies in Colorado for the past thirty years. Furthermore, a scientific examination of the dead grizzly thickened the plot considerably by indicating that she had "definitely" born cubs at some point in her life.

The Wiseman bear, its undeniable mother-status, and the looming implications of the Endangered Species Act infused the Colorado grizzly question with new urgency and emotion. In 1980, not one year after the attack, a small group of government scientists led by the highly respected Tom Beck converged on the area in an attempt to capture and radio-collar any grizzlies they could find. They found zero. The Beck Study gathered plenty of positive circumstantial evidence, including daybeds and digs and the like, but, having bagged not a single grizzly, the venture was called off a year early. Its closing immediately cast the existence of Colorado grizzlies back into the purgatory of official doubt.

The Beck Study was open to criticism, especially concerning its reliance on bait and traps, and the type of bait used (in accordance with state laws, Beck used sucker fish in his traps and grizzlies don't like sucker fish). To Douglas Peacock, the world's foremost champion of the grizzly bear, the study's failure was pre-ordained. How could such sophisticated and shy creatures be fooled with traps? Unlike their long lost brethren, who had fallen to cyanide and high-powered rifles while feeding over buckets full of tasty scraps, the San Juan grizzlies had survived so long precisely because they avoided this government chicanery.

Until the mid '90s, Peacock and biologist Dennis Sizemore led small groups of volunteers into the south San Juans, where they slowly crawled through suspected grizzly areas picking through bear scat and fresh kills. The Peacock Expeditions yielded the usual ground clutter of grizzly sign, but also tracks, credible sightings, and a seemingly irrefutable clump of grizzly hair in a piece of scat. None of it, not even the lab-tested hair sample, qualifies as absolute proof. Tom Beck explains, "There's so much distrust on all sides these days that almost any evidence short of a bear in hand is going to be stringently challenged."

The only real bear is a dead bear. Until another shows up, a fourteener's worth of circumstantial evidence suggests that the grizzlies are still up there. Alive. Clearly they do not wish to be bothered. Given the existence throughout the region of livestock folks who would hunt down or shoot on sight anything with sharp teeth, especially grizzlies, and given the tendency of biologists to swarm over any suspected grizzly territory brandishing radio collars, it is not hard to see how the San Juan bears' continued privacy might be a good thing.

25

Treasure Mountain Out-and-Back

Ride Specs

Start: From the Treasure Mountain Trail's unceremonious trailhead on FS 667
Length: 11.0-miles out-and-back
Approximate Riding Time: 1–3 hours
Technical Difficulty: Moderate: basically smooth, skinny singletrack
Physical Difficulty: Moderate: short, with just a little tough climbing
Trail Surface: 100% singletrack
Lay of the Land: Relatively pristine forest in the under-populated region between Pagosa Springs and Wolf Creek Pass
Elevation Gain: 2,128 feet
Land Status: National forest and private land (stay on the trail)
Other Trail Users: Hikers, equestrians, and hunters (in season). Expect skittish horses with inexperienced riders. Yield to equestrians by moving a good distance off the trail.

Getting There

From Pagosa Springs: Drive east on U.S. 160 for nine miles, and then turn right (south) on FS 667 (East Fork Road). Drive seven miles up this road and find the start of the Treasure Mountain Trail on the left side of the road. The trail is not always signed.

The real treasure of the Wolf Creek area is the Treasure Mountain Trail. With its smooth surface and fast turns, this prime singletrack has much in common with the perennial favorites of Southwest Colorado, among them the Hermosa Trail (Rides 20 and 21) and the section of Colorado Trail west of Molas Pass (Ride 19). Better still, Treasure Mountain has somehow managed to avoid excessive use by mountain bikers, perhaps due to its slightly stealthy hiding place in the lonely backcountry east of Pagosa Springs. (Unfortunately, while being nicely untracked, it's also quite a bit shorter than either of those other trails I mentioned.) The Treasure Mountain Trail's amazing lack of painful, Colorado climbs and rough technicality keeps it accessible to novices, but the turns will be savored best by experienced riders.

I know this trail doesn't show up in any other guidebook, and none of your friends have heard of it. Trust me on this one. You can thank me later, by sending gifts. Hunting dogs, gold nuggets, and durable mountaineering-style sunglasses are especially appreciated.

Rising from the wide valley and the dirt road that follows the East Fork of the San Juan River (Forest Service Road 667), the Treasure Mountain Trail angles easily up

a bright south-facer where riders will be nuked by the sun in the summer. Ponderosa pine provides a meager patchwork of shade early, but, exhibiting the usual and comforting rise through eco-zones, the trail soon veers into a cool, shady cove topped by aspen, fir, and spruce. Aspen leaves flutter to the forest floor like butterflies, covering the late-season trail with a soft, golden blanket. The first mile of this out-and-back is through private property, so please stay on the trail to help ensure it will remain open to the public.

Within a few miles from the start, this track is buried in the thick of the San Juan National Forest, winding through a backcountry parcel that is hyper-popular with hunting outfitters but neglected by cyclists. In the fall you'll notice a long line of the outfitters' white-tented, coffee-brewing base camps set up alongside the East Fork, as well as minor tent cities inside the national forest. If you're one of those grizzled old-schoolers who is always grumbling that the outback is clogged with mountain bikers, ride Treasure Mountain during hunting season and witness the hunter's plight. Looking for solitude deep in the woods, hoping for quiet, placidity, and other conditions that make for a successful hunt—he finds the forest crawling not with elk but

Treasure Mountain Trail.

129

with other hunters, all decked out in the requisite orange vests. (Mountain bikers, as well, might feel more secure wearing day-glow accessories. At least, keep that antler hat buried in your pack.)

Remarkably, this track ascends all the way to its intersection with the Windy Pass Trail, more than four miles, across several minor drainages and through countless serene meadows and clearings, without any truly difficult or steep pitches. Ride trails around here on a regular basis and you learn to expect certain things, like being crushed under the Iron Nazi Boot of Gravity. But this stretch, while climbing about 1,500 feet in 4.1 miles, seems refreshingly flat. To continue with the mellow, gentle, and curvy theme, hang a left at the intersection here (mile 4.1) and cruise up the excellent Windy Pass Trail.

[On a side note, adventurous souls may opt to continue straight up the Treasure Mountain singletrack. This trail climbs steadily across Treasure Mountain and over the imaginatively-named Treasure Pass, headed for a link-up with Wolf Creek Pass Road. With the Continental Divide Trail up there as well, you won't have to think too hard coming up with some intriguing options for epic loops. This upper segment of the Treasure Mountain Trail won't kill you with climbing, but the forest will let you know who's boss. Watch for early- and late-summer snow cover, and huge, snarling deadfalls doing the Horizontal Bop across the singletrack. The forest cops don't get up here too often with their chainsaws.]

The Windy Pass Trail winds around for another carefree mile, then, at mile 5.3, heads straight up a hoof-trampled, sun-bathed slope to the low saddle called Windy Pass. This climb can seem a bit harsh compared to the rest of the ride. You should tackle it anyway, because it's only 0.2 mile long and the views from Windy Pass are cool. (The saddle is a prime spot from which to view the autumn sea of colors—red, yellow, orange, purple—in the valley below the gray chaos of peaks.) There is also a

MilesDirections

0.0 START riding up the Treasure Mountain Trail from the informal trailhead on FS 667.

1.2 Enter the National Forest.

2.6 Keep right as a game trail shoots off to the left.

4.1 Take a left onto the Windy Pass Trail. *[Option. You can continue climbing on the Treasure Mountain Trail. See ride description above.]*

5.3 The singletrack gets steeper on approach to Windy Pass.

5.5 Arrive at the easy summit, a good turn-around point.

11.0 Back at the trailhead, the ride is unfortunately complete.

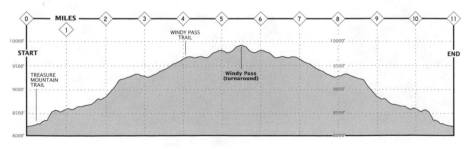

promising-looking singletrack spur up there that heads north into an aspen stand, climbs harshly, then—word to the wise—disappears. From Windy Pass, your easiest option by far is to head back the way you came. To complete a loop using U.S. Route 160 would mean dropping to the pavement on three miles of extremely technical deep-trough singletrack, which is not everybody's idea of a good time (see Ride 24, a clockwise version of such a loop, which requires three miles of fairly brutal climbing).

Ride Information

Trail Contacts:
San Juan National Forest, Durango, CO
(970) 247–4874

Schedule:
Mid May through October, due to weather

Maps:
USGS maps: Wolf Creek Pass, CO •
USFS maps: San Juan National Forest

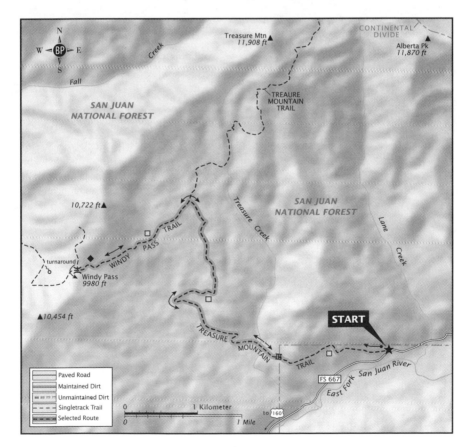

North Glade Loop

Ride Specs

Start: From the dead end of Foothills Drive

Length: 20.1-mile loop

Approximate Riding Time: 2.5–5 hours

Technical Difficulty: Moderate to Difficult: basically smooth, with thousands of dips and turns

Physical Difficulty: Moderate to Difficult: lots of tiny hills provide a different sort of workout

Trail Surface: 85% singletrack/widetrack, 9% dirt roads, and 6% paved road

Lay of the Land: Awesome trails through the sandy piñon-juniper foothills north of Farmington, NM

Elevation Gain: 1,674 feet

Land Status: BLM land and easement through private land

Other Trail Users: Motorists (motorcycles, ATVs, trucks on the dirt roads, and speed demons on the short section of highway)

Getting There

From Durango: Drive south on U.S. 550 about 45 miles to the northern outskirts of Farmington. Look for signs pointing the way to San Juan Community College. At a major intersection, take a right onto Piñon Hills Boulevard, then an immediate right onto Foothills Drive. Drive up Foothills until it dead-ends. The trail begins here, headed northeast. There are a few spaces at the dead-end to park, although there is no parking allowed there on weekdays before 5 P.M. If it is a weekday, or there are no spaces available, park a block or two down the adjacent Colibri Drive.

A fter winter settles into Durango, and the array of trails is neutralized by an ocean of mud, the local mountain bikers' thoughts turn to the desert. Dry, sandy, mudless. Sure, Durangoans could pile in the VW microbus and drive several hours to Moab and the stunningly beautiful Canyonlands, but why would they do such a thing when the amazing singletracks of northern New Mexico are less than an hour away? Drab Farmington, New Mexico, of all places, with its network of old motorcycle trails, blows Moab off the map from a trail rider's standpoint. It's hard to believe until you go see for yourself.

Through a sandy forest of short, shrubby piñon and juniper trees north of Farmington, a number of exciting singletrack routes are available, in an area called The Glade. (The network is also commonly referred to as Road Apple, after a popular race that is staged there.) This loop tours the northern half of The Glade, on some incredibly sweet trails.

A *glade* is technically an open area in a forest. The piñon-juniper woodland around Farmington is more like a little forest in the middle of a giant open area. Farmington Glade is the name for the unforested valley between the two modest ridges. In general, the trails run along the tops of the ridges.

Start from the unsigned, informal trailhead at the top of Foothills Drive and head northeast on a hardened widetrack. This is the Kinsey Trail. Almost immediately, a

132

On the Imperial Walkers Trail.

MilesDirections

0.0 START riding northeast on a widetrack from the dead-end of Foothills Drive. This is the Kinsey Trail. Almost immediately, bust a left onto a more adventurous singletrack, the Kinsey Junior Trail. *[Option. Stay on the Kinsey Trail. Both trails will take you where you want to go, Kinsey with less fanfare, more speed. Kinsey Junior is far more adventurous.]*

0.5 Stay left here.

0.7 Cross a road. *[FYI. There are hundreds of gas company roads and buried pipelines crossing our route. It is certain that there will be even more by the time this book goes to print.]*

0.9 Take a right as the trail spills out onto a doubletrack.

1.1 At a gas well, go right on a small road, then take a quick left onto a bigger road.

1.3 Veer right into another clearing at a gas well. Head straight across the clearing and find the singletrack again on the other side. There may be signs marking the trail, but don't count on it. Someone has been pulling up signs in the area. (If you find the single-track here, congratulations, you have just nav-igated the most confusing portion of this loop. If, on the other hand, you become hopelessly lost, just head east and eventually you will run into the obvious Kinsey Trail.)

2.9 Take a right onto a doubletrack.

3.3 Take a right, back onto singletrack.

3.4 Cross the doubletrack you were just on.

3.8 Cross another half-road, then rejoin the Kinsey Trail.

4.0 Cross Flora Vista Road.

4.1 Cross a half-road.

4.4 Stay left at an intersection with a tempt-ing track going off to the right, the Seven Sisters Trail. (See the Kinsey–Seven Sisters Loop chapter for a description of this trail.)

4.8 Stay right at another trail intersection.

5.6 Cross a road.

5.7 Veer right onto a road.

6.1 As your road joins another, head straight across, back onto singletrack.

8.1 Cross a road at a gas well, heading straight across the clearing to relocate the trail.

8.5 Cross a cattle guard.

8.8 Take a left onto the paved Aztec–La Plata Highway. Be careful, Hoss! Folks drive like maniacs through here.

10.4 Take a left onto singletrack. Some incredible trail sections lay ahead: Imperial Walkers and The Wildcat.

11.2 Cross another cattle guard.

11.9 Cross a road.

12.1 Cross another road.

13.2 Cross another road.

13.7 Another road crossing.

13.9 Cross another road, joining it briefly.

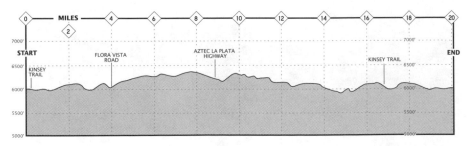

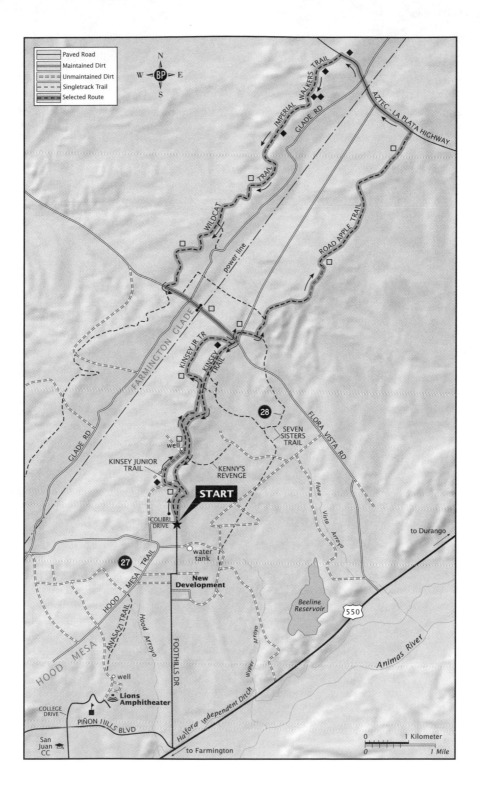

Legend
- Paved Road
- Maintained Dirt
- Unmaintained Dirt
- Singletrack Trail
- Selected Route

N
W BP E
S

IMPERIAL WALKERS TRAIL

GLADE RD

AZTEC - LA PLATA HIGHWAY

WILDCAT TRAIL

ROAD APPLE TRAIL

power line

FARMINGTON GLADE

GLADE RD

KINSEY JR TR

KINSEY TRAIL

28

SEVEN SISTERS TRAIL

FLORA VISTA RD

well

KINSEY JUNIOR TRAIL

KENNY'S REVENGE

START

COLIBRI DRIVE

to Durango

Flora Vista Arroyo

27

HOOD MESA TRAIL

water tank

New Development

HOOD MESA

ANASAZI TRAIL

Hood Arroyo

FOOTHILLS DR

Wyper Arroyo

Beeline Reservoir

550

Animas River

well

Lions Amphitheater

COLLEGE DRIVE

PIÑON HILLS BLVD

San Juan CC

Halford Independent Ditch

to Farmington

0   1 Kilometer
0   1 Mile

14.5 Stay right as the trail forks.

14.9 Cross a road.

15.7 Take a left onto Flora Vista Road and re-cross the valley.

16.1 Pass through a gate and close it behind you.

16.8 Back in familiar territory, take a right onto the Kinsey Trail and haul ass all the way back to the trailhead. *[Option. Veer right at about mile 17.0 onto the rustic Kinsey Jr., for more action.]*

17.5 Cross a cattle guard.

17.6 Go straight at an intersection with another trail.

17.7 Take a right at another singletrack inter-section.

17.9 Stay left at another singletrack intersec-tion.

18.5 Stay left as the Junior Trail creeps up on the Kinsey Trail from the right. *[Option. It's not too late to jump on that little bugger.]*

19.0 Cross a psuedo-road.

19.5 Cross another half-road.

20.1 Spill out at the top of Foothills Drive. Unfortunately, the ride is over. I hate that.

---

little singletrack veers off to the left—let's call it Kinsey Junior. The two trails are very close together, at times running parallel along the top of the ridge, sometimes join-ing, but Kinsey Junior occasionally detours to the west over more extreme terrain. The Kinsey Trail is the older route, widened and packed down by ATVs, and very quick. Kinsey Junior is slower, has more rocks, takes a more confusing route, and demands more concentration. For experienced trail riders, I recommend tackling the Junior Trail.

The two trails converge for good at about mile 3.8, before crossing Flora Vista Road. (Flora Vista is just slightly more substantial than the hundreds of other dirt roads and doubletracks that cross the route.) After crossing Flora Vista, the trail climbs one of the few steep, rocky climbs of the day. From the top of this short climb, the trail rolls fast over miles and miles of dips and tall woop-de-do's. The trail is wide, but it's excellent. This is the Road Apple Trail itself, bringing profound joy to the lives of all who ride it. (Resist the powerful temptation to veer right at mile 4.4 onto a sweet-looking moto track. The Seven Sisters Trail is even more fun than it looks, but save it for another day—*see Ride 28: Kinsey–Seven Sisters Loop.*)

At about mile 8.5, the Road Apple Trail becomes doubletrack and cruises down to the paved Aztec-La Plata Highway. Take a left onto the highway and cross the dry valley, passing under the power lines and crossing Glade Road. A short road climb brings you up to the opposite ridge, and another ridiculously fun trail, the Imperial Walkers Trail. This old motorcycle trail has been nicely named, after the best scene from *The Empire Strikes Back*. (Keep in mind that this trail was around long before *Star Wars* was a glimmer in George Lucas' eye.) In this case, the Imperial Walkers do not shoot deadly ray gun beams, although they have been known to inject chaos into a mountain bike ride or two. These Imperial Walkers are tall, steep, chalky peaks along the ridgetop, and the trail climbs right over the top of each one. That's fun stuff for motorheads. Cyclists will have to dismount and scramble up some slippery inclines.

After the Imperial Walkers section, the trail drops into what I believe to be the best section in The Glade. Back in Denver, there used to be this famous old amusement park called Elitch Gardens. Elitch's is technically still around (under the auspices of Six Flags) but it's been moved from the old neighborhood, modernized, and had its soul sucked right out. Anyway—Elitch's, as it was known, had two top-notch wooden roller coasters back in the day. The less popular of the two coasters was The Wildcat. The Wildcat never had a long line but offered some serious excitement, attacking countless shallow rollers with great speed, tossing bodies into the air as it whipped over each little peak. Mountain bikers on this next section often experience the scary-yet-thrilling sensation of catching *involuntary air*, so I naturally started calling this strip of dirt The Wildcat after that old coaster. Don't look now, but this could be my favorite trail section of all time.

The immediate vicinity of Durango is blessed with many different types of trails, but there is nothing like the Wildcat up there. The acutely dippy, convoluted, intestinal trails in The Glade/Road Apple area, of which the Wildcat is the epitome, do share key elements with a few other famous Colorado trails: the awesome lower portion of Fruita's Edge Loop, for instance, and the lower Mount Baldy Trail near Buffalo Creek. The moto-erosion, berms, and woops are reminiscent of the trails dropping from Jones Park above Colorado Springs.

The Wildcat mellows considerably, then hits Flora Vista Road. Use Flora Vista to cross the valley, then head back to the trailhead on more rolling singletrack. This ride is so fun, it should be illegal.

Ride Information

🕐 Trail Contacts:
Bureau of Land Management, Farmington, CO (505) 599–8900 • **Trails 2000,** P.O. Box 3868, Durango, CO 81302, (970) 259–4682 or *www.trails 2000.com—Trails 2000 is a highly effective non-profit that builds and maintains trails around Durango*

🕐 Schedule:
Try it year round. It is pretty unlikely that there will be any snow or mud on the trails.

Maps:
USGS maps: Farmington North, NM; Flora Vista, NM; Adobe Downs Ranch, NM; and La Plata, NM

South Glade Loop

Ride Specs

Start: From the Lions Amphitheater parking lot
Length: 17.5-mile loop
Approximate Riding Time: 2–4 hours
Technical Difficulty: Moderate: smooth but challenging trails
Physical Difficulty: Moderate: a complete lack of tough climbs
Trail Surface: 70% singletrack/widetrack, 29% dirt roads, and 1% paved road
Lay of the Land: Sandy trails through the piñon-juniper foothills north of Farmington, NM
Elevation Gain: 1,430 feet
Land Status: BLM land and easement through private land
Other Trail Users: Motorists (motorcycles, ATVs, and gas trucks on the dirt roads)

Getting There

From Durango: Drive south on U.S. 550 about 40 miles to the northern outskirts of Farmington. Look for signs pointing the way to San Juan Community College and the Lions Amphitheater. Take a right onto Piñon Hills Boulevard. Drive for about 1.5 miles and turn right onto College Drive. Follow the signs to the Lions Amphitheater parking area. (The parking lot is gated after sundown, so it may be prudent to park along the access road outside the gate.)

Durango, already the best trail-riding spot in the universe, is made even more attractive by its close proximity to Farmington, New Mexico. Draped across the dry, bumpy foothills north of Farmington are a number of long, excellent trails. This 17.5-mile loop around the southern half of the trail network uses a few of the best sections. These trails were carved in by throttle-twisters about 40 years ago and have been raged upon by them ever since. Naturally, they have a well-chewed appearance and have been beaten into widetracks in many areas. Still, some of these sections are *unbelievably fun*. Those old motocross guys knew what they were doing.

This network is often called Road Apple, after the semi-famous Road Apple Rally race. Slightly less often, it's called The Glade. This doesn't seem at all like the sort of place where you'd find a true glade, but the valley between the two ridges is called Farmington Glade, and the trail network has been called The Glade Trail System by the BLM. So be it, *The Glade* it is.

Start from the Lions Amphitheater and head north up the dirt access road, passing the day's first natural gas well on the right (there will be hundreds). After about a half mile, angle to the right, leaving the road at some 4WD tracks, and if all goes well you'll find a nice trail twisting and bumping through the woods: the Anasazi Trail.

After just 1.5 miles of sweetness, the Anasazi dumps you out onto some established dirt roads, which you use to cross the Farmington Glade. Climb the opposite low ridge on a dirt road, then, at mile 4.4, turn right onto a fun widetrack.

This trail is straight, but extremely wavy with woop-de-do's. What was once a semi-wide motorcycle route has been made doubletrack-wide by a relatively recent development: the four-wheeled ATV. You know, those little golf carts for guys who are too drunk to stay upright on two wheels. The four-wheeled ATV is the evil arch enemy of the trail lover, especially in this desert environment where just one pass from one of these retardo-buggies makes a singletrack into a double. Signs have been placed indicating that the trails are off-limits to ATVs; apparently, they've been quite ineffective. It may be time for a well-armed citizens' posse.

Canyonlands-style formations along the loop.

MilesDirections

0.0 START from the parking lot at the Lions Amphitheater and ride back up the road, taking an immediate right onto a dirt road. A sign here points the way to "Shelters."

0.3 Pass two roads on the right, then a natural gas well.

0.6 Notice the 4WD tracks on your right. In this general area, the wide singletrack Anasazi Trail begins. Find it and rage. The trail will pass right through a clearing at another well, and along the way will cross about a dozen tiny utility roads and unauthorized 4WD doubletracks.

2.1 The Anasazi Trail ends at a dirt road, with another gas well straight across (this is the third well so far). Head northwest on the dirt road that passes to the left of the well.

2.4 Straight through an intersection with another road. *[Note. this intersection is not on the map. The most important roads and wells have been illustrated on the map, but this represents just a fraction of the total number. It would be sheer insanity to mark them all. Even if we could, the effort would be futile because new roads are being cut constantly, by gas companies and monster trucks. As long as you keep this in mind while reading the cues, everything should be all right.]*

3.1 Stay right at the fork.

3.5 Take a right (still on a dirt road).

3.9 Veer left onto another dirt road.

4.0 Cross Glade Road.

4.4 Turn right onto a widetrack trail.

4.7 Cross a little access road.

6.1 The trail briefly joins a road here, essentially a crossing.

6.7 Cross a small road.

6.9 Cross another half-road.

7.2 Cross yet another half-road.

7.3 Get ready for a sharp descent next to a barbwire fence.

7.5 At the bottom, take a sharp left at a cattle guard.

7.8 Cross a glorified doubletrack.

8.1 The trail kisses a small access road at the apex of a sweeping right-hand turn. Enjoy a truly awesome section.

9.3 The trail briefly joins a road here, turning right onto the road, then left off of it.

9.8 Turn right onto Flora Vista Road.

10.2 Cross through a gate, closing it behind you.

10.9 Turn right onto the Kinsey Trail. *[Option. After about 0.2 miles on the Kinsey, you can veer right onto a nice singletrack called the Kinsey Junior Trail. Both trails eventually end up at the same place, although this little singletrack follows a meandering, occasionally confusing route to get there.]*

11.6 Cross a cattle guard.

11.7 Go straight at an intersection with another trail.

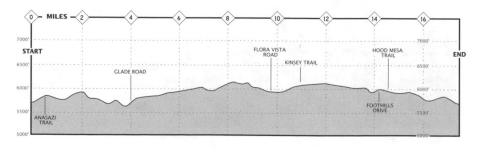

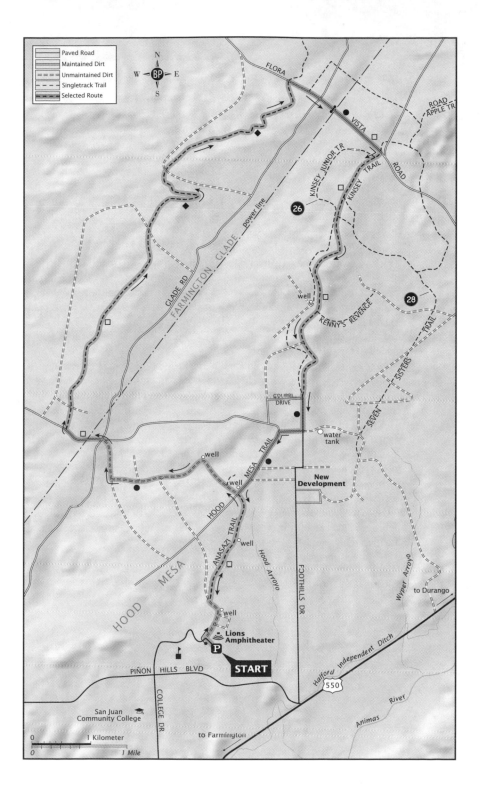

N
W   E
S

FLORA

VISTA

ROAD APPLE TR

KINSEY JUNIOR TR

KINSEY TRAIL

ROAD

GLADE RD

FARMINGTON GLADE power line

26

28

well

KENNY'S REVENGE

SEVEN SISTERS TRAIL

COLIBRI DRIVE

water tank

New Development

MESA TRAIL

HOOD

well

well

ANASAZI TRAIL

HOOD MESA

well

Hood Arroyo

FOOTHILLS DR

well

Wyper Arroyo

to Durango

Lions Amphitheater

P

START

PIÑON HILLS BLVD

COLLEGE DR

San Juan Community College

Halford Independent Ditch

550

Animas River

to Farmington

0   1 Kilometer

0   1 Mile

11.8 Take a right at another singletrack intersection.

12.0 Stay left at another singletrack intersection.

12.6 Stay left as that aforementioned singletrack creeps up on the Kinsey Trail from the right. *[Option. It's not too late to jump on that little bugger.]*

13.1 Cross a little road.

13.6 Cross another wannabe road.

14.2 Spill out at the top of Foothills Drive. Ride down Foothills on pavement.

14.6 Take a right onto Hood Mesa Trail (a road).

14.8 Take a left onto a diagonal dirt road.

15.7 Take a left onto the Anasazi Trail. Retrace your path.

17.5 End the ride back at the Lions Amphitheater.

Climb gently up the ATV track for about three miles. Then, you'll find a short but steep downhill that leads to a cattle guard, a 180-degree turn, and a short but steep climb. Topping out, the route joins one of the award-winning trail sections that has made Farmington famous. This section is known as Trey's Air Time, or just the Air Time Trail—and the name says it all. The ATVs are overmatched by the sharp dips and turns on this extremely thrilling, zero-G section. Without a doubt, this baby is made for two wheels.

Spill out onto Flora Vista Road at mile 9.8, then turn right to re-cross the valley. (For an option, continue across Flora Vista and extend the ride onto the incredible Wildcat Trail, headed toward the Imperial Walkers section.) As you reach the high point on the opposite ridge, turn right up a semi-rocky singletrack headed southwest. This is the Kinsey Trail. Shortly, a singletrack (the Kinsey Junior Trail) splits to the right from this track. Riders have the option of staying straight and high on the wide, smooth, very fast Kinsey Trail, or veering off onto Kinsey Junior, which follows a more convoluted route southward on a somewhat slower, rougher surface. Both trails eventually end up in the same place, at the dead-end of Foothills Drive, in the suburban zone.

From the top of Foothills Drive, descend for a few blocks on pavement, then turn right onto Hood Mesa Trail (not a trail but a road) and meander back to the Anasazi Trail, finishing with a flourish.

This loop through the southern Glade/Road Apple area is very lovable, but it leaves out a lot of great trails. Don't drive away from Farmington without trying the other loops described in this book (see Rides 26 and 28).

Ride Information

Trail Contacts:

Bureau of Land Management, Farmington, CO (505) 599–8900 • **Trails 2000,** P.O. Box 3868, Durango, CO 81302, (970) 259–4682 or *www.trails2000.com – Trails 2000 is a highly effective non-profit that builds and maintains trails around Durango.*

Schedule:

Try it year round. This semi-desert environment averages about a foot of snow each winter, but it melts in a heartbeat.

Maps:

USGS maps: Farmington North, NM; Flora Vista, NM; Adobe Downs Ranch, NM; and La Plata, NM

Natural gas paraphernelia all over the place.

Kinsey–Seven Sisters Loop

Ride Specs

Start: From the dead-end of Foothills Drive
Length: 10.6-mile loop
Approximate Riding Time: 1–2.5 hours
Technical Difficulty: Moderate to Difficult: serious thrills, finding the trail can be a problem at times
Physical Difficulty: Moderate: short, with gentle climbs
Trail Surface: 77% singletrack/widetrack, 15% dirt roads/doubletrack, and 8% paved road
Lay of the Land: Sandy trails through the gas well infested piñon-juniper foothills north of Farmington, NM
Elevation Gain: 908 feet
Land Status: BLM land and easement through private land
Other Trail Users: Motorists (motorcycles and ATVs)

Getting There

From Durango: Drive south on U.S. 550 about 45 miles to the northern outskirts of Farmington. Look for signs pointing the way to San Juan Community College. At a major intersection, take a right onto Piñon Hills Boulevard, then an immediate right onto Foothills Drive. Drive up Foothills until it dead-ends. The trail begins here, headed northeast. There are a few spaces at the dead-end to park, although there is no parking allowed there on weekdays before 5 P.M. If it is a weekday, or there are no spaces available, park a block or two down the adjacent Colibri Drive.

U nable to satisfy their intense love for mountain biking during the snowy winter months, mud-bogged Durangoans ventured south looking for dry trails. It was a natural progression. What they found, less than an hour away in the homely environs of Farmington, New Mexico, blew their minds: fast, rolling trails—*long trails*—that were designed solely for fun on two wheels. And yes, they were dry!

It's a different world just 1,000 feet below and 40 miles south of Durango. The sand is taking over; the desert is on the doorstep. The ubiquitous ponderosa pine and scrub oak of the Durango area is absent. Here it's all about piñon and juniper, the classic combination of arid and semi-arid zones. The *P-J Woodland*, as the ecologists say. In the P-J Woodland near Farmington, you'll find dog-sized jackrabbits, mule deer, coyotes, flocks of sheep, cattle, thousands of drab green gas wells with the accompanying access roads, and a whole bunch of excellent trails. This is one of the shorter loops available in The Glade/Road Apple trail network. The star attraction of this 10.6-mile loop is the Seven Sisters Trail, an incredible old motorcycle trail that descends from the ridge east of Flora Vista Road.

Start this one from the trailhead at the end of Foothills Drive, same as the North Glade Loop (Ride 26), and ride northeast on one of two trails that will take you to Flora Vista Road. One option is a fast, smooth widetrack called the Kinsey Trail; the

other is a more extreme singletrack with moderate rockiness that can be called the Kinsey Junior Trail. The Kinsey Junior Trail splices off from the Kinsey Trail near the trailhead and stays to the west of Kinsey for its entire length, occasionally within 20 or 30 yards of the main trail, occasionally meandering to the west over bumps and knolls. With all the access roads and doubletracks crisscrossing the zone, Kinsey Junior is hard to follow at times. Because riders on the main trail will almost certainly be glancing over at this little snake of a singletrack with a grass-is-greener uneasiness, save yourself the angst and just ride it. If you get lost, or find Kinsey Junior too severe, simply head east until you find the Kinsey Trail. The mileage cues below are for Kinsey Junior, not the Kinsey widetrack.

The Junior Trail rejoins the Kinsey Trail just south of Flora Vista Road. On the other side of Flora Vista, the main trail is called the Road Apple Trail. At mile 4.4, the Road Apple intersects with one of the most inviting trails you've ever seen, sometimes known as the Seven Sisters Trail. Along with the Wildcat and Air Time trails, this is one of the sexiest sections in The Glade system. Dipping, swooping, diving—you name it—this wide singletrack descends from the ridge in style.

Mountain bikers who are quick to criticize motorcyclists for chewing the hell out of trails should realize that ancient motocross culture created many of our favorite trails in the first place. Here is a perfect example of an old moto trail (probably dating to the '60s or early '70s) that was built with just one thing in mind. *Maximum thrills.* Enjoy the guilt-free shredding, and, if you wish, Big Air. (By the way, the four-

The top of the Seven Sisters Trail, decending from the Road Apple Trail.

MilesDirections

0.0 START riding northeast on a widetrack from the dead-end of Foothills Drive. This is the Kinsey Trail. Almost immediately, bust a left onto the Kinsey Junior Trail, a more adventurous singletrack. *[Option. Stay on the Kinsey Trail. Both trails will take you where you want to go, Kinsey with less fanfare, more speed.]*

0.5 Stay left here.

0.7 Cross a road. (There will be hundreds of similar crossings along this route. It's likely that there will be even more by the time this book goes to print.)

0.9 Take a right as the trail spills out onto a doubletrack. This next section is somewhat chaotic and requires a *zen* approach to route-finding.

1.1 At a gas well, go right on a small road, then take a quick left onto a bigger road.

1.3 Veer right into another clearing at a gas well. Head straight across the clearing and find the singletrack again on the other side. There may be signs marking the trail, but don't count on it. Someone has been pulling up signs in the area. (If you find the single-track here, congratulations, you have just navigated successfully through a confusing network of look-alike roads and wells. If, on the other hand, you become lost, an option is to simply head east and eventually you will run into the Kinsey Trail.)

2.9 Take a right onto another doubletrack.

3.3 Take a right, back onto singletrack.

3.4 Cross a small road.

3.8 Cross another half-road, then rejoin the Kinsey Trail.

4.0 Cross Flora Vista Road. (North of Flora Vista, the trail is known as the Road Apple Trail.)

4.1 Cross a small road.

4.4 You probably won't need too much coaxing to turn right onto this nice looking single-track. This is the Seven Sisters Trail.

5.0 Cross Flora Vista Road again, joining it for a brief 0.05-mile stretch.

5.8 New gas company roads have obliterated the track here, and the route has been made quite confusing as a result. At the time of this writing, you need to turn right onto a fresh road here, then, just 0.05 mile later, veer left at a Y-intersection onto another half-road. This road leads you directly to the continuation of the wide singletrack. Note, however, that this layout of roads and gas line cuts is ever-changing. Use The Force, Luke.

6.1 Veer left at a Y-intersection with another trail. *[Option. Take a right here and climb back to the main trail on the ridge.]*

6.5 Join a widetrack.

6.6 Cross a road. *[Option. This road connects to a trail called Kenny's Revenge, which climbs back up to the ridge.]*

7.2 Cross a road.

7.5 Cross another.

7.6 Cross another.

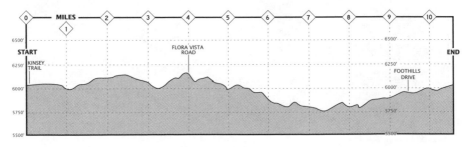

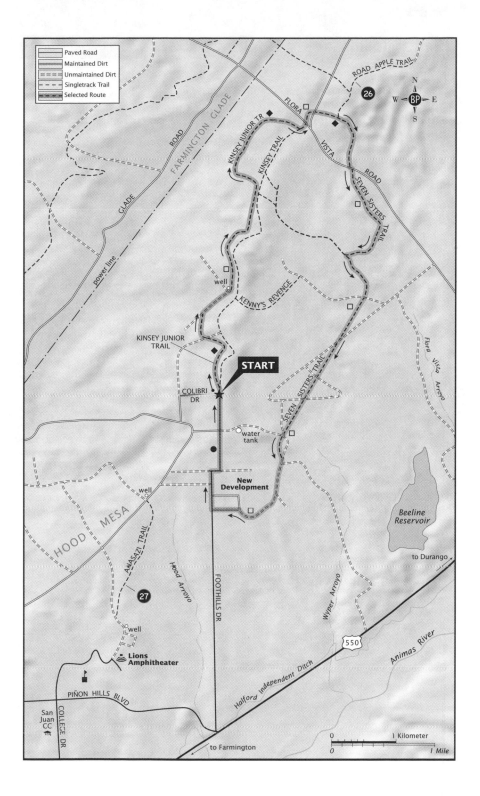

Legend

- Paved Road
- Maintained Dirt
- Unmaintained Dirt
- Singletrack Trail
- Selected Route

ROAD APPLE TRAIL

26

N
W · BP · E
S

FARMINGTON GLADE

FLORA

KINSEY JUNIOR TR

KINSEY TRAIL

GLADE ROAD

VISTA ROAD

SEVEN SISTERS TRAIL

power line

well

KENNY'S REVENGE

KINSEY JUNIOR TRAIL

START

COLIBRI DR

water tank

Flora Vista Arroyo

SEVEN SISTERS TRAIL

New Development

Beeline Reservoir

to Durango

HOOD MESA

well

ANASAZI TRAIL

Hood Arroyo

FOOTHILLS DR

27

well

Lions Amphitheater

PIÑON HILLS BLVD

San Juan CC

COLLEGE DR

to Farmington

Wyper Arroyo

550

Halford Independent Ditch

Animas River

0   1 Kilometer
0   1 Mile

8.1 Cross two more.

8.3 Join a road here, staying right of the gas well.

8.6 Veer right at a fork in the road.

8.9 Veer right, beneath the power lines. Residential development is ongoing in this area, so be ready to employ some additional flexibility with route-finding.

9.2 Take a left, still following the power lines.

9.3 Take a left.

9.4 Take a right onto Foothills Drive.

10.6 End the ride back at the top of Foothills Drive.

---

wheeled ATV, not the motorcycle, is the enemy of the mountain biker; ATVs make singletracks into roads.)

Seven Sisters crosses back over Flora Vista, lousy with woop-de-do's, then plows through a washed-out low point where the route is desecrated by new utility roads. The gas companies clearly have the run of the place, and any road they want to make through this BLM land, they make. In addition, every buried gas line makes a straight widetrack or doubletrack gash through the fragile woodland. This creates a problem with route-finding all over the map near Farmington. There are more natural gas wells in this area than there are stars in the sky, and each well seems to have at least two roads connecting. Using the wells as reference points will be occasionally useful but mostly confusing (the most strategically important wells and roads have been drawn on the map, but this represents just a small fraction of the total number). It may help to imagine the wells and roads as part of the landscape, like rock outcroppings, arroyos, and juniper trees.

With good luck and favorable karma, you will find your way through this confusing maze and end up on the arrow-straight widetrack that represents the continuation of the Seven Sisters Trail. The route runs along another buried gas line, headed southwest, perhaps toward a spectacular New Mexico sunset. Still wavy with woop-de-dos, the widetrack climbs moderately back to the residential area and the houses constructed in the Santa Fe Fauxdobe Style.

Ride Information

📞 Trail Contacts:
Bureau of Land Management, Farmington, CO (505) 599–8900

🕐 Schedule:
Try it year round. Farmington gets *some* snow, but not a whole lot.

🗺 Maps:
USGS maps: Farmington North, NM; Adobe Downs Ranch, NM; Flora Vista, NM; and La Plata, NM

Durango

Compiled here is an index of great rides in Durango and the surrounding area that didn't make the A-list this time around but deserve recognition. Check them out and let us know what you think. You may decide that one or more of these rides deserves higher status in future editions or, perhaps, you may have a ride of your own that merits some attention.

(A) Horse Gulch Road

One of the most often used connectors in the area, this moderate doubletrack is a ride in and of itself. Jump on at the dead-end of 3rd Street in southeast Durango and just ride. If you can stand not veering off onto any of a handful of tempting single-tracks leading to Telegraph and the Ridge, Horse Gulch Road will drop you (about six

miles later) onto CR 234, then, looping left, Florida Road, very near Road 071. Loop back to town on pavement, or do an out-and-back. Or, to impress your girlfriend, head up toward Haflin and Missionary Ridge.

(B) Just Haflin Loop

Speaking of Haflin...Riders looking for hills and thrills will find both on this popular outing. Ride straight out of town on Florida, headed northeast (or use the dirt Horse Gulch Road, as mentioned above). After about six miles, head left and up on Road 071 (also signed as CR 249, then 249-B). This road winds through an ever-changing maze of residential roads. It changes names several times but there will always be that little 071 sign. Road 071 dead-ends at a trailhead. From here, a rocky doubletrack chugs straight up the side of Missionary Ridge. Take a left at the telephone pole, in a clearing, and the top is just beyond. You'll be glad to see it after a tough climb. Stay left on the ridge top, pass a serious-looking radio tower, and you'll surely find the Haflin Trail rockin' and rollin' down the other side. Oh baby. Another option is to ride the 22-mile loop backward. Haflin is surprisingly manageable as a climb until the last third. Lots of unridable step-ups, though.

(C) First Fork Trail

Drive out Florida Road as if you're going to Missionary Ridge as usual. (Florida Road, by the way, is Flo-REE-duh in Durango, which may sound ridiculous until you become fully indoctrinated into the local customs.) About 3.5 miles beyond the Road 071 turn-off, turn left off of Flo-REE-duh onto CR 246. In just under two miles you will find the First Fork trailhead on your left. First Fork starts out tough, but strong riders will enjoy the solitude on this alternate singletrack route to the spine of Missionary Ridge. Anything that connects with the Missionary Ridge Trail scores points. Up there, of course, are options to Haflin, Stevens, and Red Creek, popular horse route.

(D) Missionary Ridge Road

Often used with a connecting trail as a way to bypass the steep lower portion of the Stevens Creek singletrack, this mellow dirt road can also be ridden all the way to the ridge top and beyond. This works great as an ambitious, epic adventure from town. Load up on provisions and head out on Florida or 32nd to CR 250, and ride north along the eastern edge of the Animas Valley until you find the well-marked Missionary Ridge Road veering up on your right. The road zig-zags up the slope then turns decidedly north. Look for doubletracks leading up to the trail on Lime Mesa, continuous with the Missionary Ridge Trail. Many loop options are available.

(E) Beaver Meadows–First Notch Loop

Between Pagosa and Bayfield is a huge pile of dirt roads and doubletracks, going everywhere and nowhere. These dirt roads have a certain touristy charm. The first good option east of Bayfield is Beaver Meadows Road. Non-technical, graded, and wide, this pretty road will nonetheless give you a solid workout as it climbs about 2,000 feet in eight miles. A right turn onto First Notch Road (FS 620) leads to a fast descent. Then turn right onto FS 133, a gently descending doubletrack, and the loop is completed in about 15 miles. The route can be lengthened and roughed up with more doubletrack detours, of which there are many. Be aware that the Forest Service map for this area is woefully inadequate. Begin at the intersection with FS 133 on Beaver Meadows Road. To find Beaver Meadows Road, drive east about 25 miles from Durango on U.S. 160 (past Bayfield). Turn left (north) and drive up Beaver Meadows Road for about 2.8 miles to the intersection with FS 133. Park 'n' ride. Another option is to continue climbing on Beaver Meadows Road past the FS 620 turnoff to the saddle beyond, where you may start to notice some rough trails leaving the road...interesting.

(F) First Fork Road

Not to be confused with the First Fork Trail mentioned in Honorable Mention C, First Fork is another non-technical dirt road in the area that deserves mention. This one intersects with U.S. 160 just a mile or so east of the First Notch Road junction, and about 10 miles east of Beaver Meadows Road. First Fork rises from the hamlet of Piedra and follows the Piedra River north for a good long time, then drops down to a trailhead where trails take off in every direction.

Ⓖ Colorado Trail–Dry Fork Loop from Town

This ride is a cousin of the Colorado Trail–Dry Fork–Hoffheins ride (*see Ride 9*), except this one is a true loop which begins anywhere in Durango, pops into the National Forest at either of two familiar trailheads (the lower Colorado Trail trailhead or the Dry Fork trailhead), then exits at the other. There is a good bit of pavement on either end of this 20-mile loop, but it's worth the direct, no-drive access from town. Locals are divided over which direction is best to ride, but personally I'm in love with descending the Dry Fork Trail, so I like it counter-clockwise. There is no denying that the clockwise loop is extremely fun as well, giving riders a few miles of sweet downhill cruising on a smooth single', then about four miles of rough stuff. There are big climbs in both directions, and it's a moderate-difficult ride in terms of both physical and technical challenges.

There are two crucial factors to consider before you embark on this loop. (1) The Dry Fork Trailhead and Dry Fork Road are located in the Perins Peak State Wildlife

Area, and are technically off-limits from the end of hunting season through July 15. That's a big chunk of time, but it leaves an ample window of opportunity. Most of that time belongs to the mud anyway. The closure is in effect so that wintering elk and deer may have a little peace in one of their favorite off-season haunts. This closure is not enforced with an iron fist, but it would be an understatement to say that the Division of Wildlife would appreciate your staying out of the area during that time. (2) Other trail users. These are some of the most popular singletracks in the area, especially the section of Colorado Trail below Gudy's Rest. Reign in the temptation to twist your imaginary throttle and fly.

To attack this loop counter-clockwise, start by riding up familiar 25th Street/Junction Creek Road to the main Colorado Trail trailhead, located where the pavement ends on Junction Creek Road. On the Colorado Trail, climb to Gudy's Rest, past the Hoffheins Trail turnoff, then over the top to the Dry Fork Trail. Twist down Dry Fork, which is cleverly disguised as a rocky widetrack at the top, then veer right at the Hoffheins intersection (for the Colorado Trail–Dry Fork–Hoffheins ride, turn left here and head back up on Hoffheins). The portion between the Hoffheins intersection and the Dry Fork trailhead is fun but short. Pop out onto Dry Fork Road, descend to Lightner Creek Road, then U.S. 160, back to town.

To go clockwise, ride west up U.S. 160 for about 3.4 miles, then turn right onto Lightner Creek Road and ride about one mile. Veer right off the pavement onto Dry Fork Road and climb moderately for about three miles to the Dry Fork trailhead.

There are some forks in the road along the way, but with a decent map it will be easy to find.

(H) Madden Peak

Why don't you go out and ride up a mountain for no apparent reason? Madden Peak is nearby, to assuage your Sisyphean tendencies. Drive or ride 20 miles west from Durango on U.S. 160, toward Mancos. At the top of a hill, turn right onto FS 316 (Madden Peak Road). Park at the familiar intersection with the Old Railroad Grade (leveled for Otto Mears' Rio Grande Southern back in the late 1800s, abandoned in 1952, now called FS 568) just one mile from the highway, or drive up FS 316 as far as eight miles from the highway. The end of the road is another six rough, tough miles beyond this point. There are a handful of forks along the route, so bring a map and stay on FS 316. Madden stands just a few feet shy of 12,000 feet, about 3,500 feet above the lower parking area. The road doesn't reach the summit—stash your rig and scramble to the top.

(I) Menafee Mountain

For a dirt road climb that is somewhat less painful than Madden Peak, give Menafee Mountain a shot. The road to the top of Menafee (FS 566) takes off from U.S. 160, to the southwest, just a half mile west of the turnoff for Madden Peak Road (FS 316). FS 566 is less than three miles long, and elevates a mere 1,000 feet on the way to the radio-towered peak, with a few steeper sections near the top. The scrub oak and patches of aspen make a spectacular mosaic in the fall.

(J) Dolores River Canyon

It's too bad this out-and-back canyon cruise is so far from Durango. Or is it? Highlights along this flat, riverside 4WD road include the Dolores River (a Gold Medal trout stream), sheer sandstone cliffs a la Moab, and an extended dry season. Eleven miles of moderately rocky road lead to a saddle behind the Pyramid formation, which overlooks the Dolores at a sharp left-hand bend; a good map will come in handy if you want to navigate the remaining 15 or so miles to the northern trailhead. Twenty six miles between gates leaves plenty of room for solitude.

To get to the starting point, drive to Cortez, then another 35 or so miles north from there on U.S. 666 (The Road of the Beast), almost to Dove Creek. Watch for signs that point the way north along dirt roads down to the parking area on the canyon floor. Follow the signs for the river, not the overlook.

(K) Transfer Campground

Located northeast of Mancos, Transfer Campground is the hub of an impressive network of doubletracks, dirt roads, and trails. The cycle of cutting new roads and abandoning old ones has left a jumble of half-routes in the area. The confusion has never been mapped satisfactorily by any agency, and greenhorns do well to remain glued to the main roads. Nonetheless, a variety of solid loops can be had here, for riders of almost any ability. To find Transfer Campground, drive west from Durango on U.S. 160 to Mancos, then turn right on CO 184 toward Dolores. Drive one half mile, then take a right onto CR 42 and drive 13 miles to Transfer Campground. (CR 42 becomes FS 561.) **Campers note:** Transfer is a forest service campground that is open for business from June 1 through October 10.

One of the more popular loop options uses dirt roads north of the campground and passes the Jersey Jim Lookout, an old Forest Service fire tower that is now available for nightly rentals. To try this moderate 18-miler, head north out of Transfer on FS 561 for about one mile to a fork. Go left here on FS 560 and ride for a little more than seven miles to a T-intersection with FS 556. Take a right onto FS 556 and ride for 5.5 miles, then take a right onto FS 561 and descend all the way home. The lookout stands at about mile 15. The backside of this loop hovers near 10,000 feet, with total elevation gain in the neighborhood of 1,500 feet. Additional dirt road loops, long and short, are accessed by riding out of Transfer to the east on FS 565, which is closed to vehicles. Other roads sprout off to the south, northwest, northeast, southwest, and southeast. Roads everywhere!

Trailhounds will sniff out some challenging singletracks cutting across the grid of roads and doubletracks in the vicinity of Transfer Campground. Expect long technical and unrideable sections. Try the Chicken Creek Trail, with a trailhead just north of the campground on FS 560, or the Morrison Trail (FS 610), which branches north from the Chicken Creek Trail at the bottom of its initial descent from FS 560. The well-marked Morrison leads all the way north to the Bear Creek trailhead on CO 145 (10 miles), opening up the door for a monstrous epic loop.

Ⓛ Bear Creek Trail

Tucked away on the western slope of the La Platas, rising from a lonely stretch of CO 145 between Rico and Dolores, the Bear Creek Trail is a nice valley-climbing trail that is popular with the horse folks, but is only occasionally ridden by cyclists. Moderate singletrack rises less than 2,000 feet in 12 miles beside Bear Creek, a tributary of the Dolores. Making a loop out of this one means climbing steeply out of the wide valley on one of a number of switchbackin' trails. Remember, this is just one of several Bear Creeks in southwest Colorado. To reach this Bear Creek from Durango, drive west on U.S. 160 to Mancos, then north to Dolores on CO 184. Go north from Dolores on CO 145 toward Lizard Head Pass and Telluride. Twenty miles out of Dolores, take a right onto a dirt road which leads directly to the trailhead. The trailhead is actually somewhat closer to Telluride, about 47 miles south of town on 145. As such, this ride could easily have been lumped in with the Telluride section, but there are already a few other Bear Creek Trails among that section's Honorable Mentions...

Ⓜ Colorado Trail Shuttle

A prime shuttle opportunity awaits near the upper reaches of Junction Creek Road, at the foot of the rugged peaks of the La Plata Range. *[See Ride 14 for a great reference.]* Way up there, the Colorado Trail crosses a well known but unnamed spur road off J.C. Road. To find this fortuitous crossing, drive out of town for about 16 miles on Junction Creek Road, then bust a left onto the aforementioned spur. Watch for signs. This point-to-point begins with a top-notch trail to Junction Creek, then 4.5 miles back up the other side, drainage to drainage, until the trail joins a widetrack at the top of the climb. The downhill back to the main trailhead on lower Junction Creek Road includes smooth ribbon with fast turns and natural jumps, and miles of dicey, technical goods to finish it off. A really, really fine ride. Of course, any degree of shuttle activity will shave a little bit off your soul. But I believe, in this case, that a humble appreciation of the trail and the forest through which it travels will prevent the deduction of significant points from your Karma Rating. Don't be afraid to try an out-and-back from this location, or from the lower trailhead. Just see how far you can get. Or loop it straight from town, using Junction Creek Road to the spur road, or La Plata Canyon to Kennebec (The Big Loop). "The more you drive, the less intelligent you are." (Repo Man.)

(N) Indian Trail Ridge

Some would consider this to be la crème de la dirt. Taking off from Kennebec Pass, the singletrack *[See Ride 14 for a great reference.]* Colorado Trail climbs onto the ethereal Indian Trail Ridge and flows in huge tidal waves northward. Rolling terrain on an apocalyptic scale, as each of the rollers goes about 500 feet. Human lungs only, please. Also required for this high-altitude adventure are obsessive-compulsive preparation and a steward's sensibility toward tundra and beasts. Thankfully, access is a problem. Four-wheel to the top of Kennebec, or passenger car to a spur road off Junction Creek Road (the unnamed spur is located about 16 miles above Durango on Junction Creek Road) where the Colorado Trail can be picked up a few steep, rough miles below Kennebec Pass on the east side. Just getting to the pass from here will be more than most folks can take, even though the Colorado Trail volunteers have been busy trying to neutralize the trail's bitchy attitude below Kennebec. I wish they wouldn't do that—there are plenty of easy trails close to town.

(O) Bolam Pass–Hotel Draw Loop

A 25-mile loop, highly recommended for advanced riders, with a great section of high-altitude singletrack. Start at the north Hermosa Creek trailhead, which can be found by driving about 26 miles north from Durango on U.S. 550, then turning left onto FS 578 and driving for about eight miles.

Park at the Hermosa trailhead, but start the ride by continuing up FS 578. A few miles up the road, stay right at a fork (that's Hotel Draw), and continue to the Graysill Mine, an old uranium outfit from the 1940s. About a half mile past the mine, turn left onto the Colorado Trail singletrack. Exit the ridge via Hotel Draw. In between, you will be amazed by scenery. Be kind to the alpine environment and pack warm clothing.

(P) Purgatory–Elbert Creek Loop

A 15-mile loop using dirt road, singletrack, and paved highway. Start at the Purgatory base parking area and ride up FS 578 (the main road to Hermosa Park and the upper Hermosa trailhead), then turn left onto Elbert Creek Road (FS 581). Five-plus miles up Elbert Creek Road, turn left onto the Elbert Creek singletrack and drop to the highway, looping back to Purgatory on pavement. Continuing on Elbert Creek Road would lead you to the Dutch Creek Trail, with connections to Hermosa and Jones Creek.

(Q) Harris Park Loop

A scenic, mellow dirt road/doubletrack route near Purgatory. Start from the intersection of Hermosa Park Road (FS 578) and Elbert Creek Road (FS 581), riding up Elbert Creek Road (start from the base to add some workout). Drop onto the Worlds Course singletrack (right turn), then left onto a doubletrack. Follow the signs for the Harris Park Loop, which you will notice descends nicely onto the flats (Harris Park). Hook up with Hermosa Park Road and bring it on home. Just four miles.

(R) The Ultimate Shuttle

Have a friend drop you off at the summit of Molas Pass with a backpack full of food, warm clothing, water filter, iodine pills, spare parts, and lights. Tell him "thanks, I'll see you in Durango," and start riding the Colorado Trail all the way back to town. Eighty or so miles of incredible singletrack. Those who visualize a downhill wonder-cruise are massively mistaken. Even before you reach the famous, over-hyped climb from the bridge across Junction Creek, you will be a hardened veteran of many high altitude wars, with a far-away look in your eye. Will it be possible to make the transition back into society?

(S) Molas–Silverton Loop

Of course you could shuttle this one too, but eventually you get tired of running like a mouse from U.S. 550 and its huge passes. You're a mountain biker! You eat this stuff for lunch. Believe me, if you're used to powering up the giant singletrack hills around here, then paved Molas Pass won't kill you. You laugh at Molas Pass! It is dangerous, though, in a blunt trauma sort of way—the drivers on this road are 50% drowsy truckers, 50% senile tourists—and I fret for those of you with little or no common sense about riding in traffic. But the shoulder is wide and smooth. Start this one from the Molas summit, headed northwest on the Colorado Trail. At mile 10.5, after many miles of unsurpassed singletrack cruising, bust a right, then less than one mile later, another right which puts you on the Rico-Silverton Trail at the top of a hardcore descent. Drop into Silverton on singletrack, then 4WD road, then graded dirt, then paved highway. Check out a fake gun fight, then follow the train of Winnebagos and Kenworths back up the hill. A 30-mile beauty.

(T) Silverton to Clear Lake

If you're staying in Silverton or otherwise using this old den of sin they call a town as a base, this is a great little ride. Start right from town and head up U.S. 550 toward Red Mountain Pass. After about two miles, hang a left up FS 585 (CR 7), along South Mineral Creek. Before you get to South Mineral Campground, bust a right onto FS 815. This sweet shelf road leads up to Clear Lake, or just below it anyway, climbing about 2K. Within ten miles from Silverton, you're skipping rocks across a beautiful alpine lake.

(U) Stony Pass

Another right-out-of-Silverton ride. Head north up CO 110 toward Howardsville (about four miles), then take a right onto FS 589 (CR 4). Ride up Cunningham Gulch for 1.7 miles, then veer left onto the Stony Pass Road. The pass is up there at 12,588 feet off the deck, but only about ten miles total from Silverton. Bring a camera along, definitely, and consider extending your ride into the Creede-Lake City zone, possibly as an over-nighter. Creede is about 50 miles from the top of the pass, and Rio Grande Reservoir is only about 17 miles away, with an assortment of established lakeside campgrounds. Top-notch free camping spots are everywhere along the road, however.

(V) Engineer Pass–Cinnamon Pass–Lake City Loop

Two big passes, Engineer and Cinnamon, greet you warmly on this 50-mile dirt road/4WD road loop. Both passes are in the 13,000-foot range. Accessing the western side of this loop in a 2WD vehicle is problematic. Start from a parking spot near the Picayne Gulch turnoff below Animas Forks, a 12-mile drive northeast out of Silverton on CO 110, which eventually narrows into FS 586. You'll climb like mad from this location. Less than a mile from the start, veer right up a steep 4WD road; at the next intersection, take a right for Cinnamon or go straight for Engineer. The roads are usually well-signed. (Another possible starting point is the bottom of the Engineer Pass Road on U.S. 550 near Ouray. See Ride 34 for a description of this road section.) It doesn't really matter which way you go, either pass brings equal hurt and glory. If you've got the time and cash, make reservations to stay in Lake City. The views from the pass summits are incredible. This loop is an overused 4WD-SUV route called the "Alpine Loop," so be prepared to suck some exhaust on the weekends.

(W) Fawn Gulch–Mill Creek Loop

Just one of several pavement-dirt-doubletrack loops using the town of Pagosa Springs as a start-finish. Start in town, possibly from the sizeable parking area which lies across the river from the hot springs, and ride east on U.S. 160. Watch for the smooth, inviting Fawn Gulch Road rising southward from U.S. 160 about 3 miles east of the town's edge. Fawn Gulch Road is also ominously tagged as Forest Road 666, not to be confused with Highway 666 out of Dolores. Don't expect anything too evil here, although flatlanders and some weekend warriors may find the elevation gain slightly demonic. After about one mile, turn right onto a two-track (FS 722) to begin a meandering clockwise loop that leads back to Pagosa via Willow Draw. Ride several miles of big rollers on this double', ford Mill Creek, then hang another right onto Mill Creek Road (CR 302 or FS 662) and pedal it back past the rodeo grounds and to a T-intersection with U.S. 84. Take a right and ride a short 0.3 miles to U.S. 160, then take a left and roll back into town. This 18-mile loop also works in the other direction.

(X) Reservoir Hill

This city-owned parcel sports fun singletrack and easy-climbing dirt roads, and its location right above town on the southeast side puts it within rock-throwing distance of the famed hot springs. (To find the trailhead, turn south off U.S. 160 in the heart of Pagosa at the main stoplight, as if you're going to the hot springs; cross the river, and instead of turning right into the hot springs, turn left onto San Juan Street. Go one block, then turn right on the dirt road which leads directly to the trailhead.) The terrain is moderate, with less than 500 linear feet of air space between the bottom and the top. Go here without high expectations for adventure or distance but with a need to get a quick ride in.

(Y) Chris Mountain & Turkey Springs

The section of the San Juan National Forest northwest of Pagosa teems with doubletracks and dirt roads, ranging from flat and easy to steep and painful. To reach the rough doubletrack that circumnavigates Chris Mountain—a popular destination— head west from Pagosa on U.S. 160, up the big hill, then take a right (north) on Piedra Road. Take Piedra Road for about six miles to the forest boundary and Turkey Springs Road (FS 629). Consider parking here, or hang a left onto Turkey Springs Road (FS 629), drive another 4.5 miles and park at the right fork where a doubletrack begins to chug steeply up Chris Mountain. Here begins a two-mile grunt up to another fork which marks the beginning and end of a hilly four-mile loop around the mountain. There are lots of doubletrack connectors up there, so be vigilant in your route-finding. Below Chris Mountain, several moderate and easy dirt roads and doubletracks connect to Turkey Springs Road, providing options for a variety of non-threatening routes.

A view of the Colorado Trail near Bolam Pass.

Telluride
COLORADO

Tracing the path of the cliffside Bear Creek National Recreation Trail.

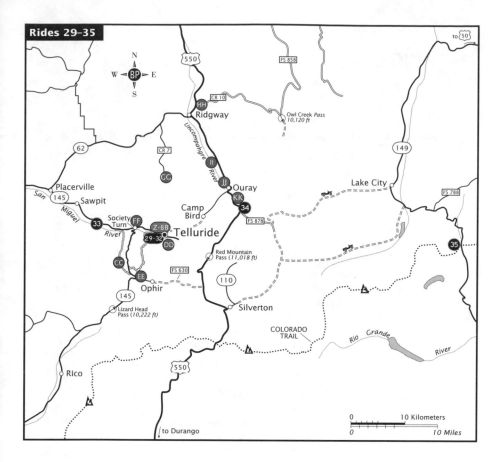

N
W — BP — E
S

550

FS 858

to 50

CR 10

Ridgway

Owl Creek Pass
10,120 ft

62

CR 7

149

Uncompahgre River

GG

II

JJ Ouray
KK

Lake City

FS 788

Placerville

San

145 Sawpit

Miguel

Society FF
Turn

33

Camp
Bird

FS 878

34

River

Z-BB

Telluride

29-32

DD

Red Mountain
Pass (11,018 ft)

FS 630

110

35

CC

EE

Ophir

145

Lizard Head
Pass (10,222 ft)

Silverton

COLORADO
TRAIL

Rio Grande
River

Rico

550

to Durango

0   10 Kilometers
0   10 Miles

The Rides

29. Imogene Pass
30. Galloping Goose
31. Wilson Mesa Long Loop
32. Western Deep Creek Loop
33. San Miguel River Ramble
34. Engineer Pass
35. Spring Creek Pass-Jarosa Mesa

Honorable Mentions

Z. Bear Creek Road
AA. West Wilson Mesa Trail
BB. Mill Creek–Deep Creek Loop
CC. Sunshine Mesa Short Loop
DD. Wasatch Trail–Bridal Veil Loop ("The Waterfall Tour")
EE. Ophir Pass
FF. Last Dollar Road
GG. West Dallas Trail
HH. Owl Creek Pass
II. East Dallas Trail
JJ. River Road
KK. Bear Creek National Recreation Trail

Telluride

Telluride

"I saw William Dafoe!"
"It's *Willem* Dafoe."
"What?"

(Just a typical conversation overheard while strolling down Main Street in Telluride, one of the world's most beautiful towns.)

These days, you never know who you might see hanging out here, especially during the summer festival season. Semi-famous Hollywood types mingle with pungent packs of nomadic *trustafarian* youngsters. Classic mid-western tourists climb out of RVs to stroll the avenue alongside an eclectic mix of full-time residents: drunken heiresses, shameless developers, artists, ski and board bums, great grandsons of prospectors turned prospectors themselves.

One look around this place and you know why people come here, and why they stay. Especially in the early summer when the various waterfalls are really flowing, the jaw-dropping view is pure magic. Rugged mountains guard Telluride on three sides, shading the village in wonderfully inconvenient isolation. One lone spur of paved highway wanders up the San Miguel Valley from the west, then dead-ends against the wall of the box canyon. The only direct access from the north, south, or east is by way of small planes or well-equipped 4WD vehicles. If you were a falcon, you could *fly* over the range from Telluride to the beautiful Victorian town of Ouray in a cool half hour—by passenger car, the trip between these two neighboring towns takes half a day. Getting to Telluride takes commitment, and getting out, once the mountains get a grip on you, takes even more. *Why leave*, you ask yourself, and then your mind goes blank.

Certainly, not everyone can feel welcome in a place that exists for the precious few, and Telluride has become one of those places. The thin air is buzzing with a slightly more rustic version of that cool attitude and strange energy reserved for high-end ski towns. You feel it in Aspen, you feel it in St. Moritz, and you feel it here: *big money in a small place*. It will infuse you with low-grade excitement or annoy the crap out of you, depending largely on the size of your wallet and access to friends' condos. Travelers on a tight budget may find themselves in a headlong down-valley retreat toward more reality-based economies, cursing Telluride's Aspenesque exclusivity and absurd prices. (The San Juan mountain towns of Ouray, Silverton, Rico, and Lake City feature similar alpine splendor without the mad opulence.)

It's doubtful many of Telluride's various hangers-on and passers-through are aware of its bloody history as battleground for an intense labor war. In a similar fashion to most other towns of Southwest Colorado, Telluride sprouted in 1880 as an accompaniment to the fledgling mining operations scattered on the steep slopes above the San Miguel River. About 20 years later, the box canyon was rocked by a prolonged spate of bombings and murders as owners and workers scrapped bitterly over terms of employment in the mines. The town was eventually occupied by government troops. When train conductors bellowed to passengers on the inbound Rio Grande Southern "To-Hell-You-Ride!" it was more than a play on words—it was a warning. Today, it's strange to sit on Colorado Avenue and consider Telluride's journey from violent,

hard-knock mining camp to ski resort sprinkled with *latte*-sipping film stars. But there it is. You wouldn't believe it if the evidence wasn't right there in front of you, wearing leather pants.

In general, people don't flock to Telluride to ride bikes. They come here to do other things, like ski, board, four-wheel, take pictures of waterfalls, sit around, and drink—not necessarily in that order. Telluride's relative anonymity in the cycling world is much appreciated by the handful of hard-core trail riders who live here. Isolation is a key ingredient in the Telluride trail experience. Within about an hour's ride from town, mountain bikers can exile themselves into the dark corners of the Uncompahgre National Forest, where elk bugle and squawk with impunity. Here, on the steep lower slopes of Mount Sneffels, and across the flowing splendor of Wilson Mesa, mountain bikes reach their full potential as tools for adventure, and mountain bikers find pure joy. Climbing the steep walls east of town and reaching far beyond through an ocean of peaks, a number of intense jeep roads are just begging to be ridden. These old mining roads make up for their lack of technical challenges with awesome view and insane workouts.

And Telluride even holds a few nice surprises for the novice cyclist as well, believe it or not. The singletrack River Trail and a paved bike path cruise the valley floor beside the San Miguel, the Bear Creek Path climbs modestly to a scenic waterfall, and the Galloping Goose Trail follows an old railroad grade away from the resort on gentle terrain. Unfortunately, the River Trail and parts of the Goose are jeopardized by current plans to develop the valley floor west of town. If this potential Vail-ization of Telluride fills you with fear and loathing, you are not alone: many of the town's residents have banded together in an attempt to halt the development, and an angry conflict has been brewing. One possible outcome of the "War for the Floor" is that the land will be purchased and kept open by a quasi-public conglomerate involving some of Telluride's fabulously wealthy residents. As usual, money talks. For the time being at least, with these gentle trails connecting the village to backcountry adventure, Telluride is one of the most cycling-friendly towns anywhere.

Telluride! It's one of those places you just have to visit. Bring your bike, and don't act too surprised if you see Willem Dafoe.

Getting around Telluride

📞 AREA CODES

The **970** area code services a large area encompassing all of Southwestern Colorado—including Durango, Pagosa Springs, and Telluride—and most of the northern half of the state as well. (The Denver/Boulder metro area uses **303** and **720**. The **719** area code services the greater south-central and southeastern part of the state, including Colorado Springs, Pueblo, Buena Vista, Leadville, Alamosa, and Del Norte.)

🚗 ROADS

For current information on statewide weather, road conditions, and closures, contact the **Colorado Department of Transportation** (CDOT) at their toll free hotline 1–877–315–ROAD. Denver metro area and out-of-state callers can access the hotline by calling (303) 639–1111. The same information can also be found by visiting CDOT's website at *www.dot.state.co.us* or *www.cotrip.org*

✈ BY AIR

The Telluride Airport (TEX), North America's highest commercial airport at 9,078 feet above sea level, is located 6 miles from Telluride, just off of Last Dollar Road. The airport is served by daily flights from Denver on United Express, and daily flights from Phoenix on American West. For more information, check its website at *www.tellurideairport.com*, or call (970) 728–5313.

To book reservations online, check out your favorite airline's website or search one of the following travel sites for the best price: *www.cheaptickets.com*, *www.expedia.com*, *www.previewtravel.com*, *www.orbitz.com*, *www.priceline.com*, *travel.yahoo.com*, *www.travelocity.com*, or *www.trip.com*—just to name a few.

🚌 SHUTTLES

A few companies provide shuttle service to and from the Telluride Airport and other destinations. Try **Telluride Express** at (888) 212–TAXI, or **Mountain Limo** ("minibar…digital sound…") at 1–888–546–6894 or (970) 728–9606. Rental cars are also available at the airport.

🚌 BY BUS

From May 24 through October 7, the "**Galloping Goose**" bus system provides free loop service around Telluride, and even sends regular shuttle buses down-valley as far as Norwood (one dollar for the Norwood bus). Call (970) 728–5700 for 24-hour shuttle information.

🚡 BY GONDOLA

Zipping passengers up the mountain to Mountain Village quickly and cleanly, **Telluride's free gondola** is always a big hit. The two-mile journey lasts about 15 minutes. Take your bike with you. The base station is located near the southern dead-end of Oak Street. Details: (970) 728–8888.

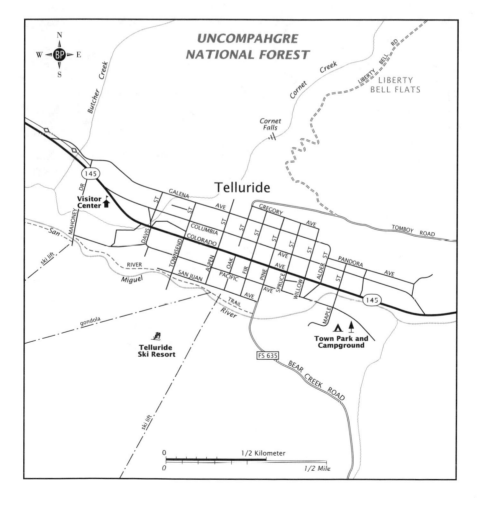

165

Imogene Pass

Ride Specs

Start: From the intersection of Oak Street and Tomboy Road in Telluride
Length: 14.5-mile out-and-back
Approximate Riding Time: 3.5–6 hours
Technical Difficulty: Moderate to Difficult: steep, rocky climbs and dangerous descending on 4WD road
Physical Difficulty: Very Difficult: a brutally steep, high-altitude climb
Trail Surface: 4WD road
Lay of the Land: Steep canyons and rocky, tundra-covered slopes of high mountains
Elevation Gain: 7,244 feet
Land Status: National forest
Other Trail Users: Hikers, joggers, and motorists (4WDs, motorcycles, and all kinds of ATVs)

Getting There

In Telluride: Park somewhere in town and hop on your bike.* To find the start, head north on Oak Street—which, by the way, can't be accessed from Colorado Avenue (CO 145) because of a little park—until the street dead-ends. On the right is the dirt Tomboy Road, where you'll begin the ride.

Parking is available on Colorado Avenue or the surrounding streets. Parking is free on Sundays but costs 50 cents per hour otherwise.

> Imogene Pass was named for Imogene Basin, which was named after Imogene Jiliff, the bride of Andrew Richardson. Richardson was an early prospector in the area.

I n a region filled with hard climbs up unforgiving mining roads, this could be the toughest. At 13,114 feet above sea level, Imogene Pass is one of the *taller* passes around, and the second half of the seven-mile approach from Telluride is heinously steep, too steep to ride for long stretches—hell, too steep to *walk* for long stretches. Enjoy.

Rising straight from Telluride, up the northern slope of the box canyon (straight toward the box), Tomboy Road at first seems innocent enough. The road elevates moderately, peppered with steep and rocky pitches, offering top-shelf views of the dueling waterfalls (Ingram, on the left, and Bridal Veil, on the right), and the town below. Your biggest problem down here is the annoying frequency of 4WDs out to conquer one of the most popular jeep routes in the *Western* Hemisphere. The ATVs are still a problem near the top, disrupting rhythm and blowing fumes, but, at that point, they're way down your list of problems. (To avoid the gas menagerie, climb the pass on a weekday.) After about 3.7 miles, the road has climbed into the old mining area near the townsite of Tomboy. It has been a slow but manageable climb so far.

Tomboy (named after founder Otis "Tomboy" Thomas) was one of a handful of behemoth mining operations that flourished for a while on the harshly steep, avalanche-terrorized slopes northeast of Telluride. The camp's unfortunate claim to fame was a sustained, bloody labor war, which took place around the turn of the 20th Century. The dispute was sparked when the ownership of the nearby

Smuggler/Union Mine (located at the top of Marshall Basin, the long couloir that's well-viewed from the top of Imogene Pass) stopped paying straight salaries to the mine's workers and began paying commission based on the amount of work done. The union went on strike. Typical of such a conflict, the company hired non-union workers after the strike, at the very same terms that had been sought by the union. The conflict escalated into the sort of violence that was sadly cliché for the times—shootings, beatings, and bombings—as union leg-breakers went after the managers and shift bosses, as well as the non-union workers. The company, likewise, tried to smash the union and keep its militant splinters away from their precious operation. This went on for years, and guys were turning up dead all over the place.

Stopping to rest near the bottom of Tomboy Road.

In 1904, Governor James Peabody dispatched federal troops and martial law was declared in Telluride; about 83 union members (plus 60 or so "sympathizers" who were culled from the town by vigilantes) were deported on the train to Montrose, and a makeshift fort was tossed up on Imogene Pass to make sure they didn't try to sneak back in. The troops also imposed a strict 8 P.M. curfew, and swept the working girls out of Telluride's infamous red light district. Anyone leaving or coming into the box canyon was required to have a special pass. Telluride was a company town.

Under the imposed security, rumors circulated that union henchmen were planning to roll dynamite bombs down the mountainsides into town, poison the town's drinking water with cyanide (most likely it was already poisoned by the mining operations), and assassinate the governor. All of the rumors were partially true. Eventually, courts ruled that the angry union would have to be let back into the town as well as the mines, and uneasy compromises were reached that nobody was particularly happy with.

Telluride had quite literally been through a war, and would never be the same. Half a century of bitter silence and a few decades' worth of rich, happy skiers gave rise

to the comforting misconception that this was always a peaceful little town.

From the Tomboy site, where pieces of old buildings clutter the avalanche chutes, your fate is apparent. Here is a fine vantage point to consider those next three miles of road shooting up the mountainside at a ridiculous angle. Here you might see a distant parade of jeeps whining up the incline in four-wheel low, as the cold alpine wind whips up, and wonder: *How tough am I?* On a hill like this, you could find out. The climbing from here on is at least as harsh as it looks from below: a torturous, rock-spitting war of attrition. A lot of turning around has been done from this point.

MilesDirections

0.0 START riding up Tomboy Road from its lower terminus, at the end of North Oak Street in Telluride.

3.7 Arrive at the lower end of the Tomboy mining area, a fine spot for carbo infusion. Above this point, the road steepens like crazy, and even the strongest cyclists will be pushing much of the time. Typical for steep 4WD routes above treeline, Tomboy Road splits into multiple spurs at numerous points. All of the roads reconverge on their way to the pass. Just pick your poison—all the routes are equally brutal.

7.1 Arrive at the Imogene Pass summit (13,114 feet). Ever been this high on a bike before? To avoid a likely conglomeration of

shivering jeepers continue straight past the sign and the old shack and find a rustic, technical trail headed out to a more secluded promontory.

7.3 The trail becomes unrideable. Turn around here, after scrambling for the rest of your winter gear. *[**Option**. From the top of the pass, Ouray can be had easily, about 10 miles down the other side. This makes a great point-to-point shuttle, or a hardcore overnighter. There are hot springs there. From Ouray, the ascent up Imogene is even tougher.]*

14.5 Arrive back in Telluride. You deserve food. You deserve beer. *But can you afford it?*

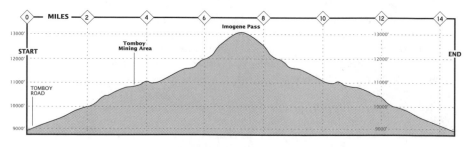

Should you reach the summit, or anywhere near it, you'll always need to be prepared for paranormal high altitude weather phenomena. Large winds and small temperatures. Strange forms of precipitation (ice pellets are a favorite). Don't get caught in a lightning storm. I could go on and on. *Pack your winter riding gear*—odds are you'll be wearing everything you packed on top of the pass, even in high summer.

The descent back to old Tomboy is a knuckle-breaker and brain-shaker, surfing dangerously over big, loose chunks. Below the townsite, the ride mellows considerably.

Ride Information

🕿 Trail Contacts:
Uncompahgre National Forest, Norwood, CO (970) 327–4261 or *www.fs.fed.us/r2/gmug*

🕑 Schedule:
Open year round, but best from June through September, due to weather. Expect winter conditions year round on the pass summit, and pack accordingly.

Ⓢ Fees/Permits:
No fees or permits are required

Ⓝ Maps:
USGS maps: Telluride, CO; Ironton, CO • **USFS maps:** *Uncompahgre National Forest*

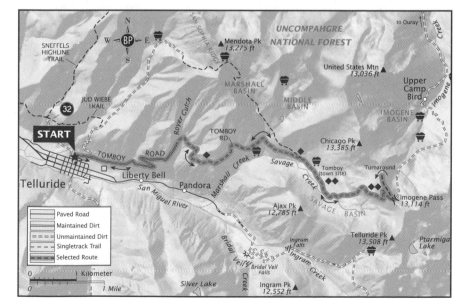

Galloping Goose

Ride Specs

Start: From the River Trail trailhead off Mahoney Drive in Telluride
Length: 29.4-mile out-and-back
Approximate Riding Time: 2.5–5 hours
Technical Difficulty: Moderate: gently graded singletrack with occasional technical sections
Physical Difficulty: Moderate: long, but without tough climbing
Trail Surface: 60% singletrack/widetrack and 40% dirt/4WD roads (you'll also cross a bit of pavement)
Lay of the Land: Forested hillside above the South Fork River and lush valley floor near Telluride
Elevation Gain: 4,972 feet
Land Status: National forest and private land
Other Trail Users: Hikers, joggers, and motorists

Getting There

In Telluride: Park somewhere in town and hop on your bike.* Head south, toward the ski hill, to the San Miguel River from Colorado Avenue (CO 145). There, next to the river, you will find a wide, gravel path. This is the River Trail. Turn right (west) onto the path and head slightly downhill to the starting point at Mahoney Drive. Mahoney Drive is the last paved street crossed by the River Trail as it heads out of town toward CO 145.

Parking is available on Colorado Avenue or the surrounding streets. Parking is free on Sundays but costs 50 cents per hour otherwise.

Launching directly from the town of Telluride, on flat terrain, this gem of a ride features some of the most easily accessible singletrack in Southwest Colorado. The out-and-back route featured here includes two surviving sections of the historic Rio Grande Southern (RGS) railroad grade. The mileage is substantial, but the conspicuous lack of brutal climbing—typical for abandoned railroad cuts—makes the miles fly by. The general theme is fast cruising on a wide trail. Novices should take note that an abbreviated version of this ride, cutting the total distance down to 13 miles, is a traditional and loveable option.

Start by zipping down the River Trail. This groomed, city-sponsored widetrack runs along the San Miguel River, as it cruises through town, running through the backyards of condos and restaurants. Soon after the San Miguel leaves town and heads down-valley, the accompanying River Trail narrows into a thin, hard-packed ribbon, twisting through the riverside brush. This is private property, but the corporate ownership allows passage on the trail for the time being. Please stay on the marked trails as the singletrack splits a few times along this first stretch. (The upper forks head up into the trees and offer more challenging terrain. These dicey upper options are highly recommended for advanced riders, but all the mileage below corresponds to the lower route). After about three miles of enjoyable winding stuff and

probable mud pits, with some brief, technical twisting onto the wooded hillside, the River Trail runs smack into CO Route 145.

On the west side of CO Route 145, our route joins the Galloping Goose Trail as it follows the old RGS railroad grade. This ledge was carved in the late 19th Century by raging capitalist Otto Mears—well, actually it was carved by guys he hired—as part of his vast system of toll roads and rails that connected nearly all of the mining camps of southwest Colorado. This line was used heavily for about three decades to haul supplies and passengers into Telluride and ore and passengers out. As the mining industry shriveled, the need for the railroad steadily declined. The tracks were finally removed in 1952.

The Goose Trail above Ilium.

171

MilesDirections

0.0 START from the intersection of the River Trail and Mahoney Drive, and begin riding west (down-valley) on the River Trail.

0.9 Cross the widetrack which leads up to Mountain Village.

1.3 The trail forks. Go right. *[Option. The upper fork offers a more technical and strenuous challenge, then quickly rejoins the lower trail at mile 1.6.]*

1.6 The trails converge.

2.6 The trail splits again. Stay right. *[Option. Once again, the upper trail is a tough and interesting option. This fork intersects with CO 145 just a few ticks uphill of the lower trail's point of intersection with CO 145.]*

3.2 Cross CO 145 (the road to Lizard Head Pass and Rico—please be careful), then ride up the road just opposite (Lawson Hill Road). The start of the Galloping Goose Trail is right there across from the gas station, on the north side of Lawson Hill Road.

3.6 Stay right on the Galloping Goose as a doubletrack comes in from the left.

6.4 The Goose spills out onto South Fork Road (FS 625). Take a right onto this road. *[Option. Lots of folks turn around right here, to make an all-singletrack 13-miler. There are many other options available from this intersection. The trail is the best way to get back to town, in my opinion. As your attorney, I advise you to avoid looping back north via the highway—Keystone Hill is not too cool.]*

6.9 Turn left onto Sunshine Mesa Road (The sign here reads "Road 63J," but on some maps this road is often marked as FS 623). The intersection is located just before the Ilium Episcopal Camp.

10.2 Before Sunshine Mesa Road takes a sharp right and begins to climb more steeply, take a left onto the Galloping Goose widetrack.

12.9 The Goose swoops down and crosses Wilson Creek on a bridge.

13.0 Intersect with a 4WD road. Take a right (going up) to continue the Goose route. From this point, the route climbs moderately on 4WD roads, doubletrack, and bits of nice singletrack. *[Option. From this intersection, one could take a left down the 4WD road to Ames and the South Fork Road, which could then be looped back down to the lower section of the Goose trail, a very popular option; or you could simply turn around here, if you wish to avoid the moderate climbs at the end of the route.]*

13.8 Stay right as a private road intersects from the left.

13.9 Take a sharp right to continue the Galloping Goose route (a little singletrack cuts the corner here).

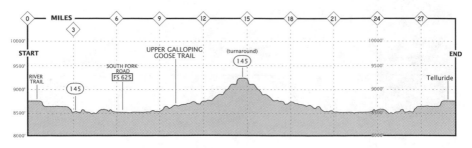

14.2 Take a left and head up another bit of sweet trail.

14.4 The route crosses beneath CO 145.

14.7 After a nice section of singletrack, the trail intersects with CO 145. Turn around and retrace your tracks. *[Option. A popular option is to cruise down the highway to the South Fork Road, then use that to access the lower portion of Galloping Goose. In my opinion, it is* much more fun to cruise back down the trail, even though you sacrifice the strange psychological comfort of completing a loop.]*

29.4 Arrive back in Telluride, at the intersection of the River Trail and Mahoney Drive.

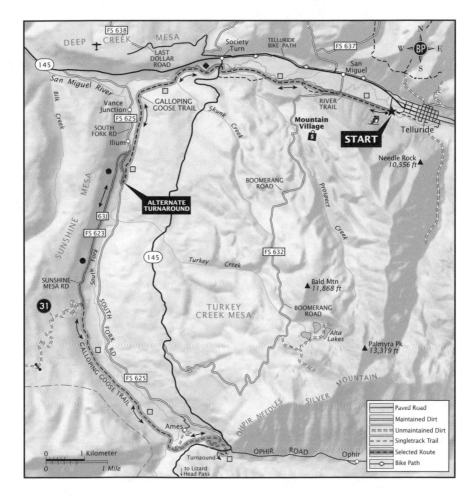

During the era of decline, in the early 1930s, the Galloping Goose was born in the office of some delusional, over-worked railroad manager. The Galloping Goose was a last-ditch effort, a desperate response to the economic realities that had been steadily choking the railroads to death. Next to the stately locomotives, which symbolize mining's Gilded Age, the comical, rattletrap Geese remind us of fleeting wealth and the boom-bust cycle. (Someday, folks will think the same way about Y-shaped bicycles.) There were actually many of these Geese—no two were alike but they were all funky-looking contraptions, quite literally *thrown* together, fabricated from oblong, bus-like shells and the chassis of Cadillacs. Needing just a single operator, the lightweight Goose was meant to haul light cargo, mail, and a dwindling number of passengers cheaply, if not safely. Though the Goose had a tendency to jump the old narrow gauge tracks with alarming frequency, no deaths were ever reported. If you'd like to lay your eyes on an actual Galloping Goose, and I know that you would, there's one sitting on Main Street in Telluride. It has been made into a very small and odd branch of a bank. (There are just three Geese left in the whole graceless gander. One is here in Telluride, another is in the town park in Dolores, and the third survives at the Railroad Museum near Golden.)

Clearly, Otto Mears' old railroad grade has reached its apotheosis of usefulness in the new millennium, as a mountain bike trail. Telluridians and visitors to town are lucky to have this strip of dirt so readily available. The Goose is a big smile as it *hauls ass* down a wide, straight ledge, then funnels into a somewhat precariously hanging singletrack with sweet, tiny turns. Watch for other beings along this tight section above the South Fork River Valley and the Ilium Episcopal Camp. At about mile 6.4—*too soon*—the trail spills out onto South Fork Road, making a natural turn-around point for beginners or folks who are already late for work. An out-and-back from Telluride to this point makes a 13-miler composed almost entirely of nice, gentle singletrack.

The extended route then travels up the easy portion of Sunshine Mesa Road (Road 63J), which was also part of the old railroad grade, and continues with still more Galloping Goose. The trail is pretty wide, but a bit rockier up here, looking down on the serene South Fork River Valley. The straight trail gains elevation softly for more than two miles, then does some moderate singletrack winding before crossing Wilson Creek on a nice bridge. Soon thereafter, the route joins a 4WD road at mile 13.0. For the next 1.7 miles, the Goose route consists of a semi-chaotic mix of 4WD roads and challeng-

> "Telluride" is actually an obscure term from chemistry, describing the compound of the element tellurium "with an electroposi-tive element or group." Tellurium is a rare, crystalline element that is found in combina-tion with gold or silver.

ing singletracks that stair-step up to CO Route 145. The main route is marked with signs. There are several options for bailouts and loops, but I like the straight out-and-back, all the way to the highway.

These trails rarely force you into your tree-climbing gears, but they still can't be classified as easy, not in good conscience. There are plenty of roots and loose rocks to keep the technical difficulty level hovering in the moderate zone. After the turn-around point, the speedy cruise down the rock-strewn upper Goose grade has pinch-flat written all over it, so keep those tires pumped up.

Back in town, you might do a doubletake after checking your odometer, because that sure didn't feel like a 30-miler.

Ride Information

🕐 Trail Contacts:
Uncompahgre National Forest, Norwood, CO (970) 327–4261 or *www.fs.fed.us/r2/gmug*

🕐 Schedule:
Open year round, but best from June through mid October, due to weather.

💲 Fees/Permits:
No fees or permits are required

🅝 Maps:
USGS maps: Telluride, CO; Gray Head, CO; Mount Wilson, CO • **USFS maps:** *Uncompahgre National Forest*

Wilson Mesa Long Loop

Ride Specs

Start: From the River Trail trailhead off Mahoney Drive in Telluride

Length: 41.0-mile loop

Approximate Riding Time: 4–8 hours

Technical Difficulty: Moderate to Difficult: challenging singletrack with a bit of everything

Physical Difficulty: Difficult: tough miles on Wilson Mesa

Trail Surface: 60% singletrack/widetrack, 36% dirt roads or doubletrack, and 4% paved roads

Lay of the Land: Deeply forested, rolling terrain flowing at the base of the spectacular San Miguel Mountains, bordering the Lizard Head Wilderness

Elevation Gain: 6,312 feet

Land Status: National forest, BLM, and private land

Other Trail Users: Hikers, equestrians, and motorcyclists (rare)

Getting There

In Telluride: Park somewhere in town and hop on your bike.* Head south, toward the ski hill, to the San Miguel River from Colorado Avenue (CO 145). There, next to the river, you will find a wide, gravel path. This is the River Trail. Turn right (west) onto the path and head slightly downhill to the starting point at Mahoney Drive. Mahoney Drive is the last paved street crossed by the River Trail as it heads out of town toward CO 145.

Parking is available on Colorado Avenue or the surrounding streets. Parking is free on Sundays but costs 50 cents per hour otherwise.

ardcore traildogs with tree-hugging tendencies will love this long, memorable tour of the gorgeous Wilson Mesa and vicinity. At 41 miles, this is one of the most serious rides available from Telluride, and requires advanced skills, fitness, and thorough preparation, in addition to the usual load of food, tools, clothing, and water (also carry a water filter or iodine pills, preferably both, through this cow-infested forest). There are no extra long climbs, but lots of smaller ones. Typically slow trail conditions on Wilson Mesa can be frustrating, but they're offset by sublime scenery and encounters with large beasts.

This dirt epic embarks directly from Telluride, utilizing the fast, fun, and super convenient River Trail–Galloping Goose combination. After six miles of speedy singletrack, riders are deposited near the bottom of Sunshine Mesa Road (Road 63J), by the Ilium Episcopal Camp. Conquer Sunshine Mesa Road, which is at first straight and easy, then steeper and twisting as it climbs through a private aspen forest. It was along this stretch that my dad saw a bobcat or lynx cross the road. (You could chop about 15 miles off this loop by driving your car to the end of Sunshine Mesa Road, but you'll lose a very gentle and fast 15 miles, and many two-wheel drives will not be able to handle the road conditions.)

Sunshine Mesa Road (Road 63J) dead-ends conveniently at Lizard Head Trail (Trail 505). Cruise past the gate and up the gentle widetrack toward the crook of the canyon. Ignore the intersection with the Wilson Mesa Trail (Trail 421) on the right. This trail shortcuts over to where you'll eventually end up, but offers less novelty and adventure than the route described here. Our widetrack degenerates and thins as it crosses numerous talus slopes, then crosses Bilk Creek on a plank. For the next few miles, the singletrack has an experts-only feel. On the other side of the water, pick up the thin trail headed harshly downhill through a series of switchbacks. At the bottom of this pitch, the roar of a waterfall beckons. The handsome and impressive Mule Falls cannot be properly viewed without an off-trail bushwhack through a half-acre of extra-thick plant material.

Mule Falls on Bilk Creek.

177

MilesDirections

0.0 START from the intersection of the River Trail and Mahoney Drive, and begin riding west (down-valley) on the River Trail.

0.9 Cross Boomerang Road, the widetrack that leads up to Mountain Village.

1.3 The trail forks. Go right. *[Option. The upper fork offers a more technical and strenuous challenge, then quickly rejoins the lower trail at mile 1.6.]*

1.6 The trails converge.

2.6 The trail splits again. Stay right. *[Option. Once again, the upper trail is tougher and more interesting. This fork intersects with CO 145 just a few ticks south of the lower trail's point of intersection with CO 145.]*

3.2 Cross CO 145 (the road to Lizard Head Pass and Rico), then ride up the road just opposite (Lawson Hill Road). The start of the Galloping Goose Trail is right there across from the gas station, on the north side of Lawson Hill Road.

3.6 Stay right on the Galloping Goose as a doubletrack comes in from the left. This spur leads to private property.

6.4 The Goose spills out onto South Fork Road (FS 625). Take a right onto this road.

6.9 Turn left onto Sunshine Mesa Road (The sign here reads "Road 63J," but on some maps this road is often marked as FS 623). The intersection is located just before the Ilium Episcopal Camp.

10.2 Sunshine Mesa Road takes a sharp right and begins to climb more steeply. Pass the intersection with the upper Galloping Goose Trail. The road climbs through a very nice aspen forest (private land), moderately rocky and steep, then levels before ending at the trailhead.

12.5 Arrive at the trailhead and dead-end of Sunshine Mesa Road. Continue past the gate and up the wide Lizard Head Trail (Trail 505).

13.2 Ignore the intersection with the Wilson Mesa Trail swooping down on the right. *[Option. Less adventurous souls can use the Wilson Mesa Trail to shortcut down to mile 16.9. This will remove a few miles and significant technicality from the loop.]*

13.7 The widetrack thins, gets pretty rustic as it traverses talus slopes.

14.4 If you can ride all this through here, you're real good.

14.6 Cross Bilk Creek on a plank. On the other side, take a right (going down), still on the Lizard Head Trail (Trail 505). *[FYI. The left fork leads directly into the Lizard Head Wilderness Area—off-limits to your capitalist-imperialist mechanism.]* This next section of singletrack descends sharply through dangerous switchbacks, and requires advanced skills.

15.1 Sneak a peak at the loud Mule Falls on the right. Begin an extended section through an enchanted forest, with several creek crossings.

16.9 Take a left at the intersection with the Wilson Mesa Trail (Trail 421), at the opening to a wet meadow. From this point, the trail is called the Wilson Mesa Trail. [*Bailout. Turn right onto the Wilson Mesa Trail and climb back onto Sunshine Mesa. This trail will pop out onto the Lizard Head Trail near the trailhead.*]

17.3 A sign here indicates five miles until Silver Pick Road, but it's really about four and a half miles.

17.8 Fork right as the trail approaches the shore of Lake Jake. This may seem like an important intersection. The left fork, however, is a cow-trail to oblivion.

18.4 Cross a cattle gate and begin a long, challenging section of sharp rollers.

21.7 The trail spills out onto Silver Pick Road (FS 622). Take a right and cruise down this road.

24.0 Take a left at the intersection, continuing down Silver Pick Road (FS 622) as it follows Big Bear Creek down to the highway and the San Miguel River.

28.0 The road surface turns to pavement.

28.1 Before intersecting with CO 145, turn right onto the dirt doubletrack that runs beside the San Miguel River.

30.7 The doubletrack peters out at a minor industrial area, forcing you up onto CO 145. Ride the highway for a mile until South Fork Road (FS 625).

31.8 Take a right onto South Fork Road (FS 625).

34.4 Take a left onto the Galloping Goose Trail; begin the gentle climb back toward town.

41.0 Arrive back in Telluride at the intersection of the River Trail and Mahoney Drive.

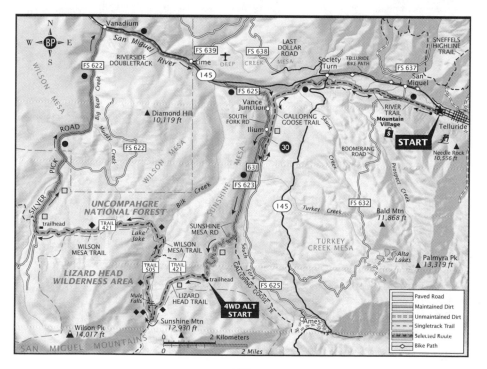

179

Near mile 16.9, the trail joins the Wilson Mesa Trail (Trail 421) at the opening of a wide, meadowed valley. This is the dip between Sunshine Mesa on the right and Wilson Mesa on the left, with Bilk Creek meandering down the middle. To the south (behind you) tower the San Miguel Mountains, among them: Wilson Peak, El Diente, Mount Wilson, Gladstone, Lizard Head, etc. To the north (straight ahead), the jagged Thirteeners that make up the Mount Sneffels massif do their share of towering. Beautiful. Ignore the ATV tracks cross-valley on your right. Our trail traverses the left rim of the grassy expanse before heading left and up to begin a sustained climb onto Wilson Mesa. Climbing into the woods again, the trail hugs the shore of Lake Jake, with its recently depleted water level. I imagine the lake being slurped up by the hordes of cows whose tracks are everywhere and whose giant heads keep popping up from the tall grasses. Is this Switzerland?

Telluride wasn't always called Telluride. Before 1881 the town was called Columbia, but was renamed because the Postal Service could not come to grips with the fact that two different mining camps had the same name. The other Columbia was in California.

If you're waiting for the hill to top out, you may be disappointed by this trail's continuous up-and-down attitude after climbing aboard Wilson Mesa. The trail dives into several drainages, then sharply out, with rolling sections in between. Trail conditions are a serious issue along this route, unfortunately. It seems this trail could potentially be fast and thrilling, but each time I've ridden this length, the surface has been muddy and slick, and trashed by intermittent cow parades. Those hooves are the size of dinner plates! And what about those shockingly huge cow pies! I found myself walking many sections which otherwise would have been fast and fun.

The forced slow-down is a mixed blessing. The Wilson Mesa Trail, directly bordering the wilderness area, provides an unbeatable opportunity to socialize with elk and other wildlife, if you take the time. Once, while creeping ultra-slowly away from the aptly named Muddy Creek in the granny, through a lush, dark forest, I heard the tell-tale crack of a branch very close by. Still as a statue, I watched as a huge elk buck with a massive velvety rack stepped into view, his head buried in the succulent greenery. He was so close I could have spit on the big fella, less than 10 feet away. He lingered for a minute or two, oblivious, feeding and snorting with contentment. Then he caught my (strong) scent and casually disappeared without making a sound. Big ol' badass buck.

The trail pops out on Silver Pick Road (Forest Service Road 622) at a proper trailhead. The next six-plus miles are all gently downhill on dirt roads to CO Route 145. Instead of riding on the highway, take the pleasant Riverside Doubletrack as far as it will take you, then ride pavement the rest of the way to South Fork Road. From there, it's an easy spin up to the singletrack which ushers you gently back to town.

Ride Information

Trail Contacts:
Uncompahgre National Forest, Norwood, CO (970) 327–4261 or *www. fs.fed.us/r2/gmug*

Schedule:
Open year round, but best from June through September, due to weather.

Fees/Permits:
No fees or permits are required

Maps:
USGS maps: Telluride, CO; Gray Head, CO; Mount Wilson, CO; Little Cone, CO • **USFS maps:** *Uncompahgre National Forest*

Western Deep Creek Loop

Ride Specs

Start: From the intersection of Colorado Avenue (CO 145) and Fir Street in downtown Telluride
Length: 18.6-mile loop
Approximate Riding Time: 3–6 hours
Technical Difficulty: Difficult: challenging singletrack with a variety of obstacles
Physical Difficulty: Difficult: tough miles, nothing for free
Trail Surface: 70% singletrack, 10% paved bike path, 10% dirt road or doubletrack, and 10% paved road
Lay of the Land: *Steep*, aspen-covered slopes at the base of the mighty Mount Sneffels massif, which consists of a multitude of jagged 12,000- and 13,000-foot peaks. The high trail provides intense views of the San Miguel range and the mountains north of Telluride. One of the nicest looking rides around.
Elevation Gain: 4,450 feet
Land Status: National forest
Other Trail Users: Hikers, joggers, and equestrians

Getting There

In Telluride: Park somewhere in town and hop on your bike.* Begin the ride from the intersection of Colorado Avenue (CO 145) and Fir Street in downtown Telluride. The intersection is right in Telluride's central business district. Fir Street divides the 100 block and 200 block of West Main.

Parking is available on Colorado Avenue or the surrounding streets. Parking is free on Sundays but costs 50 cents per hour otherwise.

FYI
During Prohibition in Telluride, one could purchase a drink almost anywhere, including the courthouse.

Here is an 18.6-mile loop that feels more like 40, but you just might love it. This route climbs out of the San Miguel Valley on Last Dollar Road to an adventurous singletrack trail that traverses the steep slopes at the base of Mount Sneffels. This upper (western) section of the Deep Creek Trail (Trail 418) is seldom attempted by two-wheeled travelers, as opposed to the heavily traveled and highly manageable section of the same trail that lies east of Mill Creek Road.

On the western Deep Creek Trail—also known as the Sheep Creek Trail in some circles, due to its close proximity to Sheep Creek, and the fact that Deep Creek is nowhere in sight—a midsection of rideable ribbon is bookended by long, hike-a-bike ascents. And when you're trudging up one of 'em, with your little Italian shoes popping off and rolling down the hill, you understand too damn well why cyclists don't attempt this route very often. Stay positive with the knowledge that walking allows you to become more intimate with this top-notch corner of the world. In a setting of unreal beauty, you see, hear, and smell more, and sneak up on more animals than you would otherwise. Also, a tough, long walking section is a natural barrier that keeps all but the heartiest individuals away from the nice segments beyond, eliminating the

need for razor wire and landmines. When you're finally up there, cruising on some rollers, glimpsing snow-covered peaks through the aspens, it belongs to you alone.

From its western trailhead off Last Dollar Road, Deep Creek Trail's barrier is a straight, steep chute carved through the lush understory of a green, aspen-dominated forest. During the 1,200-foot grind up this chute, notice that almost every tree in the vicinity has been scraped and scarred by elk and mule deer. There are supposedly about 375,000 elk bucks living in North America, and it seems that most of them have been loitering on this hillside, rubbing the crap out of these trees. To an elk or mule deer, compulsive antler-rubbing brings many positive results: It keeps the rack

View from Last Dollar Road.

183

MilesDirections

0.0 START from the intersection of Colorado Avenue (CO 145) and Fir streets in downtown Telluride. Head west, down-valley, on Colorado Avenue (CO 145). At the western edge of town, join the paved bike path that is just off the north side of the road.

1.5 The paved path crosses Mill Creek Road.

3.3 Carefully cross over CO 145 and begin riding up the paved Last Dollar Road. Let the climbing begin!

3.5 Ignore the singletrack on the right. This is a nice-looking trail that will steer you onto private land.

4.5 Hey! Those luxury home sites up there—aren't they in the avalanche path?

5.4 Veer right as the pavement ends on Last Dollar Road. *[**FYI.** The left fork leads directly to the airport.]*

6.4 Turn right into the parking area of the Deep Creek trailhead. The Deep Creek Trail (Trail 418) starts as a ridable singletrack climb.

6.9 The trail tops out and veers left onto a mellow widetrack.

7.5 At the three-point intersection, take a right across Sheep Creek onto the Deep Creek Trail (Trail 418). The trail begins to climb in a somewhat harsh fashion.

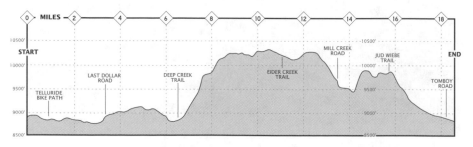

7.9 Resist the strong temptation to turn right (across the muddy creek) onto a flat trail that follows an irrigation ditch. So inviting! Unfortunately for you, your route stays left here, and goes straight up. It's hike-a-bike time.

8.7 Near the top of the big climb, veer left onto rolling doubletrack. [*FYI. The right fork heads immediately to gated private property.*].

8.9 The route becomes singletrack again, and begins to cruise sweetly downhill through the aspens, but don't get too excited. Soon you will be dealing with a string of sharp ups-and-downs.

11.2 Pass the subtle intersection with the Eider Creek Trail on the right. [*Option. This trail descends to Mill Creek Road and offers an alternative route back to town.*]

12.3 At the top of a long climb, on a fantastic ridge, pass the intersection with the Sneffels Highline Trail (Trail 434) coming in from the left. Begin a tough, switchbacked descent to Mill Creek.

13.7 Intersect with Mill Creek Road and cross Mill Creek. For the next few miles, the single-track is fast, winding, and fairly flat as it follows

the rim above Telluride. [*Option. If you're looking for a quick, painless return to the valley floor, head right here down Mill Creek Road.*]

15.8 The Deep Creek Trail (Trail 418) ends as you arrive at a T-intersection. Take the right fork, known as the Jud Wiebe Trail (Trail 432). The inviting left fork is the eastern terminus of the Sneffels Highline Trail (Trail 434).

15.9 Turn left at an intersection with a 4WD road to remain on the Jud Wiebe Trail. [*Option. Take a right here to cruise back down to town.*]

17.3 Turn right onto a widetrack (still the Jud Wiebe Trail) that climbs briefly before bombing down to Tomboy Road.

18.2 The Jud Wiebe Trail runs into Tomboy Road. Take a right, headed down.

18.4 Back in Telluride. Turn left onto Oak Street as Tomboy Road ends. Roll down Oak for a few blocks, then turn left and ride one block to Fir Street. Coast down to your original starting point at the intersection of Fir Street and Colorado Avenue.

18.6 End the ride and address your many aches and pains.

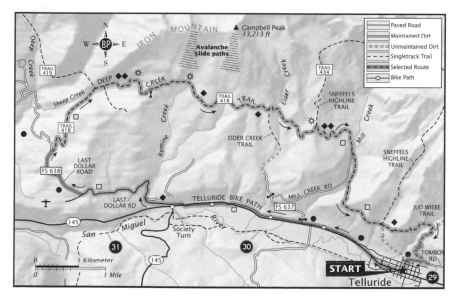

Old and new antler scars on aspen trees.

polished, removes the velvet from a new set, strengthens the neck, and gives the libidinous buck an (insufficient) outlet for his primal craziness during the rut. Maybe you, too, would like to take a moment to polish your powerful rack on a nearby aspen trunk.

After about a half-mile hike, the incline eases to the point where you can crawl aboard your rig. The trail soon joins some rolling doubletrack, then, perhaps filling you with joy, begins to descend smoothly. But not for long. This trail hears your appeals but never grants a full reprieve. Occasional soft rollers are more of a tease than a theme. Sharp, technical descents lead to chain-breaking climbs and back again. Dangerous switchbacks test your concentration, equipment, and *huevos*. At every turn, a stream crossing...avalanche chutes...timber crossings. If you're a strong, skilled trail rider with an urge for adventure and hot sauce for blood, this one is for you. If you're a novice or intermediate hoping for some moderate cruising through the woods, this trail will persecute you—stick to the section below Mill Creek.

> The ski area above Telluride was designed by French World Champion Emile Allais.

The trail eventually climbs to an intersection with the hiker-only Sneffels Highline Trail, then bombs down a long, switchbacked descent to Mill Creek. From here, the route follows easier, more popular trails back into Telluride. The very enjoyable lower Deep Creek Trail provides a nice bird's-eye view of town, as well as a proper warm-down from the day's carnage. The Jud Wiebe Trail forces more climbing but nicely delays your return to the painful realities of civilization.

Ride Information

Trail Contacts:
Uncompahgre National Forest, Norwood, CO (970) 327–4261 or www.fs.fed.us/r2/gmug

Schedule:
Open year round, but best from mid June through September, due to weather and snowmelt

Fees/Permits:
No fees or permits are required

Maps:
USGS maps: Telluride, CO; Gray Head, CO • **USFS maps:** *Uncompahgre National Forest*

Below Mill Creek, the trail cruises over the town.

San Miguel River Ramble

Ride Specs

Start: From the intersection of Silver Pick Road and an unnamed doubletrack that runs beside the San Miguel River, just off CO 145 about eight miles west of Telluride

Length: 4.7-mile out-and-back

Approximate Riding Time: 25 minutes–one hour

Technical Difficulty: Easy: uneventful double-track

Physical Difficulty: Easy: flat and short

Trail Surface: Doubletrack

Lay of the Land: BLM-managed strip of greenery between CO 145 and the pleasant but polluted San Miguel River

Elevation Gain: 365 feet

Land Status: BLM land

Other Trail Users: Hikers and walkers

Getting There

From Telluride: Drive west on CO 145 for about eight miles to the intersection with Silver Pick Road (FS 622). Turn left onto Silver Pick Road and then park about a half block from the intersection, where the gated doubletrack will be obvious.

During the 1880s in Telluride, one could buy a residential plot for one dollar. A prime corner lot on the main drag went for about 25 bucks.

F ar above Telluride, in a gorgeous array of alpine basins, huge drifts of pure white snow begin to melt, sending thousands of rivulets into dozens of brooks and creeks, which drop in crystal waterfall formation over gray cliffs, meeting at the valley floor to become the San Miguel River.

The San Miguel then chugs through a gauntlet of mine tailings and various industrial refuse on its way to Telluride, where it picks up the usual baggage associated with neo-booming tourist towns: sewage, detergent, real estate flyers, empty bottles of Patron and Fat Tire Ale. By the time it reaches Vanadium, a crossroads named for the radioactive metal that was extracted from these hills and used in nuclear warheads, the San Miguel is one abused, pissed-off waterway.

Man has been unkind to the San Miguel, especially during the mining boom of the 19th century, when the drainage was infused with lethal doses of cyanide from the extraction process. But the San Miguel, displaying remarkable pluck for a river, still puts on a happy face for the tourists every morning. On the face of things, it's a nice-looking river. It's not giving off fumes or anything. Fishermen will be tempted by the sparkling water and the hint of moderate-sized trout. Don't eat the little buggers or the heavy metals that sicken these fish will make *you* sick as well. (If you must snag fish, try Woods Lake, on the west side of Wilson Mesa, or the Dolores River

downstream, where the concentration of toxins is apparently not enough to sabotage the river's classification as a Gold Medal trout stream.)

The San Miguel is able to fully perform most of its other stream duties, including soaking the feet of weary travelers and gurgling pleasantly. The river does so well, in fact, that you may forget entirely about the highway that hums with traffic over your shoulder, the tops of trucks barely visible above the embankment.

This simple riverside ramble is not overtly spectacular compared to other rides in the area, but I felt it should be featured because it is one of the few truly easy dirt rides available around Telluride—land of the steeps—and because it provides an alternative to the popular, overcrowded Bear Creek Path. The Bear Creek Path, on the east side of Telluride, is a pretty ride, and one of the only other mellow options, but the frequency of other users there kills the mood (*see Honorable Mention Z on page 204*). The Bear Creek Path is definitely not to be confused with the Bear Creek National Recreation Trail (*see Honorable Mention KK on page 207*), which is about as hardcore as it gets.

San Miguel River.

The road is shockingly flat.

MilesDirections

0.0 START from the intersection of Silver Pick Road and the gated Riverside Doubletrack, just south of CO 145.

2.3 Turn around where the doubletrack ends.

4.7 Arrive back where you began. *[**Option.** Across Silver Pick Road, the no-motors doubletrack continues westward for a mile or two, with pretty much the same results.]*

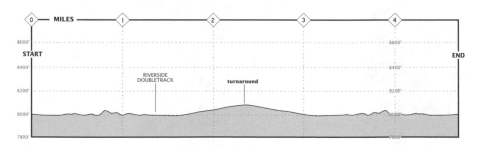

The riverside doubletrack.

Ride Information

📞 Trail Contacts:
Bureau of Land Management, Uncompahgre Resource Area, Montrose, CO (970) 240–5300

🕐 Schedule:
Open year round, but try it May through October. Expect highly erratic weather-related possibilities or prohibitions from year to year.

💲 Fees/Permits:
No fees or permits are required

🅽 Maps:
USGS maps: Grey Head, CO • **USGS maps:** *Uncompahgre National Forest*

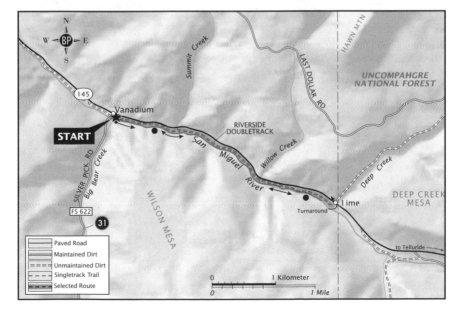

Engineer Pass

Ride Specs

Start: From the beginning of Engineer Mountain Road (FS 878), where it intersects with U.S. 550

Length: 19.6-mile out-and-back

Approximate Riding Time: 3–6 hours

Technical Difficulty: Moderate: occasionally chunky and steep sections make for a dangerous descent if you're not careful, and slow climbing

Physical Difficulty: Difficult: relentless, high-altitude grind

Trail Surface: 4WD road

Lay of the Land: High altitude jeep road with an incredible panorama of peaks and ridges

Elevation Gain: 7,068 feet

Land Status: National forest

Other Trail Users: Motorists (4WDs, motorcycles, and ATVs)

Getting There

From Telluride (with 4WD vehicle): Four-wheelers can use one of the dirt pass short-cuts out of Telluride, Ophir or Imogene. Imogene is the direct route, but a serious one, which should be attempted only by confident, well-equipped drivers. The route over Ophir Pass south of Telluride will be better for the majority of folks. Start by heading west out of Telluride on the CO 145 Spur for 3.3 miles, then turn left (south) on CO 145 at Society Turn, now headed toward Lizard Head Pass. About seven miles south from Society Turn, take a left onto the Ophir Pass Road (FS 630). The road is primarily wide, graded, and easy, with a few stream crossings and a scattering of narrow, rocky sections. The approach to the Ophir summit is about six miles of dirt; four miles down the other side brings you to U.S. 550. Take a left (north) on U.S. 550 and drive up and over spectacular Red Mountain Pass. Park at the well-marked turn-off for Engineer Mountain Road (FS 878), on the right, about nine miles from the top of Red Mountain Pass. *[**Note.** On the maps it appears that a third 4WD route (the Black Bear Pass Road) is available headed east out of Telluride. Don't even think about it! This is a treacherous shelf road that for safety reasons is reserved as a one-way for descending vehicles. Attempting to four-wheel up Black Bear Pass from Telluride is one of the most severe faux pas that could possibly be committed in Southwest Colorado.]*

From Telluride (with 2WD vehicle): Drive west on CO 145 about 20 miles to Placerville, then turn right onto CO 62 and drive over the Dallas Divide to Ridgway. At Ridgway, turn right onto our old friend U.S. 550, headed south. Staying on U.S. 550, drive through Ouray and begin climbing the approach to Red Mountain Pass. Park at the well-marked turn-off for Engineer Mountain Road (FS 878), 3.8 miles from Ouray. This all-pavement trip is in the neighborhood of 60 miles—the consolation for it being longer is that it's an unbelievably gorgeous drive, world-famous for its beauty.

This towering ascent to the treeless heights of the San Juans presents cyclists with the most stunning alpine vistas available from any popular vantage point in these mountains. From the summit of Engineer Pass, a glance in any direction reveals—along with your true small-ness—an endless sea of jagged, glacier-spotted peaks.

The views come at a price. For the legions of four-wheelers on this route, the price is a gallon of gas, and an hour or so of sitting on their ass (that rhymes!). These days, the old school jeepers are joined on the southwestern trails by an equal number of shiny new SUVs. This situation could have you yearning for the old days, when the SUVs were just for show. (It seems to me that the chintzier late-model trucks could be chewed to bits by terrain any more extreme than the moderate terrain on this route. I mean, would you really want to go four-wheelin' in a truck that has a $4,000 plastic bumper and tires that unravel *on the highway*? You might never make it back.) For you cyclists, who may be gawked at by Hummerloads of summering Texans, the

> "Son, I think your idea of fun and my idea of fun are two different things."
>
> —an unidentified Texan jeeper at the top of the pass

price of conquering Engineer Pass is much higher and will include, no doubt, many hours in the saddle and tremendous soreness in the general leg area. This is a seriously strenuous ride. If you're looking for a workout, you've found it here.

Rising from the Uncompahgre River Gorge and the so-called Million Dollar Highway (U.S. Route 550), Forest Service Road 878 starts off fairly steep and very rough. Two-wheel-drive cars and trucks are eliminated from the game early. *Damn*, you're probably thinking near the bottom, *I hope it isn't like this the whole way*. In fact, not long after the first inhospitable pitch, the road flattens and smooths considerably. At mile 2.5, you'll switch left at the turnoff for Poughkeepsie Gulch Road, an ultra-boggy 4WD route that cuts south in the general direction of Silverton. The middle

MilesDirections

0.0 START riding up Engineer Mountain Road (a.k.a. Mineral Creek Road, Engineer Pass Road, or FS 878) from its start on U.S. 550.

2.5 Stay left at the fork. The right fork follows the Uncompahgre River up Poughkeepsie Gulch; the left fork follows Mineral Creek toward Mineral Point.

5.9 Pass Mineral Point and the weird rest stop and bathroom structure.

7.2 Pass the intersection with the connector to the Cinnamon Pass road on the right. The climb steepens.

9.5 Pass the turnoff to Oh-My-God! Point on the left. [**Side-trip.** This one's worth it.]

9.8 You're on the summit of Engineer Pass. Soak in the views then head back down. [**Options.** From this high point, you have earned a few intriguing possibilities. You could continue down the back side to Lake City, which lies about 17 miles farther east, less than two hours away on smoother road. Or consider making this ride into a super-adventurous loop by following the "trail" west from

Engineer Pass into the Bear Creek drainage. Down by the creek you may or may not find an extremely rustic singletrack that drops head-long for several miles before traversing the cliffs of Bear Creek Canyon. It's mostly unrideable, with high probability of injurious wrecks on the rideable sections. This singletrack, The Bear Creek National Recreation Trail, combines the danger of Moab's Portal Trail and Durango's Haflin Canyon with jaw-dropping alpine splendor. Truly, there's nothing like it. The Forest Service has understandably deemed this trail unsafe for horses, motors, and bikes (a sign near the bottom says "Hikers Only"), but a technicality has left it open and legal for non-motorized mechanized travel. That's you. I have a sneaking suspicion that the trail will be closed to bikes upon any rational review by the forest feds, so, if you have a wild hair somewhere and want to give it a shot, please call the Ouray Ranger District first to check the status. The number is (970) 240-5300. No confusion.]

19.6 Arrive back at U.S. 550.

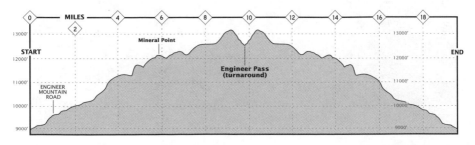

miles to timberline and Mineral Point are steady, with occasional problem sections. Looking back across the dozens of basins and canyons draining into the Uncompahgre, an impressive skyline is revealed: Mount Sneffels and the Wilson Mountains (featuring Lizard Head and El Diente, a.k.a. *the Tooth*).

Mineral City was a glorified mining camp that stood on the relatively gentle slope behind the present-day bathroom facilities (mile 5.9), the area that has since become known as Mineral Point. During the 1870s, the town boasted a population of 200 or so miners and shopkeepers, and produced an impressive amount of ore, which was packed over Engineer Pass to Lake City. Any official traces of the town disappeared by 1899, and today very little evidence exists to prove Mineral City was ever there (aside from the Forest Service marker). A true ghost town.

After cruising the flats near Mineral Point, ignoring any unfortunate, freshly cut spurs into the brutalized (by mining and 4WDs) wetlands, pass the connector to the Cinnamon Pass Road at mile 7.2. Cinnamon is Engineer's sister pass to the south, and also somewhat of a monster that has been photographed famously with road cuts through 15-foot drifts in mid summer. Both passes lead to Lake City.

After passing the Cinnamon Pass turn-off, the road steepens and switches several times on its final, painful approach to the summit. But this last pitch could really be much worse *(see Ride 29: Imogene Pass on page 166)*. There are no brain-rattling false summits. The road passes Oh-My-God! Point, a scenic cul-de-sac that is dutifully visited by each and every motorized tourist, then quickly and mercifully tops out. From the summit, at about 12,800 feet, a knowledgeable local can point out most of the high peaks of the San Juans.

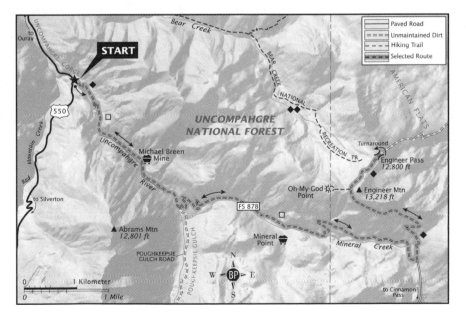

Altitude adds a whole new world of hurt to this 10-mile climb. As you approach the 13,000-foot mark, chances are very good that you'll feel some sort of altitude-induced nausea and dementia. Drinking a bucketful of water can help ward off the condition, but nothing short of frenzied descending will cure it. Speaking long term, it would take a few months of high-altitude living and riding to fully adjust.

Alpine weather is an additional challenge. When we were up here last, in mid summer, there was a light rain near the start that turned to frozen pellets at about 11,000 feet. A light breeze became an icy gale. We headed beneath a gnarled, dripping *Krummholz* tree for a quick change into all of our available gear. Hypothermia was a real possibility, depending on what the weather was going to do. We considered turning back but then spots of sun appeared, skimming across the wide couloirs.

Red Mountain Pass

"People who know about the highway are scared of it, and people who aren't scared of it are stupid."
—Bob Morss, former snowplow operator

Connecting Ouray and Silverton with a thin strip of pavement above the Uncompahgre Gorge, Red Mountain Pass is the most impressive and frightening among Colorado's many excellent paved passes. The classic and well-known Independence Pass in central Colorado, which connects Aspen and CO Route 82 near Leadville, gives Red Mountain a little competition; Wolf Creek Pass, between Pagosa Springs and the San Luis Valley, is positively tame by comparison.

Some Coloradans may enjoy hauling flatlanders up Red Mountain Pass just to see their faces while bombing down the very narrow and somewhat hairy north side into Ouray (heh, heh). Whatever your motivation, driving over Red Mountain is an end in itself, and any devoted tourist in the general vicinity should make the trip.

Driving the pass requires a healthy dose of caution, and, especially in the winter and spring, luck. With the exception of a few Alaskan roads, Red Mountain Pass is the most avalanche-prone stretch of pavement in the United States—specifically, the section crossing the East Riverside Avalanche Path, which is only partially protected by a snowshed. Each of the four separate incidents of motorists being blasted into the Uncompahgre Gorge by snowslides occurred in February or March, when the condition of the snowpack is most conducive to slides, and each occurred near the East Riverside Avalanche Path. The victims include a minister and his two daughters, and three snowplow operators who died while trying to keep the road clear.

The most recent victim, snowplow operator Eddie Imel, was hit by a slide just 200 feet from the snowshed. It has been obvious to everyone that an expansion of the shed could solve the problem, but state transportation officials have found the cost prohibitive. The necessary 1000-foot extension, 2000 tons or so of reinforced concrete, would reportedly cost around 15 million to build. Instead, the Colorado Department of Transportation relies on vigilant forecasting and four 105-millimeter Howitzers to blast the slide area. Until the snowshed is extended, many wise locals will refuse to drive Red Mountain Pass during avalanche season.

Share the road with a hundred Jeeps.

Teasing us. Before we knew it, it was a sunny day. Then, of course, it rained again, on and off, until the finish of the ride. That's typical for an a-typical day in the Colorado mountains.

Forget about trying to predict the weather on Engineer Pass. Instead, imagine the most miserable winter conditions ever seen, then pack all the gear you would like to have in such a scenario. Gore-Tex, wool, and polypropylene make a nice combination. You definitely want to remember gloves and hats. Sure, most summer days will be sunny and beautiful from start to finish, but you never know for certain, and the stakes are high. Preparation is the key to your success and safety here. Like the (real) four-wheelers with their jacks, skid plates, and winches, you can go anywhere with the proper gear. (Or, almost anywhere—occasional abandoned vehicles in Poughkeepsie Gulch, buried to the glass in mud, suggest the vincibility of the whole winch idea.)

Ride Information

Trail Contacts:
Uncompahgre National Forest, Ouray Ranger District, Montrose, CO (970) 240–5300

Schedule:
Open year round, but best from mid June to mid October. Be prepared for winter conditions year round.

Fees/Permits:
No fees or permits are required

Maps:
USGS maps: Ironton, CO; Handies Peak, CO; and Wetterhorn Peak, CO • **USFS maps:** *Uncompahgre National Forest*

Black Bears in Colorado

Black bears are under the gun in the Colorado mountains. Every year, between 500 and 1,000 Colorado black bears are killed in violent confrontations with man—that's 5–10% of the state's total bear population. Several hundred are shot by hunters, and many are run down on the highways. Others are shot legally by ranchers, or by state wildlife officers acting on the "Two Strikes and You're Out" rule. Under this rule, bears with a propensity to bother folks or mess up property are tranquilized and moved about 50 miles away from the area in question; if the bear ever comes back (strike two), it is destroyed.

Adding to the ugliness of this slaughter is the relative harmlessness of the typical black bear. According to Melody Miller, the Colorado Division of Wildlife's District Manager for the Durango area, black bears can be unpredictable, and their potential deadliness needs to be respected, but mostly they are very shy, even gentle in their dealings with man. Miller notes that in the last 34 years in Colorado, only three human deaths can be attributed to attacks by bears, in just two separate incidents. Both attacks came after the bears themselves were attacked. In the first case, an elderly couple was camping in Rocky Mountain National Park, and a black bear invaded their camp and started licking bacon grease off their grill. The gentleman sidled up behind the bear and whacked it on the head with a skillet! At that point, the enraged bear turned and killed the man and his wife. In the other case, a black bear killed a guy after he shot at the bear and missed, grazing its shoulder. Manslaughter at best. Other violent bear incidents have been few and far between. Last year, someone was charged for real by a mother bear with cubs in the San Luis Valley, but escaped basically unharmed. That's about it for black bear attacks in Colorado in the modern era. Clearly, the animals are getting a bad rap.

For the bears, some years are worse than others due to weather anomalies. In 1999, an early frost hit southwest Colorado, which ruined the yield of bear staples like blackberries, chokecherries, and acorns. (A similar situation occurred in 2000 in northern and central Colorado.) Southwest Colorado is prime bear habitat that produces some of the biggest black bears in the world, but in 1999 the big, hungry bears were forced to roam from their favored gambel oak stands to find food. Everywhere they went, they ran into people—campgrounds, garbage dumps, suburbs—and some of the bears learned to survive on the leftovers of civilization. Most of those bears are dead now.

Many people have the false impression that bears are lazy scavengers that enjoy launching regular raids into suburbia. Perhaps influenced by childhoods spent watching Yogi Bear cartoons, we imagine the beasts sneaking around look-

ing for picnic baskets, intending to snatch pies from windowsills. In fact, bears prefer their traditional stomping grounds and traditional acorns and berries—they prefer to remain far away from the nearest human—and the movement of bears en masse into populated areas is a sign of hunger and desperation in the unpopulated areas. When a bear rips the trunk off your car to get at a sack of trash, that's a last resort. It's natural for these occasional food shortages to hit certain areas, and it's natural for the bears to roam to other areas looking for food. What is highly unnatural is that the bears are corralled into an ever-shrinking area of wilderness, surrounded on all sides by high-strung suburbanites and trigger-happy ranchhands. If you're a bear, it's like the siege of Stalingrad up there.

If this pattern continues, the Colorado black bear will go the way of the Colorado grizzly.

When they don't smell anything good, hungry bears simply move on, and potential conflicts are avoided. With that in mind, here's what you can do to prevent the unnecessary death of black bears:

- Keep your camp clean.
- Burn grease off grills.
- Store your trash with your food, then lock the whole package in the trunk of your vehicle, or hang it in a tree about ten feet off the ground and five feet away from the main tree trunk. Pack out all garbage.
- Don't sleep in your cooking clothes, and don't sleep near the area where you've been cooking and eating. Keep food and food smells away from your sleeping bag.
- If you live in the area, keep your garbage locked in a closed garage or shed. If none is available, use a bear-proof trash container and empty it regularly. Keep the trash can clean. Don't feed your pets outside or store their food outside. Don't feed the bears. And finally, change your attitude: try not to be so offended by the "invasive" actions of desperate black bears. Rather, learn to accept that they live here too, and understand that there are proven methods to help keep them on their side of the woods and us safely on ours.

Spring Creek Pass– Jarosa Mesa

Ride Specs

Start: From the Spring Creek Pass summit parking area
Length: 16.6-mile out-and-back
Approximate Riding Time: 2–4 hours
Technical Difficulty: Moderate: rocky
Physical Difficulty: Moderate: mellow slopes, for the most part, but high altitude
Trail Surface: Doubletrack
Lay of the Land: Gently rolling, high altitude grassland with amazing views
Elevation Gain: 3,019 feet
Land Status: National forest
Other Trail Users: Motorists (4WDs) and equestrians

Getting There

From Telluride: Getting to Spring Creek Pass from Telluride in the typical passenger vehicle requires that you drive around a horde of serious peaks. Start by driving west to Placerville on CO 145, then turn right onto CO 62, cross the Dallas Divide, and descend into Ridgway. At Ridgway, take a left onto U.S. 550, going north. At Montrose, take a right onto U.S. 50 and drive across dry country to the Blue Mesa Reservoir, then take a right across the water onto CO 149. Drive south to Lake City, and about 20 miles south of Lake City to the Spring Creek Pass parking area. Total miles: approximately 170. *[**Note.** Several popular 4WD routes connect Telluride and Lake City. Most of these will cut the mileage in half, but the overall time for these dirt routes will be about the same or longer as that for the paved route.]*

Spring Creek Pass, tucked away on the lonely stretch of highway between Creede and Lake City, provides a pleasant opportunity for all but the most timid cyclists. Launching directly from the rest area on top of the modest pass, this route stair-steps up flowing terrain to the magical Jarosa Mesa, via doubletrack that is occasionally fast and smooth but is primarily festooned with buffed-out rock gardens. With the exception of one little bit of steep walking (about 30 steps), all the climbs are moderate in severity, as is the overall sense of the physical effort required for this ride—the loose, steep section that rises from the parking area is not representative of what lies beyond. Riding a bike up onto the bright Jarosa Mesa, with its backcountry aura and ethereal views, tends to give the impression that one has gained a lot from relatively little effort. This is a rare sensation in the steep San Juans and should be savored.

Within one mile from the start, the route sheds its forest cover and enters a wide clearing, foreshadowing the openness to come. An area of this sort, with patches of dense forest juxtaposed with large open areas, provides an excellent opportunity to observe wild beasts—especially elk—and to consider the so-called *edge effect*. This term describes the likeliness of large mammals to gather near the forested edges of clearings. Along the edges, grazing animals can enjoy chomping the more succulent greenery found in the sunny open area, but can still escape quickly into the dark

safety of the forest, where a thick piney canopy provides cover but also prevents the growth of many tasty plants.

After three miles of rolling terrain and forgiving climbs, find yourself on the mesa proper, where the doubletrack—very rocky at this point—meanders along the flat through a sea of alpine shrubs. The farther you ride, the better the views get. The chunky, jagged ridge formed by the Wetterhorn, Matterhorn, and Uncompahgre peaks pops up and says howdy on the northwestern skyline. Other than the sheep and their taciturn rifle-toting keepers, and perhaps a few jeep trippers, there will be little on the mesa to disturb your peace.

This doubletrack is decidedly rocky at points, but I would encourage beginners to give this beautiful, accessible ride a try. The high altitude can be a challenge, but the climbs are merciful and the rocks can be helpful, too—after about two miles, the route travels over volcanic rocks that actually grip your tires and provide extra traction.

DANGER!

The Jarosa Mesa is innocent enough—that is, until an electrical storm comes along. Up on a high ridge, with few trees around to absorb the strikes—hugging a piece of steel for Christ's sake!—your chances of getting lit up are quite high. Don't get fried. If dark clouds are rolling in or thunder booms in the distance, evacuate the mesa. You have less time than you think.

Should you find yourself suddenly terrorized by near and frequent lightning strikes, ditch your bike and seek the lowest ground possible. They always told you to lie down flat, but in actuality you want to keep your heart off the ground; it's much better to crouch on the balls of your feet, minimizing the area of contact with the earth. (If all else fails, this is also a good position in which to kiss your ass goodbye.)

MilesDirections

0.0 START riding west out of the parking area on the 4WD road. The route is marked as the Colorado Trail. (This is also the Continental Divide Trail.)

0.8 The two-track spills out into a huge park.

1.0 Descend for a bit.

1.9 Notice the change to volcanic rock beneath you.

3.0 Stairstep climbs, moderate for the most part, bring you up to Jarosa Mesa.

3.7 Notice the mysterious and semi-famous grave marker tucked into the brush on your right. *[**FYI.** How old is it? Who or what is buried there? Nobody seems to know. If you figure it out, drop a line. Perhaps this is the source of the otherworldly buzz I experience on the mesa top. This grave was once marked* by a cross with nails pounded into it in an interesting and crafty fashion. This pretty marker has since become a souvenir, replaced by what seems to be, well, a clump of wood. Makes me wonder if there might be some restless soul wandering around up here.]*

4.5 More climbing.

5.4 The climbs top out again, with still more spectacular views.

6.8 The doubletrack forks. I prefer heading left and climbing moderately to a serene saddle. *[**Option.** the right spur leads directly to the top of that hill in front of you which is the high point of the entire mesa area; from its summit, you can see well into the valley below with a nice look at Lake San Cristobal.]*

Sunset from the Jarosa Mesa.

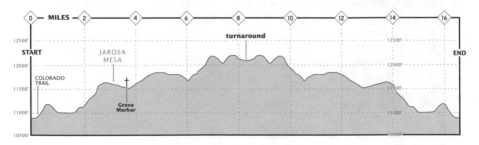

8.3 Gain the saddle, a natural turnaround point. *[Option. From this point, the route begins some serious climbing and descending, eventually rising to about 12,800 feet as it traces the Continental Divide. Adventure seekers will naturally be tempted by the possibility of riding all the way to Silverton via Minnie Gulch or Maggie Gulch, or perhaps by way of Cataract Gulch, which leaves you looking down the barrel of Cinnamon Pass. Stare at a topo before embarking on a Spring Creek to Silverton epic. For any possible version, riders must descend from the Divide, then conquer 1,000-plus feet of steep climbing before reaching one of the Silverton-bound escape chutes.]*

16.6 Arrive back at the parking area on Spring Creek Pass.

Ride Information

☎ Trail Contacts:
Rio Grande National Forest Supervisor's Office, Monte Vista, CO (719) 852–5941

◷ Schedule:
Open year round

$ Fees/Permits:
No fees or permits are required

Ⓝ Maps:
USGS maps: Slumgullion Pass, CO; Lake San Cristobal, CO • **USFS maps:** *Rio Grande National Forest Map* • **Trails Illustrated maps:** #139 and #140

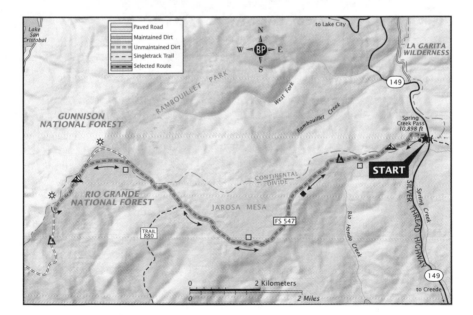

Honorable Mentions

Telluride

Compiled here is an index of great rides in the Telluride region that didn't make the A-list this time around but deserve recognition. Check them out and let us know what you think. You may decide that one or more of these rides deserves higher status in future editions or, perhaps, you may have a ride of your own that merits some attention.

(Z) Bear Creek Road

Launching directly from Telluride, this hyper-popular widetrack path/road ushers tourists, families, runners, bears, and cyclists through a scenic forest into the mist at the base of Bear Creek Falls. The creekside trip is about 2.5 miles each way, with connections at the top to the tough Wasatch Trail. Access the Bear Creek road from the southern dead-end of Pine Street. (Not to be confused with the Bear Creek National Recreation Trail south of Ouray.)

(AA) West Wilson Mesa Trail

The Wilson Mesa Long Loop (*see Ride 31*), a 41-mile loop from Telluride, uses many miles of the Wilson Mesa Trail, but it leaves untouched a sizable section west of Silver Pick Road. Access the rest of this rollicking expert's trail from the trailhead near the top of Silver Pick Road (FS 622), or from Fall Creek Road (FS 618), at a trailhead near Wood's Lake. Both roads are reached by driving west from Telluride on CO 145, toward Placerville.

(BB) Mill Creek-Deep Creek Loop

This loop is another very popular, moderate route that leaves right from downtown Telluride, only this one hits some pretty sweet singletrack. The total loop is less than seven miles if you leave out the Jud Wiebe extension. Head down-valley on the bike path for 1.5 miles, then take a right onto Mill Creek Road. Climb another 1.5 miles up steep Mill Creek and turn right onto the Deep Creek singletrack. (Turning left here would take you into some fairly serious terrain.) Cruise back to Telluride on a gentle but rewarding section of winding trail that hangs nicely over the town. This segment is much easier to handle than the portion of the same trail west of Mill Creek, as described in the Western Deep Creek Loop chapter, but it's still hazardous at speed due to hiking families. Yuppie Crossing!

(CC) Sunshine Mesa Short Loop

This short singletrack loop can be reached by riding straight from Telluride on the Galloping Goose to Ilium, then climbing Sunshine Mesa Road to the trailhead; or, drive west from town on 145, then up South Fork Road to Ilium, Sunshine Mesa Road and the trailhead. Sunshine Mesa Road could be too rough for passenger cars in spots, however. From the Sunshine Mesa trailhead, ride up the Lizard Head Trail, a gentle widetrack, until you find a tempting single' corkscrewing down on your right. Use this trail to cut across to Bilk Creek and another link-up with the Lizard Head Trail. Turn left and follow Bilk Creek through a deep, green forest to a hidden waterfall, where the trail switches up a steep climb. At the top of the hill, cross Bilk Creek and loop back down to the start. The singletrack is the border to the Lizard Head Wilderness along much of this route, always an added bonus.

(DD) Wasatch Trail-Bridal Veil Loop ("The Waterfall Tour")

Begin a difficult, adventurous loop by riding up the mellow and popular Bear Creek Road, accessed from the southern dead-end of Pine Street in Telluride. From the top of Bear Creek Road, in the mist of Bear Creek Falls, the Wasatch Trail (FS 508) climbs harshly for about a mile, forcing riders to hike and push. This seems to piss a lot of people off. Then the ascent calms down enough to keep 'em hooked. The high-point is well within reach, at an impressive 13,000-foot pass. Descend the east side into Bridal Veil Basin on a rough 4WD road, and connect with the infamous Black Bear Road near Bridal Veil Falls.

(EE) Ophir Pass

Yet another large, beautiful pass with a utilitarian mining heritage. Ophir is modestly tall at 11,743 feet above sea level. The 2,500-foot climb from CO 145 is straightforward and mellow until the ascent's final third, where it gets pretty heinous. Find the road from Telluride by driving west on CO 145 and turning left at Society Turn, heading for Lizard Head Pass. At a big, sweeping right-hander on the highway, take a left onto FS 630. Park there and ride. This pass links CO 145 with U.S. 550 south of Red Mountain Pass, and is often used by four-wheelers as part of a big round loop from Ophir to Ouray over Imogene to Telluride. Cyclists can tackle this loop in two days.

(FF) Last Dollar Road

Last Dollar Road rises from CO 145 at Society Turn, just 3.3 bike path-serviced miles west of Telluride. Last Dollar is paved at the bottom, where it ascends sharply. After passing the airport, the road loses its pavement and contours around the western slope of the Mount Sneffels massif (Hastings Mesa), through some very expensive and very gorgeous real estate. At its north end, Last Dollar Road connects with CO 62 near the Dallas Divide. There are some sizable climbs involved as the road net-gains 2,000 feet in about 15 miles. Overall the route is moderate and non-technical. Getting back to Telluride from here will be an out-and-back affair, unless you're using Last Dollar as the runway for an insane epic. (For you crazies, a giant loop can be conjured using Last Dollar Road, the West Dallas Trail (see Ride GG below), and Imogene Pass (Ride 29). Check a map, and don't let your mouth write any checks your legs can't cash.)

GG) West Dallas Trail

Drifting across the north side of Mount Sneffels, hanging around 9,600 feet, this singletrack/doubletrack route offers a memorable cruise in a sublime setting. To find it from Ouray, drive north on U.S. 550 to Ridgway, then head west on CO 62 toward the Dallas Divide for about five miles. Turn left onto Dallas Creek Road (CR 7), headed south. Drive up this road until it ends, then start riding west on a dirt road there, looking for signs which confirm you are on the right track. This road essentially becomes the Dallas Trail. Consider a nice-sized loop using CR 7, the Dallas Trail, and CR 9 (West Dallas Creek Road).

HH) Owl Creek Pass

Jump on CR 10 one mile north of Ridgway and head east to enjoy this moderate, 15-mile climb to the top of Owl Creek Pass. Fork left at mile 2.6, then right at mile 3.9. Soon you will be in the shadow of Courthouse Mountain and Chimney Peak, which bears a striking resemblance to Chimney Rock near Pagosa Springs. The pass summit, at 10,114 feet, seems really low to veterans of other area passes, which tend to be much steeper, if not as long. There may even be some trails up there (hint, hint). Continuing over the top of Owl Creek Pass would take you eventually to Cimarron, on U.S. 50 west of Gunnison.

II) East Dallas Trail

Searching frantically for rideable singletrack near Ouray, cyclists may find themselves on this trail, and may soon decide that it's too damn steep and not worth the trouble. The eastern segment of the long Dallas Trail teases you with barely ride-

able switchbacks from its trailhead (located on the River Road just north of Ouray—see Ride JJ on the following page), even throws down a couple easy, rolling sections before heading straight up. Some folks may find the workout and the views, both of which are amazing, worth the supreme effort. The trail works nicely as a descent, but it's hard to locate the top-out from the confusing network of residential roads southwest of Ridgway.

⒥ River Road

Here is a mellow 10-mile long dirt road linking Ouray and Ridgway. The narrow road is west of the Uncompahgre River, and is easy to locate as it takes off from northwest Ouray. Head west on 7th Avenue, then take a right after the bridge. (As you begin to head north, stay right but don't cross back over the river. You'll pass the trailhead for the steep Dallas Trail on your left.) The River Road is notably flat, doin' that old railroad grade thang.

ⓚ Bear Creek National Recreation Trail

This has to be one of the greatest *hiking* trails anywhere. As a mountain bike route, the B.C.N.R.T. is certainly problematic, on many levels. From an obvious trailhead on U.S. 550 a few miles above and south of Ouray, this trail switch- backs up loose shards of talus that break like dinner plates under mountain bike tires. Then the trail cuts a path across a sheer cliff, on a narrow shelf. Just walking this sec- tion is a bit dangerous. The trail is naturally off-limits to horses and motors, and it should probably be off-limits to bikes as well, but at the time of this writing it's still a legal option. Before you try it, call the Ouray Ranger District (970)

240–5300) and double-check the status, please. Then call 'em back an hour later and triple-check it. This trail is (sort of) accessible from the summit of Engineer Pass. See the Engineer Pass chapter for a description of that adventurous, dangerous option. One thing I must say: don't even think about shuttling to the top of the pass. You've got to earn this one, by riding up the pass under your own power.

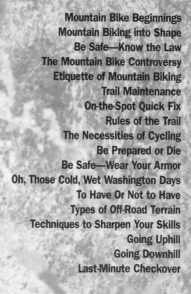

The Art of Mountain BIKING

The Art of Mountain Biking

Welcome to the new generation of bicycling! Indeed, the sport has evolved dramatically from the thin-tired, featherweight-frame days of old. The sleek geometry and lightweight frames of racing bicycles, still the heart and soul of bicycling worldwide, have lost much ground in recent years, unpaving the way for the mountain bike, which now accounts for the majority of all bicycle sales in the U.S. And with this change comes a new breed of cyclist, less concerned with smooth roads and long rides, who thrives in places once inaccessible to the mortal road bike.

The mountain bike, with its knobby tread and reinforced frame, takes cyclists to places once unheard of—down rugged mountain trails, through streams of rushing water, across the frozen Alaskan tundra, and even to work in the city. There seem to be few limits on what this fat-tired beast can do and where it can take us. Few obstacles stand in its way, few boundaries slow its progress. Except for one—its own success. If trail closure means little to you now, read on and discover how a trail can be

here today and gone tomorrow. With so many new off-road cyclists taking to the trails each year, it's no wonder trail access hinges precariously between universal acceptance and complete termination. But a little work on your part can go a long way to preserving trail access for future use. Nothing is more crucial to the survival of mountain biking itself than to read the examples set forth in the following pages and practice their message. Then turn to

the maps, pick out your favorite ride, and hit the dirt!

MOUNTAIN BIKE BEGINNINGS

It seems the mountain bike, originally designed for lunatic adventurists bored with straight lines, clean clothes, and smooth tires, has become globally popular in as short a time as it would take to race down a mountain trail.

Like many things of a revolutionary nature, the mountain bike was born on the west coast. But unlike Rollerblades, purple hair, and the peace sign, the concept of the off-road bike cannot be credited solely to the imaginative Californians—they were just the first to make waves.

The design of the first off-road specific bike was based on the geometry of the old

Schwinn Excelsior, a one-speed, camel-back cruiser with balloon tires. Joe Breeze was the creator behind it, and in 1977 he built 10 of these "Breezers" for himself and his Marin County, California, friends at $750 apiece—a bargain.

Breeze was a serious competitor in bicycle racing, placing 13th in the 1977 U.S. Road Racing National Championships. After races, he and friends would scour local bike shops hoping to find old bikes they could then restore.

It was the 1941 Schwinn Excelsior, for which Breeze paid just five dollars, that began to shape and change bicycling history forever. After taking the bike home, removing the fenders, oiling the chain, and pumping up the tires, Breeze hit the dirt. He loved it.

His inspiration, while forerunning, was not altogether unique. On the opposite end of the country, nearly 2,500 miles from Marin County, east coast bike bums were also growing restless. More and more old, beat-up clunkers were being restored and modified. These behemoths often weighed as much as 80 pounds and were so reinforced they seemed virtually indestructible. But rides that take just 40 minutes on today's 25-pound featherweights took the steel-toed-boot-and-blue-jean-clad bikers of the late 1970s and early 1980s nearly four hours to complete.

Not until 1981 was it possible to purchase a production mountain bike, but local retailers found these ungainly bicycles difficult to sell and rarely kept them in stock. By 1983, however, mountain bikes were no longer such a fringe item, and large bike manufacturers quickly jumped into the action, producing their own versions of the off-road bike. By the 1990s, the mountain bike had firmly established its place with bicyclists of nearly all ages and abilities, and now command nearly 90 percent of the U.S. bike market.

There are many reasons for the mountain bike's success in becoming the hottest two-wheeled vehicle in the nation. They are much friendlier to the cyclist than traditional road bikes because of their comfortable upright position and shock-absorbing fat tires. And because of the health-conscious, environmentalist movement of the late 1980s and 1990s, people are more activity minded and seek nature on a closer

front than paved roads can allow. The mountain bike gives you these things and takes you far away from the daily grind—even if you're only minutes from the city.

MOUNTAIN BIKING INTO SHAPE

If your objective is to get in shape and lose weight, then you're on the right track, because mountain biking is one of the best ways to get started.

One way many of us have lost weight in this sport is the crash-and-burn-it-off method. Picture this: you're speeding uncontrollably down a vertical drop that you realize you shouldn't be on—only after it is too late. Your front wheel lodges into a rut and launches you through endless weeds, trees, and pointy rocks before coming to an abrupt halt in a puddle of thick mud. Surveying the damage, you discover, with the layers of skin, body parts, and lost confidence littering the trail above, that those unwanted pounds have been shed—*permanently*. Instant weight loss.

There is, of course, a more conventional (and quite a bit less painful) approach to losing weight and gaining fitness on a mountain bike. It's called the workout, and bicycles provide an ideal way to get physical. Take a look at some of the benefits associated with cycling.

Cycling helps you shed pounds without gimmicky diet fads or weight-loss programs. You can explore the countryside and burn nearly 10 to 16 calories per minute or close to 600 to 1,000 calories per hour. Moreover, it's a great way to spend an afternoon.

No less significant than the external and cosmetic changes of your body from riding are the internal changes taking place. Over time, cycling regularly will strengthen your heart as your body grows vast networks of new capillaries to carry blood to all those working muscles. This will, in turn, give your skin a healthier glow. The capacity of your lungs may increase up to 20 percent, and your resting heart rate will drop significantly. The Stanford University School of Medicine reports to the American Heart Association that people can reduce their risk of heart attack by nearly 64 percent if they can burn up to 2,000 calories per week. This is only two to three hours of bike riding!

Recommended for insomnia, hypertension, indigestion, anxiety, and even for recuperation from major heart attacks, bicycling can be an excellent cure-all as well as a great preventive. Cycling just a few hours per week can improve your figure and sleeping habits, give you greater resistance to illness, increase your energy levels, and provide feelings of accomplishment and heightened self-esteem.

BE SAFE—KNOW THE LAW

Occasionally, even the hard-core off-road cyclists will find they have no choice but to ride the pavement. When you are forced to hit the road, it's important for you to know and understand the rules.

Outlined below are a few of the common laws found in Colorado's Vehicle Code book.

- **Bicycles are legally classified as vehicles in Colorado.** This means that as a bicyclist, you are responsible for obeying the same rules of the road as a driver of a motor vehicle.
- **Bicyclists must ride with the traffic—NOT AGAINST IT!** Because bicycles are considered vehicles, you must ride your bicycle just as you would drive a car—with traffic. Only pedestrians should travel against the flow of traffic.
- **You must obey all traffic signs.** This includes stop signs and stoplights.
- **Always signal your turns.** Most drivers aren't expecting bicyclists to be on the roads, and many drivers would prefer that cyclists stay off the roads altogether. It's important, therefore, to clearly signal your intentions to motorists both in front and behind you.
- **Bicyclists are entitled to the same roads as cars (except controlled-access highways).** Unfortunately, cyclists are rarely given this consideration. This rule, however, is often over-interpreted to mean that cyclists can just take a lane and ride out in the middle of the road. In Colorado anyway, this is not true. Cyclists are entitled to a three-foot strip on the right side of the road in most situations. I've never been able to fully understand the very complicated Colorado version of this law—even after several hours of court-ordered traffic school.
- **Be a responsible cyclist.** Do not abuse your rights to ride on open roads. Follow the rules and set a good example for all of us as you roll along.

THE MOUNTAIN BIKE CONTROVERSY

Are Off-Road Bicyclists Environmental Outlaws? Do We have the Right to Use Public Trails?

Mountain bikers have long endured the animosity of folks in the backcountry who complain about the consequences of off-road bicycling. Many people believe that the fat tires and knobby tread do unacceptable environmental damage and that our uncontrollable riding habits are a danger to animals and to other trail users. To the contrary, mountain bikes have no more environmental impact than hiking boots or horseshoes. This does not mean, however, that mountain bikes leave no imprint at all. Wherever man treads, there is an impact. By riding responsibly, though, it is possible to leave only a minimum impact—something we all must take care to achieve.

Unfortunately, it is often people of great influence who view the mountain bike as the environment's worst enemy. Consequently, we as mountain bike riders and environmentally concerned citizens must be educators, impressing upon others that we also deserve the right to use these trails. Our responsibilities as bicyclists are no more and no less than any other trail user. We must all take the soft-cycling approach and show that mountain bicyclists are not environmental outlaws.

ETIQUETTE OF MOUNTAIN BIKING

When discussing mountain biking etiquette, we are in essence discussing the soft-cycling approach. This term, as mentioned previously, describes the art of minimum-impact bicycling and should apply to both the physical and social dimensions of the sport. But make no mistake—it is possible to ride fast and furiously while maintaining the balance of soft-cycling. Here first are a few ways to minimize the physical impact of mountain bike riding.

- *Stay on the trail.* Don't ride around fallen trees or mud holes that block your path. Stop and cross over them. When you come to a vista overlooking a deep valley, don't ride off the trail for a better vantage point. Instead, leave the bike and walk to see the view. Riding off the trail may seem inconsequential when done only once, but soon someone else will follow, then others, and the cumulative results can be catastrophic. Each time you wander from the trail you begin creating a new path, adding one more scar to the earth's surface.
- *Do not disturb the soil.* Follow a line within the trail that will not disturb or damage the soil.
- *Do not ride over soft or wet trails.* After a rain shower or during the thawing season, trails will often resemble muddy, oozing swampland. The best thing to do is stay off the trails altogether. Realistically, however, we're all going to come across some muddy trails we cannot anticipate. Instead of blasting through each section of mud, which may seem both easier and more fun, lift the bike and walk past. Each time a cyclist rides through a soft or muddy section of trail, that part of the trail is permanently damaged. Regardless of the trail's conditions, though, remember always to go over the obstacles across the path, not around them. Stay on the trail.
- *Avoid trails that, for all but God, are considered impassable and impossible.* Don't take a leap of faith down a kamikaze descent on which you will be forced to lock your brakes and skid to the bottom, ripping the ground apart as you go.

Soft-cycling should apply to the social dimensions of the sport as well, since mountain bikers are not the only folks who use the trails. Hikers, equestrians, cross-country skiers, and other outdoors people use many of the same trails and can be easily spooked by a marauding mountain biker tearing through the trees. Be friendly in the forest and give ample warning of your approach.

- *Take out what you bring in.* Don't leave broken bike pieces and banana peels scattered along the trail.
- *Be aware of your surroundings.* Don't use popular hiking trails for race training.
- *Slow down!* Rocketing around blind corners is a sure way to ruin an unsuspecting hiker's day. Consider this—If you fly down a quick singletrack descent at 20 mph, then hit the brakes and slow down to only six mph to pass someone, you're still moving twice as fast as they are!

Like the trails we ride on, the social dimension of mountain biking is very fragile and must be cared for responsibly. We should not want to destroy another person's enjoyment of the outdoors. By riding in the backcountry with caution, control, and responsibility, our presence should be felt positively by other trail users. By adhering to these rules, trail riding—a privilege that can quickly be taken away—will continue to be ours to share.

TRAIL MAINTENANCE

Unfortunately, despite all of the preventive measures taken to avoid trail damage, we're still going to run into many trails requiring attention. Simply put, a lot of hikers, equestrians, and cyclists alike use the same trails—some wear and tear is unavoidable. But like your bike, if you want to use these trails for a long time to come, you must also maintain them.

Trail maintenance and restoration can be accomplished in a variety of ways. One way is for mountain bike clubs to combine efforts with other trail users (i.e. hikers and equestrians) and work closely with land managers to cut new trails or repair existing ones. This not only reinforces to others the commitment cyclists have in caring for and maintaining the land, but also breaks the ice that often separates cyclists from their fellow trailmates. Another good way to help out is to show up on a Saturday morning with a few riding buddies at your favorite off-road domain ready to work. With a good attitude, thick gloves, and the local land manager's supervision, trail repair is fun and very rewarding. It's important, of course, that you arrange a trail-repair outing with the local land manager before you start pounding shovels into the dirt. They can lead you to the most needy sections of trail and instruct you on what repairs should be done and how best to accomplish the task. Perhaps the most effective means of trail maintenance, though, can be done by yourself and while you're riding. Read on.

ON-THE-SPOT QUICK FIX

Most of us, when we're riding, have at one time or another come upon muddy trails or fallen trees blocking our path. We notice that over time the mud gets deeper and the trail gets wider as people go through or around the obstacles. We worry that the problem will become so severe and repairs too difficult that the trail's access may be threatened. We also know that our ambition to do anything about it is greatest at that moment, not after a hot shower and a plate of spaghetti. Here are a few on-the-spot quick fixes you can do that will hopefully correct a problem before it gets out of hand and get you back on your bike within minutes.

Muddy Trails. What do you do when trails develop huge mud holes destined for the EPA's Superfund status? The technique is called corduroying, and it works much like building a pontoon over the mud to support bikes, horses, or hikers as they cross. Corduroy (not the pants) is the term for roads made of logs laid down crosswise. Use small-and medium-sized sticks and lay them side by side across the trail until they cover the length of the muddy section (break the sticks to fit the width of the trail). Press them into the mud with your feet, then lay more on top if needed. Keep adding sticks until the trail is firm. Not only will you stay clean as you cross, but the sticks may soak up some of the water and help the puddle dry. This quick fix may last as long as one month before needing to be redone. And as time goes on, with new layers added to the trail, the soil will grow stronger, thicker, and more resistant to erosion. This whole process may take fewer than five minutes, and you can be on your way, knowing the trail behind you is in good repair.

Leaving the Trail. What do you do to keep cyclists from cutting corners and leaving the designated trail? The solution is much simpler than you may think. (No, don't hire an off-road police force.) Notice where people are leaving the trail and throw a pile of thick branches or brush along the path, or place logs across the opening to block the way through. There are probably dozens of subtle tricks like these that will manipulate people into staying on the designated trail. If executed well, no one will even notice that the thick branches scattered along the ground in the woods weren't always there. And most folks would probably rather take a moment to hop a log in the trail than get tangled in a web of branches.

Obstacle in the Way. If there are large obstacles blocking the trail, try and remove

them or push them aside. If you cannot do this by yourself, call the trail maintenance hotline to speak with the land manager of that particular trail and see what can be done.

We must be willing to sweat for our trails in order to sweat on them. Police yourself and point out to others the significance of trail maintenance. "Sweat Equity," the rewards of continued land use won with a fair share of sweat, pays off when the trail is "up for review" by the land manager and he or she remembers the efforts made by trail-conscious mountain bikers.

RULES OF THE TRAIL

The International Mountain Bicycling Association (IMBA) has developed these guidelines to trail riding. These "Rules of the Trail" are accepted worldwide and will go a long way in keeping trails open. Please respect and follow these rules for everyone's sake.

- **Ride only on open trails.** Respect trail and road closures (if you're not sure, ask a park or state official first), do not trespass on private property, and obtain permits or authorization if required. Federal and state wilderness areas are off-limits to cycling. Parks and state forests may also have certain trails closed to cycling.
- **Leave no trace.** Be sensitive to the dirt beneath you. Even on open trails, you should not ride under conditions by which you will leave evidence of your passing, such as on certain soils or shortly after a rainfall. Be sure to observe the different types of soils and trails you're riding on, practicing minimum-impact cycling. Never ride off the trail, don't skid your tires, and be sure to bring out at least as much as you bring in.
- **Control your bicycle!** Inattention for even one second can cause disaster for yourself or for others. Excessive speed frightens and can injure people, gives mountain biking a bad name, and can result in trail closures.
- **Always yield.** Let others know you're coming well in advance (a friendly greeting is always good and often appreciated). Show your respect when passing others by slowing to walking speed or stopping altogether, especially in the presence of horses. Horses can be unpredictable, so be very careful. Anticipate that other trail users may be around corners or in blind spots.
- **Never spook animals.** All animals are spooked by sudden movements, unannounced approaches, or loud noises. Give the animals extra room and time so they can adjust to you. Move slowly or dismount around animals. Running cattle and disturbing wild animals are serious offenses. Leave gates as you find them, or as marked.
- **Plan ahead.** Know your equipment, your ability, and the area in which you are riding, and plan your trip accordingly. Be self-sufficient at all times, keep your bike in good repair, and carry necessary supplies for changes in weather or other conditions. You can help keep trails open by setting an example of responsible, courteous, and controlled mountain bike riding.
- **Always wear a helmet when you ride.** For your own safety and protection, a helmet should be worn whenever you are riding your bike. You never know when a tree root or small rock will throw you the wrong way and send you tumbling.

Thousands of miles of dirt trails have been closed to mountain bicycling because of the irresponsible riding habits of just a few riders. Don't follow the example of these offending riders. Don't take away trail privileges from thousands of others who work hard each year to keep the backcountry avenues open to us all.

THE NECESSITIES OF CYCLING

When discussing the most important items to have on a bike ride, cyclists generally agree on the following four items.

Helmet. The reasons to wear a helmet should be obvious. Helmets are discussed in more detail in the Be Safe—Wear Your Armor section.

Water. Without it, cyclists may face dehydration, which may result in dizziness and fatigue. On a warm day, cyclists should drink at least one full bottle during every hour of riding. Remember, it's always good to drink before you feel thirsty—otherwise, it may be too late.

Cycling Shorts. These are necessary if you plan to ride your bike more than 20 to 30 minutes. Padded cycling shorts may be the only thing preventing your derriere from serious saddle soreness by ride's end. There are two types of cycling shorts you can buy. Touring shorts are good for people who don't want to look like they're wearing anatomically correct cellophane. These look like regular athletic shorts with pockets, but have built-in padding in the crotch area for protection from chafing and saddle sores. The more popular, traditional cycling shorts are made of skin-tight material, also with a padded crotch. Whichever style you find most comfortable, cycling shorts are a fairly important item for long rides.

Food. This essential item will keep you rolling. Cycling burns up a lot of calories and is among the few sports in which no one is safe from the "Bonk." Bonking feels like it sounds. Without food in your system, your blood sugar level collapses, and there is no longer any energy in your body. This instantly results in total fatigue and light-headedness. So when you're filling your water bottle, remember to bring along some food. Fruit, energy bars, or some other forms of high-energy food are highly recommended. Candy bars are not, however, because they will deliver a sudden burst of high energy, then let you down soon after, causing you to feel worse than before. Energy bars are available at most bike stores and are similar to candy bars, but provide complex carbohydrate energy and high nutrition rather than fast-burning simple sugars.

BE PREPARED OR DIE

Essential equipment that will keep you from dying alone in the woods:

Be Prepared Or Die

- Spare Tube
- Tire Irons: See the Appendix for instructions on fixing flat tires.
- Patch Kit
- Pump
- Money: Spare change for emergency calls.
- Spoke Wrench
- Spare Spokes: To fit your wheel. Tape these to the chain stay.
- Chain Tool
- Allen Keys: Bring appropriate sizes to fit your bike.
- Compass
- First-Aid Kit
- Rain Gear: For quick changes in weather.
- Matches
- Guidebook: In case all else fails and you must start a fire to survive, this guidebook will serve as excellent fire starter!

To carry these items, you will need a backpack. If you're carrying lots of equipment, you may want to consider a set of panniers. These are much larger and mount on either side of each wheel on a rack. Many cyclists, though, prefer not to use a pack at all. They just slip all they need into their jersey pockets, and off they go. Of course, these are the guys who are always asking to borrow my tools for trailside repairs.

BE SAFE—WEAR YOUR ARMOR

While on the subject of jerseys, it's crucial to discuss the clothing you must wear to be safe, practical, and—if you prefer—stylish. The following is a list of items that will save you from disaster, outfit you comfortably, and most important, keep you looking cool.

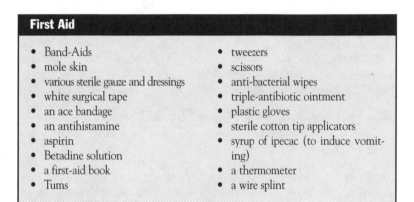

First Aid

- Band-Aids
- mole skin
- various sterile gauze and dressings
- white surgical tape
- an ace bandage
- an antihistamine
- aspirin
- Betadine solution
- a first-aid book
- Tums

- tweezers
- scissors
- anti-bacterial wipes
- triple-antibiotic ointment
- plastic gloves
- sterile cotton tip applicators
- syrup of ipecac (to induce vomiting)
- a thermometer
- a wire splint

Helmet. A helmet is an absolute necessity because it protects your head from complete annihilation. It is the only thing that will not disintegrate into a million pieces after a wicked crash on a descent you shouldn't have been on in the first place. A helmet with a solid exterior shell will also protect your head from sharp or protruding objects. Of course, with a hard-shelled helmet, you can paste several stickers of your favorite bicycle manufacturers all over the outer shell, giving companies even more free advertising for your dollar.

Shorts. Let's just say Lycra cycling shorts are considered a major safety item if you plan to ride for more than 20 or 30 minutes at a time. As mentioned in The Necessities of Cycling section, cycling shorts are well regarded as the leading cure-all for chafing and saddle sores. The most preventive cycling shorts have padded "chamois" (most chamois is synthetic nowadays) in the crotch area. Of course, if you choose to wear these traditional cycling shorts, it's imperative that they look as if someone spray painted them onto your body.

Gloves. You may find well-padded cycling gloves invaluable when traveling over rocky trails and gravelly roads for hours on end. Long-fingered gloves may also be useful, as branches, trees, assorted hard objects, and, occasionally, small animals will reach out and whack your knuckles.

Glasses. Not only do sunglasses give you an imposing presence and make you look cool (both are extremely important), they also protect your eyes from harmful ultraviolet rays, invisible branches, creepy bugs, dirt, and may prevent you from being

217

The Art of Mountain Biking

caught sneaking glances at riders of the opposite sex also wearing skintight, revealing Lycra.

Shoes. Mountain bike shoes should have stiff soles to help make pedaling easier and provide better traction when walking your bike up a trail becomes necessary. Virtually any kind of good outdoor hiking footwear will work, but specific mountain bike shoes (especially those with inset cleats) are best. It is vital that these shoes look as ugly as humanly possible. Those closest in style to bowling shoes are, of course, the most popular.

Jersey or Shirt. Bicycling jerseys are popular because of their snug fit and back pockets. When purchasing a jersey, look for ones that are loaded with bright, blinding, neon logos and manufacturers' names. These loudly decorated billboards are also good for drawing unnecessary attention to yourself just before taking a mean spill while trying to hop a curb. A cotton T-shirt is a good alternative in warm weather, but when the weather turns cold, cotton becomes a chilling substitute for the jersey. Cotton retains moisture and sweat against your body, which may cause you to get the chills and ills on those cold-weather rides.

OH, THOSE COLD, WET COLORADO DAYS

If the weather chooses not to cooperate on the day you've set aside for a bike ride, it's helpful to be prepared.

Tights or leg warmers. These are best in temperatures below 55 degrees. Knees are sensitive and can develop all kinds of problems if they get cold. Common problems include tendinitis, bursitis, and arthritis.

Plenty of layers on your upper body. When the air has a nip in it, layers of clothing will keep the chill away from your chest and help prevent the development of bronchitis. If the air is cool, a Polypropylene or Capilene long-sleeved shirt is best to wear against the skin beneath other layers of clothing. Polypropylene or Capilene, like wool, wicks away moisture from your skin to keep your body dry. Try to avoid wearing cotton or baggy clothing when the temperature falls. Cotton, as mentioned before, holds moisture like a sponge, and baggy clothing catches cold air and swirls it around your body. Good cold-weather clothing should fit snugly against your body, but not be restrictive.

Wool socks. Don't pack too many layers under those shoes, though. You may stand the chance of restricting circulation, and your feet will get real cold, real fast.

Thinsulate or Gortex gloves. We may all agree that there is nothing worse than frozen feet—unless your hands are frozen. A good pair of Thinsulate or Gortex gloves should keep your hands toasty and warm.

Hat or helmet on cold days? Sometimes, when the weather gets really cold and you still want to hit the trails, it's tough to stay warm. We all know that 130 percent of the body's heat escapes through the head (overactive brains, I imagine), so it's important to keep the cranium warm. Ventilated helmets are zdesigned to keep heads cool in the summer heat, but they do little to help keep heads warm during rides in sub-zero temperatures. Cyclists should consider wearing a hat on extremely cold days. Capilene Skullcaps are great head and ear warmers that snugly fit over your head beneath the helmet. Head protection is not lost. Another option is a helmet cover that covers those ventilating gaps and helps keep the body heat in. These do not, how-ever, keep your ears warm. Some cyclists will opt for a simple knit cycling cap sans the helmet, but these have never been shown to be very good cranium protectors.

All of this clothing can be found at your local bike store, where the staff should be happy to help fit you into the seasons of the year.

TO HAVE OR NOT TO HAVE—Other Very Useful Items

Though mountain biking is relatively new to the cycling scene, there is no short-age of items for you and your bike to make riding better, safer, and easier. We have rummaged through the unending lists and separated the gadgets from the good stuff, coming up with what we believe are items certain to make mountain bike riding eas-ier and more enjoyable.

Tires. Buying yourself a good pair of knobby tires is the quickest way to enhance the off-road handling capabilities of your bike. There are many types of mountain bike tires on the market. Some are made exclusively for very rugged off-road ter-rain. These big-knobbed, soft rubber tires virtually stick to the ground with unfor-giving traction, but tend to deteriorate quickly on pavement. There are other tires made exclusively for the road. These are called "slicks" and have no tread at all. For the average cyclist, though, a good tire somewhere in the middle of these two extremes should do the trick.

Toe Clips or Clipless Pedals. With these, you will ride with more power. Toe clips attach to your pedals and strap your feet firmly in place, allowing you to exert pressure on the pedals around the entire pedal stroke. They will increase your pedal-ing efficiency by 30 percent to 50 percent. Clipless pedals, which liberate your feet from the traditional straps and clips, have made toe clips virtually obsolete. Like ski bindings, they attach your shoe directly to the pedal. They are, however, much more expensive than toe clips. Clipless pedals and toe clips take a little getting used to, but they're definitely worth the trouble.

Bar Ends. These clamp-on additions to your original straight bar will provide more leverage, an excellent grip for climbing, and a more natural position for your hands. Be aware, however, of the bar end's propensity for hooking trees on fast descents, sending you, the cyclist, airborne. Opinions are divided on the general usefulness of bar ends. Typically, folks love their new bar ends when they put them on, then a sea-son or two later they take them off and say "man, my bike sure feels good without those bar ends."

Back Pack. These bags are ideal for carrying keys, extra food and water, guidebooks, foul-weather clothing, tools, spare tubes, and a cellular phone, in case you need to call for help.

Suspension Forks. For the more serious off-roaders who want nothing to impede their speed on the trails, investing in a pair of suspension forks is a good idea. Like

tires, there are plenty of brands to choose from, and they all do the same thing—absorb the brutal beatings of a rough trail. The cost of these forks, however, is sometimes more brutal than the trail itself.

Bike Computers. These are fun gadgets to own and are much less expensive than in years past. They have such features as trip distance, speedometer, odometer, time of day, altitude, alarm, average speed, maximum speed, heart rate, global satellite positioning, etc. Bike computers will come in handy when following these maps or to know just how far you've ridden in the wrong direction.

Water Pack. This is quickly becomming an essential item for cyclists pedaling for more than a few hours, especially in hot, dry conditions. The most popular brand is, of course, the Camelback, and these water packs can carry in their bladder bags as much as 100 ounces of water. These packs strap onto your back with a handy hose running over your shoulder so you can be drinking water while still holding onto the bars on a rocky descent with both hands. These packs are a great way to carry a lot of extra liquid on hot rides in the middle of nowhere.

TYPES OF OFF-ROAD TERRAIN

Before roughing it off road, we may first have to ride the pavement to get to our destination. Please, don't be dismayed. Some of the country's best rides are on the road. Once we get past these smooth-surfaced pathways, though, adventures in dirt await us.

Rails-to-Trails. Abandoned rail lines are converted into usable public resources for exercising, commuting, or just enjoying nature. Old rails and ties are torn up and a trail, paved or unpaved, is laid along the existing corridor. This completes the cycle from ancient Indian trading routes to railroad corridors and back again to hiking and cycling trails.

Unpaved Roads are typically found in rural areas and are most often public roads. Be careful when exploring, though, not to ride on someone's unpaved private drive.

Forest Roads. These dirt and gravel roads are used primarily as access to forest land and are generally kept in good condition. In Southwestern Colorado, many of these forest roads are incredibly steep and rough old mining roads that are only accessible to 4WD vehicles and mountain bikes. They are almost always open to public use.

Singletrack can be the most fun on a mountain bike. These trails, with only one track to follow, are often narrow, challenging pathways through the woods. Remember to make sure these trails are open before zipping into the woods. (At the time of this printing, all trails and roads in this guidebook were open to mountain bikes.)

Open Land. Unless there is a marked trail through a field or open space, you should not plan to ride here. Once one person cuts his or her wheels through a field or meadow, many more are sure to follow, causing irreparable damage to the landscape.

TECHNIQUES TO SHARPEN YOUR SKILLS

Many of us see ourselves as pure athletes—blessed with power, strength, and endless endurance. However, it may be those with finesse, balance, agility, and grace that get around most quickly on a mountain bike. Although power, strength, and endurance do have their places in mountain biking, these elements don't necessarily form the complete framework for a champion mountain biker.

The bike should become an extension of your body. Slight shifts in your hips or knees can have remarkable results. Experienced bike handlers seem to flash down technical descents, dashing over obstacles in a smooth and graceful effort as if pirouetting in Swan Lake. Here are some tips and techniques to help you connect with your bike and float gracefully over the dirt.

BRAKING

Using your brakes requires using your head, especially when descending. This doesn't mean using your head as a stopping block, but rather to think intelligently. Use your best judgment in terms of how much or how little to squeeze those brake levers.

The more weight a tire is carrying, the more braking power it has. When you're going downhill, your front wheel carries more weight than the rear. Braking gently with the front brake will help keep you in control without going into a skid. Be careful, though, not to overdo it with the front brakes and accidentally toss yourself over the handlebars. And don't neglect your rear brake! When descending, shift your weight back over the rear wheel, thus increasing your rear braking power as well. This will balance the power of both brakes and give you maximum control.

Good riders learn just how much of their weight to shift over each wheel and how to apply just enough braking power to each brake, so not to "endo" over the handlebars or skid down a trail.

If you're one of those beginners who is convinced that a pair of ultra-powerful, fine-tuned brakes will transform you instantly into a World Cup champion downhiller, you're barking up the wrong tree. Other factors—like experience, good vision, and confidence—are far more important. Riders who possess these qualities don't have to think much about their brakes.

GOING UPHILL—Climbing Those Treacherous Hills

Shift into a low gear. Before shifting, be sure to ease up on your pedaling so there is not too much pressure on the chain. With that in mind, it's important to shift before you find yourself on a steep slope, where it may too late. Find the gear best for you that matches the terrain and steepness of each climb.

Stay seated. Standing out of the saddle is often helpful when climbing steep hills on a bike, but you may find that on dirt, standing may cause your rear tire to lose its grip and spin out. Climbing is not possible without traction. As you improve, you will likely learn the subtle tricks that make out-of-saddle climbing possible. Until then, have a seat.

Lean forward. On very steep hills, the front end may feel unweighted and suddenly pop up. Slide forward on the saddle and lean over the handlebars. Think about putting your chin down near your stem. This will add more weight to the front wheel and should keep you grounded. It's all about using the weight of your head to your advantage. Most people don't realize how heavy their noggin is.

221

Relax. As with downhilling, relaxation is a big key to your success when climbing steep, rocky climbs. Smooth pedaling translates into good traction. Tense bodies don't balance well at low speeds. Instead of fixating grimly on the front wheel, look up at the terrain above, and pick a good line.

Keep pedaling. On rocky climbs, be sure to keep the pressure on, and don't let up on those pedals! You'll be surprised at what your bike will just roll over as long as you keep the engine revved up.

GOING DOWNHILL—The Real Reason We Get Up in the Morning

Relax. Stay loose on the bike, and don't lock your elbows or clench your grip. Your elbows need to bend with the bumps and absorb the shock, while your hands should have a firm but controlled grip on the bars to keep things steady. Breathing slowly, deeply, and deliberately will help you relax while flying down bumpy singletrack. Maintaining a death-grip on the brakes will be unhelpful. Fear and tension will make you wreck every time.

Use Your Eyes. Keep your head up, and scan the trail as far forward as possible. Choose a line well in advance. You decide what line to take—don't let the trail decide for you. Keep the surprises to a minimum. If you have to react quickly to an obstacle, then you've already made a mistake.

Rise above the saddle. When racing down bumpy, technical descents, you should not be sitting on the saddle, but hovering just over it, allowing your bent legs and arms to absorb the rocky trail instead of your rear. Think jockey.

Remember your pedals. Be mindful of where your pedals are in relation to upcoming obstacles. Clipping a rock will lead directly to unpleasantness. Most of the time, you'll want to keep your pedals parallel to the ground.

Stay focused. Many descents require your utmost concentration and focus just to reach the bottom. You must notice every groove, every root, every rock, every hole, every bump. You, the bike, and the trail should all become one as you seek singletrack nirvana on your way down the mountain. But if your thoughts wander, however, then so may your bike, and you may instead become one with the trees!

LAST-MINUTE CHECKOVER

Before a ride, it's a good idea to give your bike a once-over to make sure everything is in working order. Begin by checking the air pressure in your tires before each ride to make sure they are properly inflated. Mountain bikes require about 45 to 55 pounds per square inch of air pressure. If your tires are underinflated, there is greater likelihood that the tubes may get pinched on a bump or rock, causing the tire to flat.

Looking over your bike to make sure everything is secure and in its place is the next step. Go through the following checklist before each ride.

- **Pinch the tires to feel for proper inflation.** They should give just a little on the sides, but feel very hard on the treads. If you have a pressure gauge, use that.
- **Check your brakes.** Squeeze the rear brake and roll your bike forward. The rear tire should skid. Next, squeeze the front brake and roll your bike forward. The rear wheel should lift into the air. If this doesn't happen, then your brakes are too loose. Make sure the brake levers don't touch the handlebars when squeezed with full force.

- **Check all quick releases on your bike.** Make sure they are all securely tightened.
- **Lube up.** If your chain squeaks, apply some lubricant.
- **Check your nuts and bolts.** Check the handlebars, saddle, cranks, and pedals to make sure that each is tight and securely fastened to your bike.
- **Check your wheels.** Spin each wheel to see that they spin through the frame and between brake pads freely.
- **Have you got everything?** Make sure you have your spare tube, tire irons patch kit, frame pump, tools, food, water, foul-weather gear, and guidebook.

Local Bike Shops

Durango

Hassle Free Sports.
2615 Main. (970) 295-3874.

Mountain Bike Specialists.
949 Main. (970) 247-4066. Ed Zink's shop. Zink is the Ironhorse promoter and one of the greatest all-time mountain bike advocates.

Durango Cyclery.
143 East 13th. (970) 247-0747.

Pedal The Peaks.
598 Main. (970) 259-6880.

Second Gear.
600 East 2nd. (970) 247-4511. This shop sells used sporting goods, including some bike stuff.

Rentals are also available at:

Southwest Adventures.
12th and Camino del Rio. (970) 259-0370.

Black Forest Mountain Bike Rental.
56 Ponderosa Homes Road, Vallecito Lake. (970) 884-4173.

Telluride/Ouray

Telluride Sports.
150 West Colorado. (970) 728-4477 or 1-800-828-7547.

Paragon Ski & Sport.
217 West Colorado. (970) 728-4525.

Ridgway Outdoor Experience.
102 Campbell Lane, Ridgway. (970) 626-3608. At the time of this writing there are no shops in Ouray, so this is as close as it gets. Or try the many shops up the road in Montrose.

Rentals are also available at:

The Boot Doctors.
Inn at Lost Creek, Mountain Village. (970) 728-8954.

Slopestyle.
236 West Colorado. (970) 728-9889.

Good Eats
Where to Carbo-load and Fill the Gullet

Durango

This is just a partial list of places to get a reasonably priced meal in Durango. I have ignored the many high-end restaurants, most of which are quite good I'm sure.

Durango Diner. 957 Main. (970) 247-9889. Watch for flying elbows as you attempt to consume the biggest pancakes you've ever seen in this narrow and cramped diner. Lots of green chile and spicy sausage-inspired dishes. Highly recommended! Extreme carbo-loading.

Griego's North. 2603 Main. (970) 259-3558. Cheap Mexican food is just what you need sometimes, and you'll find it at this converted Sonic on Main. Dollar tacos hit the spot. Don't leave without an armload of the excellent sopapillas.

Nature's Oasis. 1123 Camino del Rio (Camino del Rio is just another name for Main/US 160). (970) 247-1988. This natural foods grocery has a juice bar and sandwiches.

Storyville Barbeque & Woodfired Pizza. 1150 B Main Avenue. (970) 259-1475. Prime opportunities for carbo-loading in this casual, folksy tavern. Occasional live music. The little one-man pizzas are quite good.

Lori's Family Dining. 2653 Main. (970) 247-1224. Classic American fare served with a smile in this popular super-spoon. A sign on the wall states that Lori's has the friendliest waitstaff in the world, and after one visit you'll probably agree. Minimize your driving: Lori's shares a parking lot with Hassle Free Sports.

College Drive Cafe. 666 East College Drive. (970) 247-5322. Very popular with the locals. Good food, large portions, and fair prices. Rivals the Durango Diner for best breakfast burrito.

Farquahrt's Pizza Mia. 725 Main Ave. (970) 247-5442. Decent pizza and sandwiches, hard to pronounce.

City Market. Two locations: 9th and Main, 32nd and Main. Big grocery stores with good deli sandwiches.

Mama's Boy. 2659 Main Avenue. (970) 247-0060. Sterile, somewhat frightening atmosphere, but giant, tasty portions. Grab a calzone. Top-notch carbo loading.

Serious Texas Barbecue. A roadside trailer on north Main provides some of the most satisfying lunches in town. The "Texas Taco" is brisket, potatoes, cheese, onions, and hot sauce folded in a tortilla. Damn that's good!

Durango Bagel. 106 E. 5th St. (970) 385-7297. Breakfast and lunch bagel concoctions. "Voted Best Bagel in the Four Corners." I can hear the New Yorkers chuckling from here.

Gazpacho. 431 East 2nd Avenue. (970) 259-9494. Adequate food and powerful margaritas at this cantina with atmosphere.

Steamworks. *801 East 2nd Avenue. (970) 259-9200. Liquid carbo-loading. Spacious, yet crowded, neo-maxi brewpub setting, offers a little taste of cheesy lower downtown Denver right here in Durango.*

Telluride

Telluride is packed with fine dining opportunities—so I'm told. I can't even get in the front door of those places, so I'm personally unable to provide information on the town's many high-quality eateries. But folks with the means to wine and dine at restaurants like La Marmotte, Cosmopolitan, Sofio's, Cazwella's, Rustico Ristorante, or Campagna (which claims to have the best Italian food in Colorado) probably don't care what I think anyway. Pickins are slim for the hungry hobo caught in the box canyon. The following is a short, incomplete sampling of places to buy food relatively cheaply.

Baked in Telluride. *127 South Fir. (970) 728-4705. The staff may forget your order, but once you are finally served, the food will satisfy. Pizza, calzones, sandwiches, salads, baked goods. Free pizza delivery. To order, call (970) 728-4775.*

Fat Alley. *122 South Oak. (970) 728-3985. BBQ served with a full compliment of side dishes, like bourbon and fried okra. A traditional stop for the budget traveler.*

Floradora. *103 West Colorado. (970) 728-3888. Old school restaurant on Main Street (Colorado Avenue) serves moderately priced American fare. Some of the desserts are as big as your head.*

Magic Market. *225 South Pine. (970) 728-8789. Small town grocery, only instead of an old lady at the register, it's some kid with a bone in his nose.*

Cafe Vienna. *333 West Colorado. (970) 728-4504. High altitude caffeine junky needle exchange program on Main Street.*

Repair and

Mainten

Mainten

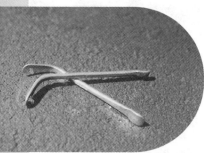

Repair and Maintenance

FIXING A FLAT

TOOLS YOU WILL NEED

- Two tire irons
- Pump (either a floor pump or a frame pump)
- No screwdrivers!!! (This can puncture the tube)

REMOVING THE WHEEL

The front wheel is easy. Simply open the quick release mechanism or undo the bolts with the proper sized wrench, then remove the wheel from the bike.

The rear wheel is a little more tricky. Before you loosen the wheel from the frame, shift the chain into the smallest gear on the freewheel (the cluster of gears in the back). Once you've done this, removing and installing the wheel, like the front, is much easier.

REMOVING THE TIRE

Step one: Insert a tire iron under the bead of the tire and pry the tire over the lip of the rim. Be careful not to pinch the tube when you do this.

Step two: Hold the first tire iron in place. With the second tire iron, repeat step one, three or four inches down the rim. Alternate tire irons, pulling the bead of the tire over the rim, section by section, until one side of the tire bead is completely off the rim.

Step three: Remove the rest of the tire and tube from the rim. This can be done by hand. It's easiest to remove the valve stem last. Once the tire is off the rim, pull the tube out of the tire.

CLEAN AND SAFETY CHECK

Step four: Using a rag, wipe the inside of the tire to clean out any dirt, sand, glass, thorns, etc. These may cause the tube to puncture. The inside of a tire should feel smooth. Any pricks or bumps could mean that you have found the culprit responsible for your flat tire.

Step five: Wipe the rim clean, then check the rim strip, making sure it covers the spoke nipples properly on the inside of the rim. If a spoke is poking through the rim strip, it could cause a puncture.

Step six: At this point, you can do one of two things: replace the punctured tube with a new one, or patch the hole. It's easiest to just replace the tube with a new tube when you're out on the trails. Roll up the old tube and take it home to repair later that night in front of the TV. Directions on patching a tube are usually included with the patch kit itself.

INSTALLING THE TIRE AND TUBE
(This can be done entirely by hand)

Step seven: Inflate the new or repaired tube with enough air to give it shape, then tuck it back into the tire.

Step eight: To put the tire and tube back on the rim, begin by putting the valve in the valve hole. The valve must be straight. Then use your hands to push the beaded edge of the tire onto the rim all the way around so that one side of your tire is on the rim.

Step nine: Let most of the air out of the tube to allow room for the rest of the tire.

Step ten: Beginning opposite the valve, use your thumbs to push the other side of the tire onto the rim. Be careful not to pinch the tube in between the tire and the rim. The last few inches may be difficult, and you may need the tire iron to pry the tire onto the rim. If so, just be careful not to puncture the tube.

BEFORE INFLATING COMPLETELY

Step eleven: Check to make sure the tire is seated properly and that the tube is not caught between the tire and the rim. Do this by adding about 5 to 10 pounds of air, and watch closely that the tube does not bulge out of the tire.

Step twelve: Once you're sure the tire and tube are properly seated, put the wheel back on the bike, then fill the tire with air. It's easier squeezing the wheel through the brake shoes if the tire is still flat.

Step thirteen: Now fill the tire with the proper amount of air, and check constantly to make sure the tube doesn't bulge from the rim. If the tube does appear to bulge out, release all the air as quickly as possible, or you could be in for a big bang.

When installing the rear wheel, place the chain back onto the smallest cog (furthest gear on the right), and pull the derailleur out of the way. Your wheel should slide right on.

LUBRICATION PREVENTS DETERIORATION

Lubrication is crucial to maintaining your bike. Dry spots will be eliminated. Creaks, squeaks, grinding, and binding will be gone. The chain will run quietly, and the gears will shift smoothly. The brakes will grip quicker, and your bike may last longer with fewer repairs. Need I say more? Well, yes. Without knowing where to put the lubrication, what good is it?

THINGS YOU WILL NEED
- One can of bicycle lubricant, found at any bike store.
- A clean rag (to wipe excess lubricant away).

WHAT GETS LUBRICATED
- Front derailleur
- Rear derailleur
- Shift levers
- Front brake
- Rear brake

- Both brake levers
- Chain

WHERE TO LUBRICATE

To make it easy, simply spray a little lubricant on all the pivot points of your bike. If you're using a squeeze bottle, use just a drop or two. Put a few drops on each point wherever metal moves against metal, for instance, at the center of the brake calipers. Then let the lube sink in.

Once you have applied the lubricant to the derailleurs, shift the gears a few times, working the derailleurs back and forth. This allows the lubricant to work itself into the tiny cracks and spaces it must occupy to do its job. Work the brakes a few times as well.

LUBING THE CHAIN

Lubricating the chain should be done after the chain has been wiped clean of most road grime. Do this by spinning the pedals counterclockwise while gripping the chain with a clean rag. As you add the lubricant, be sure to get some in between each link. With an aerosol spray, just spray the chain while pedalling backwards (counterclockwise) until the chain is fully lubricated. Let the lubricant soak in for a few seconds before wiping the excess away. Chains will collect dirt much faster if they're loaded with too much lubrication.

Index

A

B

C

D

E

F

Meet the Author

Robert Hurst is a native Coloradan who is just happy to be in one piece after working for nine years as a bike messenger in Denver. He celebrates his continued survival by spending time in the mountains, and by riding the world's most excellent trails. He still can't believe people actually get paid to write trail guides.

Author

FALCONGUIDES®

Ffrom nature exploration to extreme adventure, FalconGuides lead you there. With more than 400 titles available, there is a guide for every outdoor activity and topic, including essential outdoor skills, field identification, trails, trips, and the best places to go in each state and region. Written by experts, each guidebook features detailed descriptions, maps, and advice that can enhance every outdoor experience.

You can count on FalconGuides to lead you to your favorite outdoor activities wherever you live or travel.

MOUNTAIN BIKING

These local mountain biking guides comprehensively cover the best local riding in a region, usually around an urban area. They are small, lightweight, and fit nicely into a bike jersey pocket.

4 ¼" x 7" · paperback · maps, elevation graphs

AFALCONGUIDE

Bruce Grubbs

Mountain Biking St. George/ Cedar City

AFALCONGUIDE

Amber Travsky

Mountain Biking Jackson Hole

AFALCONGUIDE

Steve Johnson

Mountain Biking the Twin Cities